ess

# MCSE
# Readiness Review
# Exam 70-028
# Administering
Microsoft®
# SQL Server™ 7.0

PUBLISHED BY
Microsoft Press
A Division of Microsoft Corporation
One Microsoft Way
Redmond, Washington 98052-6399

Library of Congress Cataloging-in-Publication Data
Spealman, Jill.
      MCSE Readiness Review—Exam 70-028: Administering Microsoft SQL Server 7.0 /
Jill Spealman.
          p.  cm.
      ISBN 0-7356-0672-2
      1. Electronic data processing personnel--Certification.
      2. Microsoft software--Examinations--Study guides.   3. SQL server.
      I. Title.   II. Title: Exam 70-028, Microsoft SQL Server 7.0.
      QA76.3.S64   1999
      005.75'85--dc21                                            99-33262
                                                                    CIP

Printed and bound in the United States of America.

1 2 3 4 5 6 7 8 9   MLML    4 3 2 1 0 9

Distributed in Canada by Penguin Books Canada Limited.

A CIP catalogue record for this book is available from the British Library.

Microsoft Press books are available through booksellers and distributors worldwide. For further information about international editions, contact your local Microsoft Corporation office or contact Microsoft Press International directly at fax (425) 936-7329. Visit our Web site at mspress.microsoft.com.

**Acquisitions Editor:** Jeff Madden
**Project Editor:** Jocelyn Lee Markey

# Contents

# Welcome to Administering Microsoft SQL Server 7.0

Welcome to *MCSE Readiness Review—Exam 70-028: Administering Microsoft SQL Server 7.0*. The Readiness Review series gives you a focused, timesaving way to identify the information you need to know to pass the Microsoft Certified Professional (MCP) exams. The series combines a realistic electronic assessment with a review book to help you become familiar with the types of questions you will encounter on the MCP exam. By reviewing the objectives and sample questions, you can focus on the specific skills you need to improve before taking the exam.

This book helps you evaluate your readiness for the MCP Exam 70-028: Administering Microsoft SQL Server 7.0. When you pass this exam, you earn core credit toward Microsoft Certified Database Administrator (MCDBA) certification, elective credit toward Microsoft Certified Systems Engineer (MCSE) certification, and elective credit toward Microsoft Certified Systems Engineer + Internet certification. In addition, when you pass this exam you achieve Microsoft Certified Professional status.

**Note** You can find a complete list of MCP exams and their related objectives on the Microsoft Certified Professional Web site at http://www.microsoft.com/mcp.

The Readiness Review series lets you identify any areas in which you may need additional training. To help you get the training you need to successfully pass the certification exams, Microsoft Press publishes a complete line of self-paced training kits and other study materials. For comprehensive information about the topics covered in the Administering Microsoft SQL Server 7.0 exam, you might want to see the corresponding training kit—the *Microsoft SQL Server 7.0 System Administration Training Kit*.

# Before You Begin

This MCSE Readiness Review consists of two main parts: the Readiness Review electronic assessment on the accompanying compact disc, and this Readiness Review book.

# The Readiness Review Components

The electronic assessment is a practice certification exam that helps you evaluate your skills. It provides instant scoring feedback, so you can determine areas in which additional study may be helpful before you take the certification exam. Although your score on the electronic assessment does not necessarily indicate what your score will be on the certification exam, it does give you the opportunity to answer questions that are similar to those on the actual certification exam.

The Readiness Review book is organized by the exam's objectives. Each chapter of the book pertains to one of the six primary groups of objectives on the actual exam, called the *Objective Domains*. Each Objective Domain lists the tested skills you need to master to adequately answer the exam questions. Because the certification exams focus on real-world skills, the Tested Skills and Suggested Practices lists provide suggested practices that emphasize the practical application of the exam objectives.

Within each Objective Domain, you will find the related objectives that are covered on the exam. Each objective provides you with the following:

- Key terms you must know in order to understand the objective. Knowing these terms can help you answer the objective's questions correctly.

- Several sample exam questions with the correct answers. The answers are accompanied by discussions as to why each answer is correct or incorrect. (These questions match the questions you will find on the electronic assessment.)

- Suggestions for further reading or additional resources to help you understand the objective and increase your ability to perform the task or skills specified by the objective.

You use the electronic assessment to determine the exam objectives that you need to study, and then use the Readiness Review book to learn more about those particular objectives and discover additional study materials to supplement your knowledge. You can also use the Readiness Review book to research the answers to specific sample test questions. Keep in mind that to pass the exam, you should understand not only the answer to the question, but also the concepts upon which the correct answer is based.

# MCP Exam Prerequisites

No exams or classes are required before you take the Administering Microsoft SQL Server 7.0 exam. However, in addition to the administration, installation, configuration, management, and troubleshooting skills tested by the exam, you should have a working knowledge of the administration, operation, and support of hardware and software in stand-alone computers. This knowledge should include:

- How to perform common Microsoft Windows NT administrative tasks, including creating user and group accounts, assigning permissions, and sharing folders

- How to recognize networking components, including clients, servers, local area networks (LANs), protocols, services, and network operating systems

- How to install application software

- How to recognize basic computer hardware components, including memory, hard disks, CPUs, and communication and printer ports

**Note** After you have used the Readiness Review and determined that you are ready for the exam, see the "Test Registration and Fees" section in the Appendix for information on scheduling for the exam. You can schedule exams up to six weeks in advance, or as late as one working day before the exam date.

# Know the Products

Microsoft's certification program relies on exams that measure your ability to perform a specific job function or set of tasks. Microsoft develops the exams by analyzing the tasks performed by people who are currently performing the job function. Therefore, the specific knowledge, skills, and abilities relating to the job are reflected in the certification exam.

Because the certification exams are based on real-world tasks, you need to gain hands-on experience with the applicable technology in order to master the exam. In a sense, you might consider hands-on experience in an organizational environment to be a prerequisite for passing an MCP exam. Many of the questions relate directly to Microsoft products or technology, so use opportunities at your organization or at home to practice using the relevant tools.

# Using the MCSE Readiness Review

Although you can use the Readiness Review in a number of ways, you might start your studies by taking the electronic assessment as a pretest. After completing the exam, review your results for each Objective Domain and focus your studies first on the Objective Domains where you received the lowest scores. The electronic assessment allows you to print your results, and a printed report of how you fared can be useful when reviewing the exam material in this book.

After you have taken the Readiness Review electronic assessment, use the Readiness Review book to learn more about the Objective Domains that you find difficult and to find listings of appropriate study materials that may supplement your knowledge. By reviewing why the answers are correct or incorrect, you can determine if you made a simple comprehension error or if you need to study the objective topics more.

Alternatively, you can use the Learn Now feature of the electronic assessment to review your answer to each question. This feature provides you with the correct answer and a reference to the *Microsoft SQL Server 7.0 System Administration Training Kit* (purchased separately) or other resources. If you use this method and you need additional information to understand an answer, you can also reference the question in the Readiness Review book.

You can also use the Readiness Review book to focus on the exact objectives that you need to master. Each objective in the book contains several questions that help you determine if you understand the information related to that particular skill. The book is also designed for you to answer each question before turning the page to review the correct answer.

The best method to prepare for the MCP exam is to use the Readiness Review book in conjunction with the electronic assessment and other study material. Thoroughly studying and practicing the material combined with substantial real-world experience can help you fully prepare for the MCP exam.

## Understanding the Readiness Review Conventions

Before you start using the Readiness Review, it is important that you understand the terms and conventions used in the electronic assessment and book.

### Question Numbering System

The Readiness Review electronic assessment and book contain reference numbers for each question. Understanding the numbering format will help you use the Readiness Review more effectively. When Microsoft creates the exams, the questions are grouped by job skills called *objectives*. These objectives are then organized by sections known as *Objective Domains*. Each question can be identified by the Objective Domain and the objective it covers. The question numbers follow this format:

Test Number.Objective Domain.Objective.Question Number

For example, question number 70-028.02.01.003 means this is question three (003) for the first objective (01) in the second Objective Domain (02) of the Administering Microsoft SQL Server 7.0 exam (70-028). Refer to the "Exam Objectives Summary" section later in this introduction to locate the numbers associated with particular objectives. Each question is numbered based on its presentation in the printed book. You can use this numbering system to reference questions on the electronic assessment or in the Readiness Review book. Even though the questions in the book are organized by objective, you will see questions in random order during the electronic assessment and the actual certification exam.

# Using the Readiness Review Electronic Assessment

The Readiness Review electronic assessment is designed to provide you with an experience that simulates that of the actual MCP exam. The electronic assessment material mirrors the type and nature of the questions you will see on the certification exam. Furthermore, the electronic assessment format approximates the certification exam format and includes additional features to help you prepare for the real examination.

Each iteration of the electronic assessment consists of 60 questions covering all the objectives for the Administering Microsoft SQL Server 7.0 exam. (The actual certification exams generally consist of 50 to 70 questions, although fewer questions are presented if you are taking a computer adaptive test.) Just as with a real certification exam, you see questions from the objectives in random order during the practice test. Similarly to the certification exam, the electronic assessment allows you to mark questions and review them after you finish the test.

---

**Note** For more information about computer adaptive testing, refer to the "Computer Adaptive Testing" section in the appendix of this book.

---

To increase its value as a study aid, you can take the electronic assessment multiple times. Each time, you are presented with a different set of questions in a revised order; however, some questions may be repeated from exams you may have taken earlier.

If you have used one of the certification exam preparation tests available from Microsoft, then the Readiness Review electronic assessment should look familiar. The difference is that the electronic assessment covers more questions while providing you with the opportunity to learn as you take the exam.

# Installing and Running the Electronic Assessment Software

Before you begin using the electronic assessment, you need to install the software. You need a computer with the following minimum configuration:

- 486 or higher Intel-based processor (486 must be running in Enhanced Mode)

- Microsoft Windows 95 or later (including Windows NT)

- 4 MB of RAM

- 15 MB of available disk space

- CD-ROM drive

- Mouse or other pointing device (recommended)

▶ **To install the electronic assessment**

1. Insert the Readiness Review compact disc into your CD-ROM drive.

2. From the root directory of the compact disc, open the Assess folder and double-click the SETUP.EXE file.

   A dialog box appears indicating you will install the MCSE Readiness Review test.

3. Click Next.

   The Select Destination Directory dialog box appears showing a default installation directory (named C:\MP028, where C: is the name assigned to your hard disk).

4. Either accept the default or change the installation directory if needed, and then click Next.

   The electronic assessment software installs.

---

**Note** These procedures describe using the electronic assessment on a computer running Windows 95, Windows 98, or Windows NT 4.0.

---

▶ **To start the electronic assessment**

1. From the Start menu, point to Programs, point to MCSE Readiness Review, and then click (70-028) SQL Server 7.0 Administration.

   The electronic assessment program starts.

2. Click Start Test, or from the main menu, double-click the test name.

   Information about the MCSE Readiness Review series appears.

3. Click Start Test.

## Taking the Electronic Assessment

The Readiness Review electronic assessment consists of 60 multiple-choice questions, and as in the certification exam, you can skip questions or mark them for later review. Each exam question contains a reference number that you can use to refer back to the Readiness Review book, and if you want, you can pause and continue taking the exam at a later time.

Before you end the electronic assessment, you should make sure to answer all the questions. When the exam is graded, unanswered questions are counted as incorrect and will lower your score. Similarly, on the actual certification exam you should complete all questions or they will be counted as incorrect. No trick questions appear on the exam. The correct answer will always be among the list of choices. Some questions may require more than one response, and this will be indicated in the question. A good strategy is to eliminate the most obvious incorrect answers first to make it easier for you to select the correct answer.

You have 90 minutes to complete the electronic assessment. During the exam, you will see a timer indicating the amount of time you have remaining. This will help you to gauge the amount of time you should use to answer each question and to complete the exam. The amount of time you are given on the actual certification exam varies with each exam. Generally, certification exams take approximately 90 minutes to complete.

During the electronic assessment, you can find the answer to each question by clicking the Learn Now button as you review the question. You see the correct answer and a reference to the applicable section of the *Microsoft SQL Server 7.0 System Administration Training Kit* and other resources, which can be purchased separately.

## Ending and Grading the Electronic Assessment

When you click the Grade Now button, you have the opportunity to review the questions you marked or left incomplete. This format is similar to the one used on the actual certification exam. When you are satisfied with your answers, click the Grade Test button. The electronic assessment is graded, and the software presents your section scores and your total score.

---

**Note** You can always end a test without grading your electronic assessment by clicking the Quit Test button.

---

After your electronic assessment is graded, you can view a list of Microsoft Press references by clicking the Review Incorrect Answers button. You can then click OK to view the questions you missed.

## Interpreting the Electronic Assessment Results

The Section Scoring screen shows you the number of questions in each Objective Domain section, the number of questions you answered correctly, and a percentage grade for each section. You can use the Section Scoring screen to determine where to spend additional time studying. On the actual certification exam, the number of questions and the passing score will depend on the exam you are taking. The electronic assessment records your score each time you grade an exam so you can track your progress over time.

▶ **To view your progress and exam records**

1. From the electronic assessment main menu, select File, then select History, and then choose View.

2. Click View History.

   Each attempt score and your total score appears.

3. Select an attempt, and then click View Details.

   The section score for each attempt appears. You can review the section score information to determine which Objective Domains you should study further. You can also use the scores to determine your progress as you continue to study and prepare for the real exam.

## Ordering More Questions

Self Test Software offers practice tests to help you prepare for a variety of MCP certification exams. These practice tests contain hundreds of additional questions and are similar to the Readiness Review electronic assessment. For a fee, you can order exam practice tests for this exam and other Microsoft certification exams. Click on the To Order More Questions button on the electronic assessment main menu for more information.

# Using the Readiness Review Book

You can use the Readiness Review book as a supplement to the Readiness Review electronic assessment, or as a stand-alone study aid. If you decide to use the book as a stand-alone study aid, review the Table of Contents or the list of objectives to find topics of interest or an appropriate starting point for you. To get the greatest benefit from the book, use the electronic assessment as a pretest to determine the Objective Domains where you should spend the most study time. Or, if you would like to research specific questions while taking the electronic assessment, you can use the question number located on the question screen to reference the question number in the Readiness Review book.

One way to determine areas where additional study might be helpful is to carefully review your individual section scores from the electronic assessment and note objective areas where your score could be improved. The section scores correlate to the Objective Domains listed in the Readiness Review book.

## Reviewing the Objectives

Each Objective Domain in the book contains an introduction and a list of practice skills. Each list of practice skills describes suggested tasks you can perform to help you understand the objectives. Some of the tasks suggest reading additional material, while others are hands-on practices with software or hardware. You should pay particular attention to the hands-on suggestions, as the certification exam reflects real-world knowledge you can gain only by working with the software or technology. Increasing your real-world experience with the relevant products and technologies will greatly enhance your performance on the exam.

Once you have determined the objectives you would like to study, you can use the Table of Contents to locate the objectives in the Readiness Review book. When reviewing a specific objective, you should make sure you understand the purpose of the objective and the skill or knowledge it is measuring on the certification exam. You can study each objective separately, but you may need to understand the concepts explained in other objectives.

Make sure you understand the key terms for each objective. You will need a thorough understanding of these terms to answer the objective's questions correctly. Key term definitions are located in the Glossary of this book.

## Reviewing the Questions

Each odd-numbered page contains one or two questions followed by the possible answers. After you review the question and select a probable answer, you can turn to the following page to determine if you answered the question correctly. (For information about the question numbering format, see "Question Numbering System," earlier in this introduction.)

The Readiness Review briefly discusses each possible answer and provides a specific reason why each answer is correct or incorrect. You should review the discussion of each possible answer to help you understand why the correct answer is the best answer among the choices given. You should understand not only the answer to the question, but the concepts on which the correct answer is based. If you feel you need more information about a topic or if you do not understand the answer, use the Further Reading section in each objective to learn where you can find more information.

The answers to the questions in the Readiness Review are based on current industry specifications and standards. However, the information provided by the answers is subject to change as technology improves and changes.

# Exam Objectives Summary

The Administering Microsoft SQL Server 7.0 (70-028) certification exam measures your ability to implement, administer, support, and troubleshoot SQL Server 7.0. Before taking the exam, you should be proficient with the job skills presented in the following sections. The sections provide the exam objectives and the corresponding objective numbers (which you can use to reference the questions in the Readiness Review electronic assessment and book), grouped by Objective Domains.

# Objective Domain 1:  Planning

The objectives in Objective Domain 1 are as follows:

- Objective 1.1 (70-028.01.01)—Develop a security strategy.

- Objective 1.2 (70-028.01.02)—Develop a SQL Server capacity plan.

- Objective 1.3 (70-028.01.03)—Develop a data availability solution.

- Objective 1.4 (70-028.01.04)—Develop a migration plan.

- Objective 1.5 (70-028.01.05)—Develop a replication strategy.

# Objective Domain 2:  Installation and Configuration

The objectives in Objective Domain 2 are as follows:

- Objective 2.1 (70-028.02.01)—Install SQL Server 7.0.

- Objective 2.2 (70-028.02.02)—Configure SQL Server.

- Objective 2.3 (70-028.02.03)—Implement full-text searching.

# Objective Domain 3:  Configuring and Managing Security

The objectives in Objective Domain 3 are as follows:

- Objective 3.1 (70-028.03.01)—Assign SQL Server access to Windows NT accounts, SQL Server login accounts, and built-in administrator accounts.

- Objective 3.2 (70-028.03.02)—Assign database access to Windows NT accounts, SQL Server login accounts, the guest user account, and the dbo user account.

- Objective 3.3 (70-028.03.03)—Create and assign SQL Server roles. (Server roles include fixed server, fixed database, public, user-defined database, and application.)

- Objective 3.4 (70-028.03.04)—Grant to database users and roles the appropriate permissions on database objects and statements.

- Objective 3.5 (70-028.03.05)—Audit server and database activity.

# Objective Domain 4:  Managing and Maintaining Data

The objectives in Objective Domain 4 are as follows:

- Objective 4.1 (70-028.04.01)—Create and manage databases.

- Objective 4.2 (70-028.04.02)—Load data using various methods. (Methods include the INSERT statement, the SELECT INTO statement, the bcp utility, Data Transformation Services (DTS), and the BULK INSERT statement.)

- Objective 4.3 (70-028.04.03)—Back up system and user databases by performing a complete database backup, a transaction log backup, a differential database backup, and a filegroup backup.

- Objective 4.4 (70-028.04.04)—Restore system and user databases from a complete database backup, a transaction log backup, a differential database backup, and a filegroup backup.

- Objective 4.5 (70-028.04.05)—Manage replication.

- Objective 4.6 (70-028.04.06)—Automate administrative tasks.

- Objective 4.7 (70-028.04.07)—Enable access to remote data.

# Objective Domain 5:  Monitoring and Optimization

The objectives in Objective Domain 5 are as follows:

- Objective 5.1 (70-028.05.01)—Monitor SQL Server performance.

- Objective 5.2 (70-028.05.02)—Tune and optimize SQL Server.

- Objective 5.3 (70-028.05.03)—Limit resources used by queries.

# Objective Domain 6:  Troubleshooting

The objectives in Objective Domain 6 are as follows:

- Objective 6.1 (70-028.06.01)—Diagnose and resolve problems in upgrading from SQL Server 6.x.

- Objective 6.2 (70-028.06.02)—Diagnose and resolve problems in backup and restore operations.

- Objective 6.3 (70-028.06.03)—Diagnose and resolve replication problems.

- Objective 6.4 (70-028.06.04)—Diagnose and resolve job or alert failures.

- Objective 6.5 (70-028.06.05)—Diagnose and resolve distributed query problems.

- Objective 6.6 (70-028.06.06)—Diagnose and resolve client connectivity problems.

- Objective 6.7 (70-028.06.07)—Diagnose and resolve problems in accessing SQL Server, databases, and database objects.

# Getting More Help

A variety of resources are available to help you study for the exam. Your options include instructor-led classes, seminars, self-paced kits, or other learning materials. The materials described here are created to prepare you for MCP exams. Each training resource fits a different type of learning style and budget.

# Microsoft Official Curriculum (MOC)

Microsoft Official Curriculum (MOC) courses are technical training courses developed by Microsoft product groups to educate computer professionals who use Microsoft technology. The courses are developed with the same objectives used for Microsoft certification, and MOC courses are available to support most exams for the MCSE certification. The courses are available in instructor-led, online, or self-paced formats to fit your preferred learning style.

# Self-Paced Training

Microsoft Press self-paced training kits cover a variety of Microsoft technical products. The self-paced kits, which are based on MOC courses, feature self-paced lessons, hands-on practices, multimedia presentations, practice files, and demonstration software. They can help you understand the concepts and get the experience you need to prepare for the corresponding MCP exam.

To help you prepare for the Administering Microsoft SQL Server 7.0 (70-028) MCP exam, Microsoft has written the *Microsoft SQL Server 7.0 System Administration Training Kit*. With this official, self-paced training kit, you can learn the fundamentals of SQL Server administration. This kit gives you training for the real world by offering hands-on training through CD-ROM–based administrative exercises.

# MCP Approved Study Guides

MCP Approved Study Guides, available through several organizations, are learning tools that help you prepare for MCP exams. The study guides are available in a variety of formats to match your learning style, including books, compact discs, online content, and videos. These guides come in a wide range of prices to fit your budget.

# Microsoft Seminar Series

Microsoft Solution Providers and other organizations are often a source of information to help you prepare for an MCP exam. For example, many Solution Providers will present seminars to help industry professionals understand a particular product technology, such as networking. For information on all Microsoft-sponsored events, visit http://www.microsoft.com/event.

# Planning

The Planning domain examines the basic steps necessary for implementing SQL Server 7.0 in an organization. These steps include:

- Developing a security strategy
- Developing a SQL Server capacity plan
- Developing a data availability solution
- Developing a migration plan
- Developing a replication strategy

Before implementing SQL Server in your organization, you must gather the information and resources you need to make the necessary decisions regarding these steps.

## Tested Skills and Suggested Practices

- **Developing a security strategy. Consider security issues such as authentication, roles, SQL Server services, application security, and linked databases.**

  - Practice 1: Determine how authentication is set up. Learn about using authentication modes and login authentication. Learn how user logins may be set up individually or using the Windows NT group structure.

  - Practice 2: Determine the purpose of roles. Learn about role types. Determine role setup strategies—whether to set up roles corresponding to Windows NT users, Windows NT groups, SQL Server logins, or other database roles.

  - Practice 3: Identify the SQL Server services. Learn how security is provided for server services.

  - Practice 4: Determine ways to provide application security. Learn the purpose of application roles and Microsoft Transaction Server.

  - Practice 5: Determine the purpose of linked servers. Learn how security is provided for linked servers.

- **Developing a SQL Server capacity plan. Be able to plan your capacity strategy. Consider issues such as file location, filegroups, growth potential, hardware, and communication.**

  - Practice 1: Learn about primary, secondary, and transaction log files. Analyze strategies for the placement of files.

  - Practice 2: Learn about filegroups. Analyze strategies for using filegroups.

  - Practice 3: Learn how SQL Server can accommodate database growth.

  - Practice 4: Learn which RAID (redundant array of independent disks) methods can be used with SQL Server. Analyze the advantages and disadvantages of each method. Compare the use of RAID methods with the use of filegroups.

  - Practice 5: Learn the various network libraries and protocols that can be used with SQL Server. Analyze the advantages and disadvantages of each.

- **Developing a data availability solution. Be able to plan your data availability strategy. Consider uses for backup and restore operations, standby servers, and clustering.**

  - Practice 1: Learn the various backup and restore methods. Analyze the advantages and disadvantages of each method. Analyze strategies for using various combinations of backup methods. Familiarize yourself with backup and restore syntax.

  - Practice 2: Learn the function of a standby server. Read about the benefits of using a standby server over clustering. Determine if a standby server should be used in a given situation.

  - Practice 3: Learn the function of clustering. Read about the benefits of using clustering over a standby server. Determine if clustering should be used in a given situation.

- **Developing a migration plan. Be able to plan your migration strategy, including upgrading to SQL Server 7.0 and importing and exporting data in SQL Server 7.0.**

  - Practice 1: Learn about upgrading to SQL Server 7.0. Analyze the advantages and disadvantages of the one-computer and two-computer upgrade methods. Analyze the advantages and disadvantages of the named pipe and tape data transfer methods.

  - Practice 2: Learn about importing and exporting data in SQL Server 7.0. Analyze the many data transfer methods to determine their advantages and disadvantages.

- **Developing a replication strategy. Be able to plan your replication strategy, including determining replication types and models.**

  - Practice 1: Learn about replication types. Analyze the capabilities of each type.

  - Practice 2: Learn about replication models (also known as *communication topologies*). Analyze the capabilities of each model.

O B J E C T I V E   1 . 1

# Develop a security strategy.

Your security strategy determines the systems and data that users are allowed to access. Follow these steps to determine a security strategy for SQL Server:

1. Choose the appropriate authentication mode and login authentication. Assign users to SQL Server administrative capabilities using server roles.

2. Assign users to database capabilities using database roles.

3. Determine the Windows NT accounts used to run SQL Server services.

4. Plan an application security strategy.

5. Determine security requirements for linked servers.

Authentication identifies the user's login account and confirms connection with SQL Server. Two types of authentication must be determined: the authentication mode for the server, and login authentication for the user.

The two modes of authentication for the server are Mixed mode (SQL Server and Windows NT), which allows the server to use Windows NT authentication logins and/or SQL Server authentication logins, and Windows NT Only, which allows the server to use Windows NT authentication logins only.

The two types of login authentication for the user are Windows NT Authentication login and SQL Server Authentication login. With Windows NT Authentication login, the server recognizes a Windows NT login as a trusted connection. The login ID and password are passed from Windows NT to SQL Server; reentering is not required. With SQL Server Authentication login, the server requires a SQL Server login account ID and password different from the Windows NT login.

Note that using the Mixed authentication mode does not require users to enter a SQL Server login account ID and password unless the user's login account requires SQL Server Authentication.

After connection to the SQL Server, a user must be granted permission to access databases on the server. Permissions are granted by assigning users to roles, mapped to their user logins. *Roles* are administrative units within SQL Server that allow you to organize users into a unit to which you can apply permissions. Roles are used in SQL Server the way groups are used in Windows NT. Roles may contain SQL Server logins, Windows NT logins, groups, or other roles. There are four SQL Server role types.

*Fixed server roles* provide seven levels of SQL Server administrative permissions to which staff members may be assigned. Server roles can contain Windows NT users, Windows NT groups, or SQL Server logins.

*Fixed database roles* provide nine levels of administrative permissions for each database to which staff members may be assigned. Database roles can contain Windows NT users, Windows NT groups, SQL Server logins, and other database roles.

*User-defined database roles* provide a way to create a group of database users with a set of common permissions. Database roles can contain Windows NT users, Windows NT groups, SQL Server logins, and other database roles.

The *public role* provides a way to assign permissions to all users of a database. Analogous to the Everyone group in Windows NT, the public role contains every database ID in the database and is contained in every database. The public role cannot be dropped.

When SQL Server runs on Windows NT, some SQL Server components run as Windows NT services. Part of your security strategy should include determining which Windows NT accounts will be used to run SQL Server services. In a typical installation, the following components of SQL Server run as Windows NT services:

- MSSQLServer service, the database server for SQL Server

- SQLServerAgent service, the agent that runs scheduled administrative tasks

- Microsoft Search service (Windows NT only), a full-text search engine

- MSDTC (Microsoft Distributed Transaction Coordinator) service, a manager of transactions among servers

For these services to run, they must be assigned a local system, local user, or domain user Windows NT user account. These accounts are assigned during SQL Server setup. Local system and local user accounts do not have network access rights and cannot interact with other servers. For this reason, Microsoft recommends that you use a domain user account that is a member of the Administrators local group for the MSSQL Server, SQLServerAgent, and MSDTC services. Microsoft Search service is always assigned the local system account.

To control SQL Server connectivity with applications, you must determine an application security plan. *Application roles*, a new role type in SQL Server 7, provide a way to set up security for a particular application, ensuring that users gain access to SQL Server databases through specific applications only. Application roles are assigned to applications, not users, and are activated when the user enters a password for the application. The Microsoft Transaction Server, a Microsoft BackOffice product, is a tool used mainly by SQL developers to handle connectivity with multiple-tier client/server applications.

When developing a security strategy, you must also consider whether servers will be linked. Linked servers allow distributed queries, updates, commands, and transactions on many data sources across the enterprise. Servers may link when a login mapping is created at the source server between the linked servers, allowing the sending server to provide a login name and password to connect to the receiving server on its behalf. With the default mapping, a linked server configuration will pass the current security credentials of the login to the receiving server. Distributed queries are subject to the permissions set up for the data source at the receiving server. The provider detects permission violations when the query is executed.

Questions related to this objective are designed to determine if you have an awareness of these issues. To successfully answer the questions for this objective, you need a firm understanding of several key terms. For definitions of these terms, refer to the Glossary in this book.

# Key Terms

- Application role
- Authentication
- Authentication mode
- Database
- Database object
- Distributed query
- Fixed database role
- Fixed server role
- Group
- Linked server
- Local group
- Local server
- Login (account)
- Microsoft Search service
- MSDTC (Microsoft Distributed Transaction Coordinator) service
- MSSQLServer service
- Permissions
- Remote server
- Role
- Sa (system administrator) login
- Service
- SQL Mail
- SQLServerAgent service
- Stored procedure
- Structured query language (SQL)
- System administrator
- Trusted connection

**70-028.01.01.001**

You are preparing to deploy SQL Server 7.0 on a computer running Windows NT Server 4.0. You need to grant access to SQL Server to 14 users in the sales department.

The required result is to allow the 14 users to connect to SQL Server.

The first optional result is to minimize the administrative effort needed to grant SQL user access.

The second optional result is to make the user authentication process as simple as possible.

The proposed solution is to install SQL Server selecting Mixed authentication mode. Configure a Windows NT group containing the 14 users. Add the Windows NT group as a SQL Server login and grant the Windows NT group access to SQL Server using Windows NT login authentication.

What does the proposed solution provide?

A. The required result and all optional results.

B. The required result and one optional result.

C. The required result but none of the optional results.

D. The proposed solution does not provide the required result.


**70-028.01.01.002**

You want to grant server-level permission to configure linked servers. Which fixed server role should you use?

A. dbcreator

B. diskadmin

C. setupadmin

D. securityadmin

## 70-028.01.01.001

You are preparing to deploy SQL Server 7.0 on a computer running Windows NT Server 4.0. You need to grant access to SQL Server to 14 users in the sales department.

The required result is to allow the 14 users to connect to SQL Server.

The first optional result is to minimize the administrative effort needed to grant SQL user access.

The second optional result is to make the user authentication process as simple as possible.

The proposed solution is to install SQL Server selecting Mixed authentication mode. Configure a Windows NT group containing the 14 users. Add the Windows NT group as a SQL Server login and grant the Windows NT group access to SQL Server using Windows NT login authentication.

What does the proposed solution provide?

▶ **Correct Answer: A**

A. **Correct:** Since the server has been assigned the Mixed authentication mode, the 14 users in the Windows NT group can connect to SQL Server using Windows NT login authentication. Granting SQL Server access to one Windows NT group rather than to each of the 14 users minimizes administrative effort. Since users connect to SQL Server using Windows NT login authentication, the login authentication process is simple, requiring only the user's Windows NT password.

B. **Incorrect:** See the explanation for answer A.

C. **Incorrect:** See the explanation for answer A.

D. **Incorrect:** See the explanation for answer A.


## 70-028.01.01.002

You want to grant server-level permission to configure linked servers. Which fixed server role should you use?

▶ **Correct Answer: C**

A. **Incorrect:** The dbcreator (database creator) fixed server role is permitted to create and alter databases but cannot configure linked servers.

B. **Incorrect:** The diskadmin (disk administrator) fixed server role is permitted to manage disk files but cannot configure linked servers.

C. **Correct:** The setupadmin (setup administrator) fixed server role is permitted to configure linked servers and mark a stored procedure at startup.

D. **Incorrect:** The securityadmin (security administrator) fixed server role is permitted to manage server logins but cannot configure linked servers.

## 70-028.01.01.003

You want to grant database-level permission to add, modify, or drop database objects. Which fixed database role should you use?

A. db_ddladmin

B. db_datareader

C. db_datawriter

D. db_securityadmin

## 70-028.01.01.004

You want to plan the security of SQL Server deployment in your Windows NT domain environment.

The required result is to configure the proper SQL Server services login account to support communication between your local SQL Server system and remote servers using Windows NT trusted connections.

The first optional result is to allow the SQL Server administrator to set up multiserver jobs.

The second optional result is to allow the use of SQL Mail.

The proposed solution is to configure a domain user account with membership in the local Administrators Windows NT group, apply the Password Never Expires attribute, specify all logon hours, and use the account to run both the MSSQLServer and SQLServerAgent services.

What does the proposed solution provide?

A. The required result and all optional results.

B. The required result and one of the optional results.

C. The required result but none of the optional results.

D. The proposed solution does not provide the required result.

## 70-028.01.01.003

You want to grant database-level permission to add, modify, or drop database objects. Which fixed database role should you use?

▶ **Correct Answer: A**

A. **Correct:** The db_ddladmin (DDL administrator) fixed database role is permitted to add, modify, and/or drop objects in the database.

B. **Incorrect:** The db_datareader (data reader) fixed database role is permitted to view all data in all user tables in the database.

C. **Incorrect:** The db_datawriter (data writer) fixed database role is permitted to modify all data in all user tables in the database.

D. **Incorrect:** The db_securityadmin (security administrator) fixed database role is permitted to administer roles and statement and object permissions in the database.

## 70-028.01.01.004

You want to plan the security of SQL Server deployment in your Windows NT domain environment.

The required result is to configure the proper SQL Server services login account to support communication between your local SQL Server system and remote servers using Windows NT trusted connections.

The first optional result is to allow the SQL Server administrator to set up multiserver jobs.

The second optional result is to allow the use of SQL Mail.

The proposed solution is to configure a domain user account with membership in the local Administrators Windows NT group, apply the Password Never Expires attribute, specify all logon hours, and use the account to run both the MSSQLServer and SQLServerAgent services.

What does the proposed solution provide?

▶ **Correct Answer: A**

A. **Correct:** Server-to-server communications are supported by configuring a domain user account for both MSSQLServer and SQLServerAgent service. The SQL Server Setup program selects the currently logged-in domain user account by default. Configuring a domain user account for SQLServerAgent service ensures that multiserver jobs are allowed. Configuring a domain user account for MSSQLServer service ensures that SQL mail is allowed.

B. **Incorrect:** See the explanation for answer A.

C. **Incorrect:** See the explanation for answer A.

D. **Incorrect:** See the explanation for answer A.

## 70-028.01.01.005

You are the SQL Server administrator, and it is your first month on the job. You need to make a plan for allowing various levels of access to SQL Server, while grouping employees into their respective job classifications. What should you do?

A. Create Windows NT groups for each job classification and map each group to its respective database.

B. Create Windows NT groups for each job classification and map each group to the public fixed database role.

C. Create Windows NT groups for each job classification and map each group to the db_owner fixed database role.

D. Create Windows NT groups and user-defined database roles for each job classification and map the groups to the new roles.

## 70-028.01.01.005

You are the SQL Server administrator, and it is your first month on the job. You need to make a plan for allowing various levels of access to SQL Server, while grouping employees into their respective job classifications. What should you do?

▶ **Correct Answer: D**

A.  **Incorrect:** While Windows NT groups can group employees into their respective job classifications, you still need a method to allow various levels of access to SQL Server.

B.  **Incorrect:** Windows NT groups can organize employees by their respective job classifications. However, the public fixed database role is already available to every user in a database, and does not provide various levels of access to SQL Server.

C.  **Incorrect:** Windows NT groups can organize employees by their respective job classifications. However, the db_owner fixed database role allows members to perform all database activities, and does not provide various levels of access to SQL Server.

D.  **Correct:** Windows NT groups and user-defined database roles can organize employees by their respective job classifications and allow various levels of access to SQL Server.

# Further Reading

The *Microsoft SQL Server 7.0 System Administration Training* volume of the *Microsoft SQL Server 7.0 System Administration Training Kit,* Chapter 1, Lesson 4 and Chapter 11, Lesson 2, contain information about authentication modes and login authentication. Chapter 1, Lesson 4 and Chapter 11, Lesson 3 examine database access through permissions and roles. Chapter 2, Lesson 1 explains how to create SQL Server Services user accounts. Chapter 12, Lesson 3 includes information about use of the sa (system administrator) login. Lesson 4 provides information about application roles.

Use Microsoft SQL Server Books Online (free download available at http://support.microsoft.com/download/support/mslfiles/sqlbol.exe) to search for "authentication" and related areas to view information about authentication modes and login authentication. Search for "roles" for information about fixed server, fixed database, and user-defined database roles. Search for "application roles" for information about application roles. Search for "SQL server services" for information about SQL Server Services accounts.

O B J E C T I V E    1 . 2

# Develop a SQL Server capacity plan.

Developing a server capacity plan involves considering your needs regarding:

- Location of database system files

- Use of filegroups

- Plans for growth

- Physical hardware

- Communication requirements

The location of database system files affects performance. Adequate system capacity must be available to accommodate database system files. SQL Server creates databases by storing data and objects in database system files. A *primary database file* contains the startup information for the database and is used to store data. Each database has only one primary data file. A *secondary database file* holds data that does not fit in the primary data file. There can be one or multiple secondary data files located across multiple physical disks. *Transaction log files* hold the log information used to recover the database. Each database must have at least one log file.

Most databases perform well with one data file and one transaction log file. To maximize performance, create files on as many different available local physical disks as possible. Do not place the transaction log files on the same physical disk with the other files. A file cannot be used by more than one database.

Along with file location strategies discussed earlier, filegroups can improve system performance by controlling the placement of data and indexes onto multiple disks, multiple disk controllers, or RAID (redundant array of independent disks) systems. Adequate system capacity must be available when using filegroups. Filegroups assemble database files together for administrative and data allocation purposes. The system administrator can create filegroups for each disk drive, then assign specific tables, indexes, or data from a table to specific filegroups. Queries for data from the table will be spread across the disks, improving performance.

There are three types of filegroups. The *primary filegroup* contains the primary data file and any other secondary files not put into another filegroup. All pages for the system tables are allocated in the primary filegroup. User-defined filegroups are created by the user when first creating or later altering the database. The *default filegroup* contains the pages for all tables and indexes that do not have a filegroup specified when they are created. Initially, the primary filegroup is the default filegroup, but this can be changed at any time.

The location of filegroups and the files they contain affect performance. To maximize performance, create filegroups on as many different available local physical disks as possible, and place objects that compete heavily for space in different filegroups. Place different tables used in the same join queries in different filegroups; this will improve performance, due to parallel disk I/O searching for joined data. Place heavily accessed tables and the nonclustered indexes belonging to those tables in different filegroups; this will improve performance, due to parallel I/O if the files are located on different physical disks.

A file can be a member of only one filegroup. Transaction log files are never part of any filegroups. If you use multiple database files, create a second filegroup for the additional file and make that filegroup the default filegroup. This way, the primary file will contain only system tables and objects.

As a system administrator, you must provide capacity for system growth over time. SQL Server 7.0 can support terabyte databases effectively. SQL Server handles growth over time by allowing database files to expand automatically, eliminating the need for action by the system administrators. Database size can be expanded by creating secondary database files on separate physical disk drives. The transaction log can be expanded either automatically or manually. In addition to providing room for database growth, SQL Server allows for system expansion by providing the ability to move a database from one server to another.

When planning the physical hardware system capacity, you must consider employing the RAID system. RAID comprises multiple disk drives that provide higher performance, reliability, and storage capacity, as well as lower cost. While RAID is not a part of SQL Server, implementing RAID levels 0, 1, and 5 in hardware can improve SQL Server's performance.

Level 0, known as *disk striping*, uses a disk file system called a *stripe set*. Data is divided into blocks and spread (striped) in a fixed order among all disks in an array. The striping allows operations to be performed independently and simultaneously, providing excellent read/write performance. However, there is no redundancy, and this level provides no fault tolerance.

Level 1, known as *disk mirroring*, provides an identical, redundant copy of a primary disk written to the mirror disk. RAID 1 provides fault tolerance and improves read performance.

Level 5, known as *striping with parity*, stripes the data in large blocks across all the disks in an array. Fault tolerance is provided by the parity information. The data and parity information are arranged on the disk array so that the two are always on different disks. Striping with parity offers better read performance than disk mirroring.

A recommended installation technique is to configure the database on a RAID 0 drive and then place the transaction log on a RAID 1 drive. This technique provides the best disk I/O performance for the database and maintains transaction log recoverability. However, if data must be quickly recoverable, consider configuring the database on a RAID 5 disk. Since RAID 5 provides redundancy of all data on the array, it offers higher reliability and faster recovery.

Although fault-tolerant RAID implementations provide available and current data, they are not a replacement for the regular backup of servers and hard disks.

Various *network libraries* allow SQL Server to use a shared network protocol for communicating with clients. Each network library must be examined from both the client and server perspectives when developing a capacity plan.

The network libraries supported by SQL Server are:

- **Named Pipes:** Installed by default. Allows clients to connect with a named pipe over any Microsoft-supplied transport protocol. Not supported by Windows 95 or Windows 98.

- **TCP/IP:** Installed by default. Allows clients to communicate by using standard Windows Sockets across TCP/IP.

- **Multiprotocol:** Installed by default. Communicates using Windows NT remote procedure call (RPC) over Named Pipes, TCP/IP Sockets, NWLink IPX/SPX, and other IPC mechanisms.

- **NWLink IPX/SPX:** Allows Novell SPX clients to connect using Netware IPX/SPX.

- **AppleTalk:** Allows Apple Macintosh–based clients to connect to SQL Server using native AppleTalk (as opposed to TCP/IP).

- **Banyan VINES:** Allows communication across the Banyan VINES IP network protocol using Banyan VINES Sequenced Packet Protocol (SPP).

Windows NT authentication requires either the Named Pipes or the Multiprotocol network library. Windows NT encryption requires the Multiprotocol network library.

During SQL Server setup, the same network libraries must be installed on both the client and the server. A SQL Server network library requires the corresponding network protocol to be installed on both the client and server.

Questions related to this objective are designed to determine if you have an awareness of these issues. To successfully answer the questions for this objective, you need a firm understanding of several key terms. For definitions of these terms, refer to the Glossary in this book.

## Key Terms

- Database file

- Domain

- Fault tolerance

- Filegroup

- Master domain

- Mirror set

- Network library

- Primary data file

- Protocol

- RAID

- Read performance

- Resource domain

- Scalability

- Secondary data files

- Stripe set

**70-028.01.02.001**

You want to plan the deployment of SQL Server in a Windows NT domain environment. The SQL Server installation must support communication with remote Windows NT systems. In which domain should you install SQL Server?

A. Any domain

B. The master domain

C. Any resource domain

D. An untrusted domain

**70-028.01.02.002**

You are considering a purchase of SQL Server 7.0 for your Windows NT domain environment. Your supervisor is concerned about scalability of the server. How is scalability addressed in SQL Server 7.0?

A. The database size may be expanded by creating a primary database file on separate physical disks.

B. The database size may be expanded by creating secondary database files on separate physical disks.

C. The database size may be expanded by creating a primary database file on a separate physical disk.

D. The database size may be expanded by creating a secondary database file on a separate physical disk.

## 70-028.01.02.001

You want to plan the deployment of SQL Server in a Windows NT domain environment. The SQL Server installation must support communication with remote Windows NT systems. In which domain should you install SQL Server?

▶ **Correct Answer: B**

    A. **Incorrect:** Microsoft recommends that SQL Server be installed in a domain that has access to all user accounts for all domains. Any domain may not have this capability.

    B. **Correct:** The master domain is trusted by all other domains on the network, it acts as the central administrative unit for user and group accounts, and it is the best domain on which to install SQL Server.

    C. **Incorrect:** A resource domain only establishes a one-way trust relationship with the master domain, enabling users with accounts in the master database to use resources in all the other domains. You need to install SQL Server in a domain that has access to all user accounts for all domains.

    D. **Incorrect:** An untrusted domain would not allow you to communicate with linked Windows NT systems. You need to install SQL Server in a domain that has access to all user accounts for all domains.

## 70-028.01.02.002

You are considering a purchase of SQL Server 7.0 for your Windows NT domain environment. Your supervisor is concerned about scalability of the server. How is scalability addressed in SQL Server 7.0?

▶ **Correct Answer: B**

    A. **Incorrect:** The primary database file contains the startup information for the database and is used to store data. Since every database has only one primary data file, located on one physical disk, you cannot expand database size by creating a primary database file on separate physical disks.

    B. **Correct:** You can expand database size by creating secondary database files on separate physical disk drives.

    C. **Incorrect:** The primary database file contains the startup information for the database and is used to store data. Since every database has only one primary data file, located on one physical disk, you cannot expand database size by creating a primary database file on a separate physical disk.

    D. **Incorrect:** Although you can expand database size by creating a secondary database file on a separate physical disk drive, even greater database size can be achieved by creating more than one secondary database file on more than one separate physical disk drive.

**70-028.01.02.003**

Your Windows NT Server computer running SQL Server has four hard disks. The boot and system partitions reside on drive C.

The required result is to provide fault tolerance capability when one hard disk (other than C) fails.

The first optional result is to increase disk read performance.

The second optional result is to accommodate database growth.

The proposed solution is to implement RAID level 1.

What does the proposed solution provide?

A.  The required result and all optional results.

B.  The required result and one optional result.

C.  The required result but none of the optional results.

D.  The proposed solution does not provide the required result.

## 70-028.01.02.003

Your Windows NT Server computer running SQL Server has four hard disks. The boot and system partitions reside on drive C.

The required result is to provide fault tolerance capability when one hard disk (other than C) fails.

The first optional result is to increase disk read performance.

The second optional result is to accommodate database growth.

The proposed solution is to implement RAID level 1.

What does the proposed solution provide?

▶ **Correct Answer: B**

A. **Incorrect:** See the explanation for answer B.

B. **Correct:** Since RAID level 1 (disk mirroring) simultaneously writes the same data to two physical drives, fault tolerance is provided if one hard disk fails. Disk mirroring also provides increased disk read performance, since both of the drives can be read at the same time. However, because RAID 1 requires 50 percent of available disk space for the redundant copy, this method does not easily support database growth.

C. **Incorrect:** See the explanation for answer B.

D. **Incorrect:** See the explanation for answer B.

**70-028.01.02.004**

Your Windows NT Server computer running SQL Server has four hard disks. The boot and system partitions reside on drive C. You want to plan the capacity of your SQL Server installation, but you do not know how the database is structured. A RAID system is available for the server.

The required result is to provide a high level of SQL Server disk read performance.

The first optional result is to minimize the administrative duties of the SQL Server administrator.

The second optional result is to provide fault tolerance capability when one hard disk (other than C) fails.

The proposed solution is to implement RAID 5.

What does the proposed solution provide?

A. The required result and all optional results.

B. The required result and one optional result.

C. The required result but none of the optional results.

D. The proposed solution does not provide the required result.

## 70-028.01.02.004

Your Windows NT Server computer running SQL Server has four hard disks. The boot and system partitions reside on drive C. You want to plan the capacity of your SQL Server installation, but you do not know how the database is structured. A RAID system is available for the server.

The required result is to provide a high level of SQL Server disk read performance.

The first optional result is to minimize the administrative duties of the SQL Server administrator.

The second optional result is to provide fault tolerance capability when one hard disk (other than C) fails.

The proposed solution is to implement RAID 5.

What does the proposed solution provide?

▶ **Correct Answer: A**

A. **Correct:** RAID Level 5 (disk striping with parity) provides excellent disk read performance, since data is distributed among multiple drives and can be read simultaneously. Using the striping capabilities of RAID 5 requires minimal maintenance for the SQL Server administrator. Since RAID 5 adds a parity-information stripe for each disk partition in the volume, fault tolerance is provided if one hard disk fails. Although the use of filegroups could maximize disk read performance and provide fault tolerance capability, filegroups are an advanced database design technique and require definition and management by the system administrator.

B. **Incorrect:** See the explanation for answer A.

C. **Incorrect:** See the explanation for answer A.

D. **Incorrect:** See the explanation for answer A.

**70-028.01.02.005**

Your SQL Server computer has a hardware write-caching mechanism, but it was not designed for database servers. What should you do?

A. Enable write caching on the disk controllers.

B. Disable write caching on the disk controllers.

C. Ensure that the transaction log and database both reside on the same hard disk.

D. Ensure that the transaction log resides on a hard disk separate from the database.

## 70-028.01.02.005

Your SQL Server computer has a hardware write-caching mechanism, but it was not designed for database servers. What should you do?

▶ **Correct Answer: B**

A. **Incorrect:** You should disable a write-caching disk controller on your computer unless it has been specifically designed for a database. Contact your hardware vendor to determine if a write-caching disk controller is designed for use with a database server, as it can damage SQL Server data integrity.

B. **Correct:** You should disable a write-caching disk controller on your computer unless it has been specifically designed for a database. Contact your hardware vendor to determine if a write-caching disk controller is designed for use with a database server, as it can damage SQL Server data integrity.

C. **Incorrect:** To increase performance and decrease the likelihood of data loss, transaction log files and database files should be placed on *separate* physical disks. However, the location of transaction log files and database files is not related to the write-caching mechanism.

D. **Incorrect:** While transaction log files and database files should be placed on separate physical disks, the location of transaction log files and database files is not related to the write-caching mechanism.

# Further Reading

The *Microsoft SQL Server 7.0 System Administration Training* volume of the *Microsoft SQL Server 7.0 System Administration Training Kit,* Chapter 2, Lesson 1, contains information about SQL Server deployment in the Windows NT domain environment, including domains and network libraries. Chapter 5, Lesson 1 provides information about using write-caching on disk controllers. Lesson 2 contains advice on the physical location of database and log files. Lesson 3 provides information about scalability of database files. Lesson 4 supplies details on using the RAID storage system to provide fault tolerance and read performance.

See *Microsoft Windows NT Technical Support Training,* Glossary, for definitions of master and resource domains. Chapter 7 provides detailed information about RAID capabilities.

Use Microsoft SQL Server Books Online (free download available at http://support.microsoft.com/download/support/mslfiles/sqlbol.exe) to search for "files and filegroups" and "using files and filegroups" to view information about database system files, file placement, and database scalability. Search for "RAID," "fault tolerance," "developing a drive performance strategy," and related terms for information about planning the physical hardware system. Search for "communication," "network protocols," "network libraries," and related terms for information about client and server networking.

OBJECTIVE   1.3

# Develop a data availability solution.

Data availability is the accessibility of data in relation to the total amount of time the data is needed. Fast, reliable data access may provide a business with an edge over the competition. Your requirements for data access and their cost drive the solutions you must implement to provide data availability. SQL Server provides the following capabilities to support data availability:

- Backup and restore

- Standby servers

- Clustering

Planning and implementation of backup and restore procedures are the most important tasks for a system administrator. By developing and routinely implementing a backup plan, data can remain accessible and reliable.

There are four ways to back up data. *Complete database backup* records the complete database, including pages containing data and the information used to rebuild database files and filegroups. *Transaction log backup* records the transactions that have modified a database since the last complete database, differential database, or transaction log backup. *Differential backup* records only those changes made to the database since the last full database backup. *File/filegroup backup* records all pages in a specified file or filegroup.

Data can be backed up to three types of backup devices. *Tape devices* record data on tape. Tape devices are slower than disk devices but are the most cost-effective solution. *Disk devices* record data on a disk drive. Disk drives are faster than tape devices but may cost more. *Named pipe devices* are vehicles for carrying data to third-party backup software, which then writes data to tape or disk.

Backup and restoration strategies—which method of backup is used, how often a method is used, where data is stored, and the speed and cost of data restoration—must be determined by need and resources.

A *standby server* (also known as a *warm spare*) is a second server that can be brought online if the primary server fails. The standby server contains a copy of the databases on the primary server, which are maintained by performing backups of database and transaction logs on the primary server and restoring them on the standby. If the primary server or a single database fails, the system administrator must bring the standby server online for the databases to be available to user processes. Since the standby server only contains data from the last transaction log backup, user processes must log in to the standby and restart any tasks they were performing when the primary server failed.

When the primary server becomes available again, changes made on the standby server databases must be restored on the primary server. Otherwise, the changes made on the standby are lost when the primary server databases are backed up and restored on the standby server.

The advantages of using a standby server over clustering are less complexity, lower cost, and flexible server location requirements. Disadvantages include increased management needs for individual server management, and the loss of some data not included in transaction log backup.

You can set up a cluster of two servers to provide high data availability support for SQL Server. A *cluster* is a group of servers that can operate as a single server. The main reasons for using clustering technology are: to reduce or eliminate server downtime for mission-critical systems, to accommodate extremely heavy server usage, and to simplify management of mission-critical systems. A *server cluster* consists of two or more physical Windows NT servers (also known as *nodes*). Each node in the cluster is available to do the same work. Each node's local hard drive contains a copy of Windows NT Enterprise Edition and Clustering Service and is networked to one or more external shared drives containing application and data files. Each physical Windows NT server is networked to a common backbone and to a common network so that each server in the cluster can communicate and detect whether or not another server has failed.

Instead of connecting to one of the physical servers, clients connect to a SQL Server "virtual" server, which has a network name, IP address, disk array, peripherals, resources, and services (including SQL Server). The physical Windows NT Server that actually has control of SQL Server is transparent to clients. When a failure occurs, control of the services and resources migrates to a remaining physical Windows NT Server. This process is called *failover*. At failover, clients must reconnect to the same virtual server name and may experience a brief downtime. SQL Server is started automatically on the secondary node, and any transactions that were in process during the system failure are rolled back.

Questions related to this objective are designed to determine if you have an awareness of these issues. To successfully answer the questions for this objective, you need a firm understanding of several key terms. For definitions of these terms, refer to the Glossary in this book.

# Key Terms

- Backup
- Backup file
- Backup set
- Cluster
- Database backup (also known as full or complete database backup)
- Database file
- Differential database backup
- Failover
- File/filegroup backup
- Media
- Media set
- Named pipe
- Node
- Standby server
- Transaction log
- Transaction log backup

**70-028.01.03.001**

You are the SQL Server administrator. The server has two tape drives. A media set has been previously defined.

The required result is to back up the TESTS database.

The first optional result is to speed up the backup process.

The second optional result is to define all backup files as members of the existing media set.

The proposed solution is to back up the TESTS database to both tape drives using the BACKUP statement with the Medianame option.

What does the proposed solution provide?

A.  The required result and all optional results.

B.  The required result and one of the optional results.

C.  The required result but none of the optional results.

D.  The proposed solution does not provide the required result.

## 70-028.01.03.001

You are the SQL Server administrator. The server has two tape drives. A media set has been previously defined.

The required result is to back up the TESTS database.

The first optional result is to speed up the backup process.

The second optional result is to define all backup files as members of the existing media set.

The proposed solution is to back up the TESTS database to both tape drives using the BACKUP statement with the Medianame option.

What does the proposed solution provide?

► **Correct Answer: A**

A. **Correct:** Backing up the TESTS database is accomplished using the BACKUP statement. You can speed up the backup process by writing to multiple backup devices at the same time. Using the Medianame option allows you to specify all backup files as members of a media set.

B. **Incorrect:** See the explanation for answer A.

C. **Incorrect:** See the explanation for answer A.

D. **Incorrect:** See the explanation for answer A.

**70-028.01.03.002**

You are the SQL Server administrator. The server has one tape drive.

The required result is to back up the TESTS database.

The first optional result is to append the backup to a tape containing a Windows NT backup.

The second optional result is to configure the backup so it does not rewind and unload the tape after it completes.

The proposed solution is to create two new permanent backup files. Back up the TESTS database to the tape drive using the BACKUP statement with the Init and Nounload options.

What does the proposed solution provide?

A. The required result and all optional results.

B. The required result and one of the optional results.

C. The required result but none of the optional results.

D. The proposed solution does not provide the required result.

## 70-028.01.03.002

You are the SQL Server administrator. The server has one tape drive.

The required result is to back up the TESTS database.

The first optional result is to append the backup to a tape containing a Windows NT backup.

The second optional result is to configure the backup so it does not rewind and unload the tape after it completes.

The proposed solution is to create two new permanent backup files. Back up the TESTS database to the tape drive using the BACKUP statement with the Init and Nounload options.

What does the proposed solution provide?

▶ **Correct Answer: B**

A. **Incorrect:** See the explanation for answer B.

B. **Correct:** Backing up the TESTS database is accomplished using the BACKUP statement. However, the Init option overwrites the existing Windows NT backup. The Noinit option (default) appends backups to a file. The Nounload option configures the backup so it does not rewind and unload the tape after it completes.

C. **Incorrect:** See the explanation for answer B.

D. **Incorrect:** See the explanation for answer B.

## 70-028.01.03.003

You want to create a permanent backup file on a disk named testarch and perform a full database backup. Which syntax should you use?

A. USE master
EXEC sp_add_job 'disk', 'testarch',
'C:\archive\Testarch.bak'
BACKUP DATABASE TESTS TO testarch

B. USE master
EXEC sp_add_job 'testarch', 'disk',
'C:\archive\Testarch.bak'
BACKUP DATABASE TESTS TO testarch

C. USE master
EXEC sp_addumpdevice 'testarch', 'disk'
'C:\archive\Testarch.bak'
BACKUP DATABASE TESTS TO testarch

D. USE master
EXEC sp_addumpdevice 'disk', 'testarch',
'C:\archive\Testarch.bak'
BACKUP DATABASE TESTS TO testarch

## 70-028.01.03.004

Your SQL Server system has a very large database partitioned among multiple files that are modified 24 hours per day. You want to minimize the time required to back up the database. Which backup method should you use?

A. Differential backup with full database backup

B. Full database backup with transaction log backup

C. Database file backup with transaction log backup

D. Differential backup with full database backup and transaction log backup

## 70-028.01.03.003

You want to create a permanent backup file on a disk named testarch and perform a full database backup. Which syntax should you use?

▶ **Correct Answer: D**

A. **Incorrect:** The sp_add_job system stored procedure is used to create a new job. The sp_addumpdevice system stored procedure should be used to create a named backup device.

B. **Incorrect:** The sp_add_job system stored procedure is used to create a new job. The sp_addumpdevice system stored procedure should be used to create a named backup device. In addition, the device type "disk" should be followed by the logical name "testarch."

C. **Incorrect:** The device type "disk" should be followed by the logical name "testarch."

D. **Correct:** The USE function followed by "master" specifies that the backup file is created from the master database. The sp_addumpdevice system stored procedure is used to create a named backup device and the device type "disk" is followed by the logical name "testarch."

## 70-028.01.03.004

Your SQL Server system has a very large database partitioned among multiple files that are modified 24 hours per day. You want to minimize the time required to back up the database. Which backup method should you use?

▶ **Correct Answer: C**

A. **Incorrect:** Since the very large database is modified 24 hours per day and is partitioned among multiple files, providing a full database backup and a more frequent differential backup is not a complete backup method. To back up information necessary to redo changes made after a database backup was performed, you must provide a transaction log backup. In addition, differential back-ups of the entire database would not meet the minimal backup time requirement.

B. **Incorrect:** The full database backup and the transaction log backup provide all the information needed to effectively back up the system. However, you would have to perform the full database backup daily, which would not meet the minimal backup time requirement.

C. **Correct:** When the database is very large and partitioned among multiple files, or when your data-base must allow updates at all times, perform regularly scheduled complete database file backups periodically along with frequent transaction log backups. This practice provides the necessary infor-mation with minimal time investment and a smaller potential for system disruption than frequent complete database backups.

D. **Incorrect:** Providing a full database backup, a differential backup, and a transaction log backup provides all the information needed to effectively back up the system. However, you would have to perform differential backups of the entire database daily, which would not meet the minimal backup time requirement.

**70-028.01.03.005**

Your SQL Server database is 500 MB in size and is modified several times daily. The database is stored on a second hard disk and the transaction log is stored on a third hard disk. You need to choose a backup strategy to minimize the potential loss of data. You want to minimize the time required to perform the restoration process in the event your database is lost or corrupted. Which strategy should you use?

A. Differential backup with full database backup

B. Full database backup with transaction log backup

C. Database file backup with transaction log backup

D. Differential backup with full database backup and transaction log backup

## 70-028.01.03.005

Your SQL Server database is 500 MB in size and is modified several times daily. The database is stored on a second hard disk and the transaction log is stored on a third hard disk. You need to choose a backup strategy to minimize the potential loss of data. You want to minimize the time required to perform the restoration process in the event your database is lost or corrupted. Which strategy should you use?

▶ **Correct Answer: D**

    A. **Incorrect:** Since the 500-MB database is modified several times per day, providing a full database backup and a more frequent differential backup is not a complete backup method. To back up information necessary to redo changes made after a database backup was performed, you must also provide a transaction log backup.

    B. **Incorrect:** The full database backup and the transaction log backup provide all the information needed to effectively back up the system. However, you would have to perform the full database restore followed by the transaction log restore, which would not meet the minimal restoration time requirement.

    C. **Incorrect:** Since the database is not partitioned among multiple files, providing a database file backup is not necessary and would require additional administrative, backup, and restoration time.

    D. **Correct:** By restoring the most recent complete database backup and the most recent differential backup along with only the transaction log backups created since the most recent differential backup, you can fully recover the database. This strategy reduces recovery time if the database becomes damaged.

# Further Reading

The *Microsoft SQL Server 7.0 System Administration Training* volume of the *Microsoft SQL Server 7.0 System Administration Training Kit,* Chapter 8, Lesson 1 explains backup types. Lesson 2 provides information about backup and restore strategies. Chapter 9, Lesson 1 includes topics on backup devices and media sets. Lesson 2 explains the syntax for using a BACKUP statement and provides backup procedures. Chapter 10, Lesson 4 provides details on setting up a standby server.

Use Microsoft SQL Server Books Online (free download available at http://support.microsoft.com/download/support/mslfiles/sqlbol.exe) to search for "backing up and restoring databases," "database backups," "transaction log backups," "differential database backups," and related terms for backup information and strategies. Search for "using standby servers" for information about standby servers. Search for "configuring SQL server failover support" and "using SQL server failover support" for detailed information about clustering.

*SQL Server System Administration.* New Riders, Indianapolis, IN, 1999. ISBN 1-56205-955-6. Chapter 6 contains detailed information about backup strategies. Chapter 10 explains standby servers and clustering and discusses which is right for your business.

OBJECTIVE    1.4

# Develop a migration plan.

The methods of migrating existing data to SQL Server 7.0 depend upon the location of the data. Migrating data in previous versions of SQL Server involves upgrading to SQL Server 7.0; migrating data in other sources involves transferring data to SQL Server 7.0.

Using the SQL Server Upgrade Wizard, you can upgrade SQL Server version 6.*x* to SQL Server 7.0. The wizard upgrades databases you specify, transferring all data and objects, replication settings, SQL Executive settings, and many SQL Server 6.*x* configuration options. You cannot upgrade SQL Server versions 1.*x* or 4.2*x* directly to version 7.0; you must first upgrade these versions to version 6.5 and then upgrade to version 7.0.

There are two ways to perform an upgrade. The *one-computer process* upgrades SQL Server version 6.*x* to version 7.0 on the same computer. Since data is overwritten, this method is not as safe as the two-computer process. The *two-computer process* transfers data from a source computer running SQL Server version 6.*x* to another target computer running SQL Server 7.0. Since data is copied, this method is safer than the one-computer process.

There are two methods of data transfer during the upgrade. The *named pipe method* transfers data in memory directly from SQL Server 6.*x* to SQL Server 7.0. This method is safer and more reliable than tape. The *tape method* requires a Windows NT tape driver and is used when there is insufficient disk space for a named pipe transfer. Usually, SQL Server 6.*x* data is exported to tape, deleted from the disk, and then imported to SQL Server 7.0. For large databases, this method is faster than the named pipe method.

Before beginning an upgrade, you must consider which upgrade and data transfer methods best suit your application.

Since many applications (for example, mainframe, e-mail, or spreadsheets) do not use SQL Server as a primary data source, data must often be transferred to SQL

Server 7.0. SQL Server provides many methods for transferring data between and among databases, including:

- Bulk copy libraries and the bcp command prompt utility, which import and export data between SQL Server and a data file.

- The BULK INSERT statement, which imports data from a data file to SQL Server.

- Distributed queries, which select data from another data source and can also be used to specify the data to be inserted.

- Data Transformation Services (DTS), which provide import and export wizards, or DTS Designer to create a package that can be used to import or export data. The package can also transform data during the import or export process.

- The SELECT INTO statement, which creates a new table based on an existing table.

- The INSERT statement, which adds data to an existing table.

- SQL Server replication, which allows you to make duplicate copies of your data, move those copies to different locations, and synchronize the data automatically so that all copies have the same data values. Replication can be implemented between databases on the same or different servers.

Each method can accomplish varying tasks with varying levels of effort for the system administrator. Before beginning an upgrade, you must consider which import or export methods best suit your application. Considerations include source and destination data format, source and destination data location, whether import and/or export are required, whether data manipulation is required, import or export frequency, import or export method usability, and import or export method performance.

Questions related to this objective are designed to determine if you have an awareness of these issues. To successfully answer the questions for this objective, you need a firm understanding of several key terms. For definitions of these terms, refer to the Glossary in this book.

# Key Terms

- Bcp utility

- Database object

- Data transfer

- Data Transformation Services (DTS)

- Data type

- Dependencies

- Distributed query

- Distribution database

- Distributor

- Migration

- Named pipe

- Publisher

- Query

- Replication

- Replication settings

- ScriptSort order

- SQL Executive settings

- SQL Server Upgrade Wizard

- Subscriber

- Tape backup

- Tempdb

- Transaction log

- Unicode

- Unicode collation

## 70-028.01.04.001

Your company uses SQL Server 4.2 on a computer running Windows NT Server 3.51, and you want to upgrade to SQL Server 7.0.

The required result is to upgrade your database directly to version 7.0.

The first optional result is to transfer replication settings.

The second optional result is to transfer SQL Executive settings.

The proposed solution is to install Windows NT Server 4.0, apply Service Pack 4, install SQL Server 7.0, and use the SQL Server Upgrade Wizard to upgrade the version 4.2 databases directly to version 7.0.

What does the proposed solution provide?

A. The required result and all optional results.

B. The required result and one of the optional results.

C. The required result but none of the optional results.

D. The proposed solution does not provide the required result.

## 70-028.01.04.001

Your company uses SQL Server 4.2 on a computer running Windows NT Server 3.51, and you want to upgrade to SQL Server 7.0.

The required result is to upgrade your database directly to version 7.0.

The first optional result is to transfer replication settings.

The second optional result is to transfer SQL Executive settings.

The proposed solution is to install Windows NT Server 4.0, apply Service Pack 4, install SQL Server 7.0, and use the SQL Server Upgrade Wizard to upgrade the version 4.2 databases directly to version 7.0.

What does the proposed solution provide?

▶ **Correct Answer: D**

A. **Incorrect:** See the explanation for answer D.

B. **Incorrect:** See the explanation for answer D.

C. **Incorrect:** See the explanation for answer D.

D. **Correct:** You cannot use the SQL Server Upgrade Wizard to upgrade your SQL 4.2 database directly to 7.0. You must first upgrade to SQL version 6.5, then install Windows NT Server 4.0 and apply Service Pack 4. Only then can you use the SQL Server Upgrade Wizard to upgrade the SQL 6.5 database to 7.0, which includes the transfer of replication and SQL Executive settings.

**70-028.01.04.002**

You want to upgrade from SQL Server 6.5 to SQL Server 7.0. Some of your databases have cross-database dependencies. You want to delete all of the SQL Server 6.x devices. What should you do? (Choose three.)

A. Upgrade all databases.

B. Upgrade only the databases without cross-database dependencies.

C. Upgrade the databases with cross-database dependencies one at a time.

D. Upgrade the databases with cross-database dependencies simultaneously.

E. Enable the Delete 6.x Devices Before Importing Data option in the SQL Server Upgrade Wizard.

F. Disable the Delete 6.x Devices Before Importing Data option in the SQL Server Upgrade Wizard.

## 70-028.01.04.002

You want to upgrade from SQL Server 6.5 to SQL Server 7.0. Some of your databases have cross-database dependencies. You want to delete all of the SQL Server 6.x devices. What should you do? (Choose three.)

▶ **Correct Answers: A, D, and E**

A. **Correct:** Before creating databases in SQL Server 7.0, the SQL Server Upgrade Wizard provides the option to delete the SQL Server 6.x devices (files, including database files) to reclaim disk space. When you choose to delete SQL Server 6.x devices, the SQL Server Upgrade Wizard deletes all of the SQL Server 6.x devices, not just the ones that you want to upgrade. Therefore, you should upgrade all databases, including those with cross-database dependencies, at the same time.

B. **Incorrect:** Before creating databases in SQL Server 7.0, the SQL Server Upgrade Wizard provides the option to delete the SQL Server 6.x devices (files, including database files) to reclaim disk space. When you choose to delete SQL Server 6.x devices, the SQL Server Upgrade Wizard deletes all of the SQL Server 6.x devices, not just the ones that you want to upgrade. Therefore, if you upgrade only the databases without cross-database dependencies, those databases with cross-database dependencies will be deleted.

C. **Incorrect:** Before creating databases in SQL Server 7.0, the SQL Server Upgrade Wizard provides the option to delete the SQL Server 6.x devices (files, including database files) to reclaim disk space. When you choose to delete SQL Server 6.x devices, the SQL Server Upgrade Wizard deletes all of the SQL Server 6.x devices, not just the ones that you want to upgrade. Therefore, if you upgrade databases with cross-database dependencies one at a time, only one database will be upgraded and those remaining will be deleted. Databases with cross-database dependencies are migrated as a unit by SQL Server and must always be upgraded simultaneously.

D. **Correct:** Before creating databases in SQL Server 7.0, the SQL Server Upgrade Wizard provides the option to delete the SQL Server 6.x devices (files, including database files) to reclaim disk space. When you choose to delete SQL Server 6.x devices, the SQL Server Upgrade Wizard deletes all of the SQL Server 6.x devices, not just the ones that you want to upgrade. Therefore, you should upgrade all databases, including those with cross-database dependencies, at the same time. Databases with cross-database dependencies are migrated as a unit by SQL Server and must always be upgraded simultaneously.

E. **Correct:** Before creating databases in SQL Server 7.0, the SQL Server Upgrade Wizard provides the Delete 6.x Devices Before Importing Data option to delete the SQL Server 6.x devices (files, including database files) to reclaim disk space. When you choose to delete SQL Server 6.x devices, the SQL Server Upgrade Wizard deletes all of the SQL Server 6.x devices, not just the ones that you want to upgrade. Therefore, you should upgrade all databases, including those with cross-database dependencies, at the same time.

F. **Incorrect:** See the explanation for answer E.

**70-028.01.04.003**

You are the SQL Server 6.5 administrator, and you want to upgrade to SQL Server 7.0. Your database has a custom sort order. Your application fails without the custom sort order in place. How can you upgrade from the custom sort order? (Choose two.)

A. Use the sp_helprevdatabase system stored procedure.

B. Use Unicode data types if possible in SQL Server 7.0.

C. Use non-Unicode data types if possible in SQL Server 7.0.

D. Reprogram the application to operate independently of the custom sort order.

**70-028.01.04.004**

You need to plan a migration to SQL Server 7.0. There are SQL Server 6.5 Publishers and Subscribers in your Windows NT enterprise. Which practices are recommended? (Choose two.)

A. Set tempdb to 10 MB.

B. Set tempdb to 25 MB.

C. Upgrade replication servers in any order.

D. Upgrade the Replication Distributor server first.

## 70-028.01.04.003

You are the SQL Server 6.5 administrator, and you want to upgrade to SQL Server 7.0. Your database has a custom sort order. Your application fails without the custom sort order in place. How can you upgrade from the custom sort order? (Choose two.)

▶ **Correct Answers: B and D**

A. **Incorrect:** SQL Server 7.0 does not support custom sort orders. The sp_helprevdatabase system stored procedure is no longer available in SQL Server version 7.0. This system stored procedure did not assist in upgrading custom sort orders.

B. **Correct:** SQL Server 7.0 does not support custom sort orders. Microsoft recommends that you use the new Unicode data types when possible in SQL Server 7.0, since Unicode offers an expanded range of characters and may be compatible with your SQL Server 6.*x* custom sort order.

C. **Incorrect:** SQL Server 7.0 does not support custom sort orders. Microsoft recommends that you use the new Unicode data types when possible in SQL Server 7.0, since Unicode offers an expanded range of characters and may be compatible with your SQL Server 6.*x* custom sort order.

D. **Correct:** SQL Server 7.0 does not support custom sort orders. Applications that depend on a custom sort order must be reprogrammed to account for the new sort order.

## 70-028.01.04.004

You need to plan a migration to SQL Server 7.0. There are SQL Server 6.5 Publishers and Subscribers in your Windows NT enterprise. Which practices are recommended? (Choose two.)

▶ **Correct Answers: B and D**

A. **Incorrect:** See the explanation for answer B.

B. **Correct:** After you install SQL Server 7.0, and before you use the SQL Server Upgrade Wizard, you should set the tempdb size to the recommended setting of 25 MB (10 MB is the minimum value).

C. **Incorrect:** See the explanation for answer D.

D. **Correct:** When upgrading enterprise servers involved in replication, you must upgrade the Distributor before you upgrade any other servers. You can phase in the upgrading of other servers, though you must upgrade all of the replication servers before using the new replication features.

## 70-028.01.04.005

You want to migrate from Access to SQL Server 7.0.

The required result is to re-create the Access database objects in SQL Server.

The first optional result is to change the data type of a migrated database in SQL Server.

The second optional result is to minimize the maintenance of the transaction log.

The proposed solution is to write an object creation script to re-create the Access database objects, run the script, and enable the Truncate Log on Checkpoint option.

What does the proposed solution provide?

A. The required result and all optional results.

B. The required result and one of the optional results.

C. The required result but none of the optional results.

D. The proposed solution does not provide the required result.

**70-028.01.04.005**

You want to migrate from Access to SQL Server 7.0.

The required result is to re-create the Access database objects in SQL Server.

The first optional result is to change the data type of a migrated database in SQL Server.

The second optional result is to minimize the maintenance of the transaction log.

The proposed solution is to write an object creation script to re-create the Access database objects, run the script, and enable the Truncate Log on Checkpoint option.

What does the proposed solution provide?

▶ **Correct Answer: B**

A. **Incorrect:** See the explanation for answer B.

B. **Correct:** Writing and running an object creation script or using the Enterprise Manager to import the Access database allows you to re-create the database objects in SQL Server. It is not possible to change the data type in SQL Server; you should make changes to the data types before migration from Access. By enabling the Truncate Log on Checkpoint option, the transaction log is truncated, minimizing maintenance needed to control the size of the log.

C. **Incorrect:** See the explanation for answer B.

D. **Incorrect:** See the explanation for answer B.

# Further Reading

Download the white paper "Converting Databases to Microsoft Server 7.0" available under "support" at http://www.microsoft.com/sql.

The *Microsoft SQL Server 7.0 System Administration Training* volume of the *Microsoft SQL Server 7.0 System Administration Training Kit,* Chapter 3, Lesson 1 provides details on upgrading from SQL Server 4.2 and removing SQL Server 6.*x* devices during an upgrade. Lesson 2 covers the options encountered while using the SQL Server Upgrade Wizard.

Use Microsoft SQL Server Books Online (free download available at http://support.microsoft.com/download/support/mslfiles/sqlbol.exe and search for "upgrading from an earlier version of SQL Server" and "which versions can be upgraded" for information about upgrading to SQL Server 7.0. Search for "data transfer method" for details on deleting SQL Server 6.*x* devices during an upgrade. Search for "upgrading a custom sort order" for information about upgrading databases with custom sort orders. Search for "replication and upgrading" for details on upgrading a system using replication. Search for "migrating database objects from Access to SQL Server" and "data types in Access and SQL Server" for details on migrating Access to SQL Server. Search for "choosing tools to import or export data" for information about transferring data into and out of databases.

View the Microsoft Tech Talk on "Preparing for SQL Server 7.0: Setup and Upgrade" available under "support" at http://www.microsoft.com/sql.

The *Microsoft SQL Server 7.0 Resource Guide,* Chapter 19, covers the migration of Access databases to SQL Server in detail.

# Develop a replication strategy.

Replication allows you to distribute data from one SQL server to others in various locations. Using a Publisher server and a Distributor server, you can automate the distribution of data to Subscriber servers. In SQL Server 7.0, Subscribers are also permitted to update data at the Publisher. Since a replication system is complex and valuable to an organization, implementation requires careful planning of replication types and models for maximum benefit from a minimum of network resources.

Replication types provide different capabilities and attributes for latency, autonomy, data consistency, conflicts, and network resources during replication. There are three replication types. With *snapshot replication*, a picture of the entire current data (changed and unchanged) at a source server refreshes data at a destination server at scheduled intervals or on demand. With *transactional replication*, only changed data is distributed as the changes occur. Since the sequence of transactions is maintained and changes are made in one location, conflicts do not occur. With *merge replication*, multiple sites (both Publishers and Subscribers) independently make data changes, which are periodically merged together at the source server. Since the sequence of transactions is not logged and changes are made in multiple locations, conflicts may occur.

*Replication models* (also known as *communication topologies*) define the relationship and synchronization between replicas of the database. Specifically, replication models determine:

- The length of time required for data changes to get from a Publisher to a Subscriber

- Whether update failures prevent Subscribers from being updated

- The order in which data changes are sent to Subscribers

There are three main replication models. In the Central Publisher/Distributor model (default), the Publisher and the Distributor can reside on one server or on separate servers. The publication server is the primary source of all replicated data supplied to

Subscribers. The distribution server stores data before the data is replicated to the subscribing servers.

In the Central Subscriber/Multiple Publishers model, multiple Publishers replicate information into a common destination table at a Subscriber. This model allows for the consolidation of data at a central site, providing the local sites with local data only.

In the Multiple Publishers/Multiple Subscribers model, two servers publish the same data. One Publisher sends data to a Subscriber, which publishes the data to other Subscribers. This model is used when data must be sent to Subscribers over a slow or expensive communications link.

Questions related to this objective are designed to determine if you have an awareness of these issues. To successfully answer the questions for this objective, you need a firm understanding of several key terms. For definitions of these terms, refer to the Glossary in this book.

## Key Terms

- Distributor

- Merge replication

- Publication

- Publisher

- Replication

- Replication model

- Replication type

- Snapshot replication

- Subscriber

- Transactional replication

**70-028.01.05.001**

You need to plan a replication strategy for your SQL Server 7.0 installation. There are four sites that need to update data independently of each other. To synchronize the copies but not maintain transaction ordering, which replication type should you use?

A. Merge

B. Snapshot

C. Snapshot with updating Subscribers

D. Transactional with updating Subscribers

**70-028.01.05.002**

Which type of SQL Server replication is the least complex, simply refreshing the Subscriber on a scheduled basis?

A. Merge

B. Snapshot

C. Transactional

## 70-028.01.05.001

You need to plan a replication strategy for your SQL Server 7.0 installation. There are four sites that need to update data independently of each other. To synchronize the copies but not maintain transaction ordering, which replication type should you use?

▶ **Correct Answer: A**

A. **Correct:** Since the four sites need to update data independently of each other, merge replication is the best choice. Merge replication offers the highest degree of autonomy; however, it does not guarantee transactional integrity.

B. **Incorrect:** Snapshot replication takes a picture of the published data in the database at a moment in time and sends it to the Subscriber. In snapshot replication, sites cannot update data independently from each other, as data moves from Publisher to Subscriber only.

C. **Incorrect:** Snapshot replication with updating Subscribers allows Subscribers to update data but does not allow sites to make changes independently of each other. The two-phase commit protocol (2PC) used by the updating Subscribers method makes data changes dependent on all sites being able to successfully and immediately accept the transaction. If one site is unavailable, no work proceeds.

D. **Incorrect:** Transactional replication with updating Subscribers allows Subscribers to update data but does not allow sites to make changes independent of each other. The two-phase commit protocol (2PC) used by the updating Subscribers method makes data changes dependent on all sites being able to successfully and immediately accept the transaction. If one site is unavailable, no work proceeds. In addition, a key feature of transactional replication is maintaining transaction ordering.

## 70-028.01.05.002

Which type of SQL Server replication is the least complex, simply refreshing the Subscriber on a scheduled basis?

▶ **Correct Answer: B**

A. **Incorrect:** Merge replication is the most complex type of replication because it allows changes to be made independently by both the Publisher and the Subscriber and it merges the changes at a later time, using a complex algorithm to avoid conflicts.

B. **Correct:** Snapshot replication is the least complex type of replication because it simply performs a refresh of data for the Subscriber at chosen intervals, rather than when the data changes actually occur.

C. **Incorrect:** Transactional replication is more complex than snapshot replication because it provides data for the Subscriber asynchronously to Subscribers as incremental changes, while maintaining transactional consistency.

## 70-028.01.05.003

You want to develop a replication strategy. Subscribers need to receive data changes as they occur. Which type of SQL Server replication should you use?

A. Merge

B. Snapshot

C. Transactional

## 70-028.01.05.004

You want to choose a replication model for your SQL Server 7.0 enterprise. You want Subscribers to receive read-only data. Which replication model should you use?

A. Central Publisher/Distributor

B. Central Subscriber/Multiple Publishers

C. Multiple Publishers/Multiple Subscribers

## 70-028.01.05.003

You want to develop a replication strategy. Subscribers need to receive data changes as they occur. Which type of SQL Server replication should you use?

▶ **Correct Answer: C**

   A. **Incorrect:** Merge replication allows data changes to be made independently by both the Publisher and the Subscriber, and it merges the changes at a later time. Subscribers do not receive data changes as they occur.

   B. **Incorrect:** Snapshot replication performs a refresh of data changes for the Subscriber at chosen intervals, rather than when the data changes actually occur.

   C. **Correct:** Transactional replication provides data changes for the Subscriber asynchronously to Subscribers as they occur, while maintaining transactional consistency.

## 70-028.01.05.004

You want to choose a replication model for your SQL Server 7.0 enterprise. You want Subscribers to receive read-only data. Which replication model should you use?

▶ **Correct Answer: A**

   A. **Correct:** In the Central Publisher/Distributor model, the Publisher and the Distributor can reside on one server or on separate servers. The publication server (central office) is the primary source of all replicated data supplied to Subscribers (sales offices).

   B. **Incorrect:** In the Central Subscriber/Multiple Publishers model, multiple Publishers replicate information into a common destination table at a Subscriber. You want to replicate information from one source to multiple destinations. You need one Publisher (central office) and multiple Subscribers (sales offices).

   C. **Incorrect:** In the Multiple Publishers/Multiple Subscribers model, two servers publish the same data. One Publisher sends data to a Subscriber, which publishes the data to other Subscribers. This model is used when data must be sent to Subscribers over a slow or expensive communications link. You need one Publisher (central office) and multiple Subscribers (sales offices).

## 70-028.01.05.005

You want to design a replication model for your SQL Server 7.0 enterprise. Your company manufactures aircraft parts and has five regional warehouses in the United States. You need the capability to centrally monitor the inventory while allowing the manager of each warehouse to manage his/her inventory. On which replication model should you base your design?

A. Central Publisher/Distributor

B. Central Subscriber/Multiple Publishers

C. Multiple Publishers/Multiple Subscribers

## 70-028.01.05.005

You want to design a replication model for your SQL Server 7.0 enterprise. Your company manufactures aircraft parts and has five regional warehouses in the United States. You need the capability to centrally monitor the inventory while allowing the manager of each warehouse to manage his/her inventory. On which replication model should you base your design?

▶ **Correct Answer: B**

A. **Incorrect:** In the Central Publisher/Distributor model, there is one source (publication server) of all replicated data supplied to multiple destinations (Subscribers). You need multiple Publishers (managers) and a central Subscriber (central office).

B. **Correct:** In the Central Subscriber/Multiple Publishers model, multiple Publishers (warehouse managers) replicate information into one table at a Subscriber (central office). The table is partitioned to contain location-specific data as part of the primary key. Each Publisher replicates location-specific data.

C. **Incorrect:** In the Multiple Publishers/Multiple Subscribers model, two servers publish the same data. One Publisher sends data to a Subscriber, which publishes the data to other Subscribers. This model is used when data must be sent to Subscribers over a slow or expensive communications link. You need multiple Publishers (managers) but only one central Subscriber (central office).

# Further Reading

The *Microsoft SQL Server 7.0 System Administration Training* volume of the *Microsoft SQL Server 7.0 System Administration Training Kit,* Chapter 15, Lesson 3 provides details on choosing replication types. Lesson 4 covers replication models and examples of their use.

Use Microsoft SQL Server Books Online (free download available at http://support.microsoft.com/download/support/mslfiles/sqlbol.exe) to search for "replication types," "planning for replication," "site autonomy," and related areas to find detailed information about choosing replication types. Search for "topology types" and related areas for details on designing the appropriate replication model.

*SQL Server System Administration.* New Riders, Indianapolis, IN, 1999. ISBN 1-56205-955-6. Chapter 9 contains detailed information about replication.

# Installation and Configuration

The Installation and Configuration domain examines the issues involved in the installation and configuration of SQL Server. These issues include:

- Choosing the appropriate character set, sort order, and Unicode collation sequence

- Installing network libraries and protocols, services, and SQL Server clients

- Performing an unattended installation

- Upgrading from a SQL Server 6.*x* database

- Configuring SQL Mail and default ANSI settings

- Installing and configuring the Full-Text Search service

## Tested Skills and Suggested Practices

- **Installing SQL Server 7.0. Be able to install SQL Server 7.0 in a variety of situations, including on a server, on a client, with an unattended installation, and as an update from SQL Server 6.*x*.**

  - Practice 1: Review the screens in the installation process. Learn the purpose of character sets, Unicode collations, sort orders, network libraries and protocols, and SQL Server service accounts in an installation.

  - Practice 2: Learn how installation of SQL Server on a client computer is different from installation on the server. Learn about the Management Tools available in a client installation. Recognize the purpose of the Client Configuration Utility.

  - Practice 3: Determine the purpose of an unattended installation. Familiarize yourself with the various methods for creating setup initialization files. Learn procedures for performing an unattended installation.

■ Practice 4: Learn how the SQL Server Upgrade Wizard upgrades databases to SQL Server version 7.0. Differentiate between the one-computer and the two-computer upgrade processes. Compare the named pipe and tape backup data transfer methods.

■ **Configuring SQL Server. Be able to configure SQL Mail and SQLAgent Mail. Be able to configure ANSI database options.**

■ Practice 1: Perform all tasks involved in configuring mail service for SQL Server, including: 1) creating an e-mail account for SQL Server on the e-mail server, 2) configuring SQL Server to log in to Windows NT with an e-mail account, 3) installing a mail client/profile on the SQL Server, and 4) configuring SQL Mail and SQLAgentMail if desired.

■ Practice 2: Read about the purpose of each ANSI database option. Configure the ANSI database options.

■ **Implementing full-text searching. Be able to implement full-text searching, including installation, enabling for columns and tables, and index creation and management.**

■ Practice 1: Learn which setup type allows full-text search installation. Install full-text search during the setup process.

■ Practice 2: Familiarize yourself with the various methods for enabling columns and tables for full-text indexing. Enable columns and tables for full-text indexing.

■ Practice 3: Perform all tasks involved in creating and maintaining full-text indexes, including: 1) creating full-text catalogs, 2) associating tables with catalogs and index names, 3) adding columns to the index definitions, 4) establishing the full-text start-seed value for tables, and 5) populating full-text indexes in a catalog. Learn when repopulation is necessary.

OBJECTIVE 2.1

# Install SQL Server 7.0.

There are a number of ways to install SQL Server 7.0. Depending on your needs, you can install it on a server or on a client or clients. You can install SQL Server 7.0 using the SQL Server Setup Program, using setup initialization files in an unattended installation, or as an update to SQL Server 6.x. When installing SQL Server, you must consider your configuration needs, including:

- The character set
- Sort order
- Unicode collation
- Network libraries and protocols
- SQL Server service accounts

The character set determines the types of characters that SQL Server recognizes. The sort order determines how SQL Server compares, collates, and presents non-Unicode data in response to queries. The Unicode collation provides a sort order for Unicode data stored by SQL Server. It's important to choose the correct character set and sort order during installation, since changing them later requires rebuilding and reloading your databases. Network libraries and protocols determine how the SQL Server and clients communicate over the network. The SQL Server Services account specifies the server account used for SQL Server services.

To install and configure a SQL Server client, the main task is to configure the client network connection with the SQL Server. If you plan to remotely manage SQL Server from a client, you may choose to load specific SQL Server Management Tools and documentation on a client, after carefully considering the users and their needs. After loading the appropriate Management Tools, you should verify operations by running the tools. If the tools allow you to connect to SQL Server, they have been installed successfully. If you are unable to connect to SQL Server, use the Client Network utility provided to properly configure the client software to communicate with SQL Server.

To install several instances of SQL Server with identical configurations, perform an unattended installation. Unattended installations allow you to install SQL Server on a computer without having to respond to prompts. Installation settings are contained in a setup initialization file that is read by the setup program, making installation automatic. The Microsoft Systems Management Server (SMS) also allows you to perform unattended installations on multiple Windows NT servers in your enterprise. The SQL Server compact disc contains two setup initialization files. You can also create setup initialization files to automate installation options of your choice.

The Server Upgrade Wizard is provided for upgrading from SQL Server version 6.*x* to SQL Server 7.0. The wizard upgrades databases you specify, transferring replication settings, SQL Executive settings, and many other SQL Server 6.*x* configuration options. The wizard cannot consolidate databases from multiple SQL Server 6.*x* installations; you must consolidate all of the SQL Server 6.*x* databases on one server and then run the wizard to upgrade the consolidated server. You cannot upgrade SQL Server versions 1.*x* or 4.2*x* directly to version 7.0; you must first upgrade these versions to version 6.5 and then upgrade to version 7.0.

Questions related to this objective are designed to determine if you have an awareness of these issues. To successfully answer the questions for this objective, you need a firm understanding of several key terms. For definitions of these terms, refer to the Glossary in this book.

## Key Terms

- Binary sort order
- Character set
- Client
- Code page
- Diacritical mark
- Dictionary sort order
- Network library
- Protocol
- Replication settings
- Service
- Setup initialization file
- Sort order
- SQL Executive settings
- Unattended installation
- Unicode
- Unicode collation

## 70-028.02.01.001

You want to install SQL Server on an Intel-based computer running Windows NT Server with Service Pack 4 applied. All client computers in the network environment run Windows 95, Windows 98, or Windows NT. Which character set should you specify during setup?

A. Code page 437

B. Code page 850

C. Code page 1251

D. Code page 1252

## 70-028.02.01.002

You want to install SQL Server on an Intel-based computer running Windows NT Server with Service Pack 4 applied. All client computers in the network environment run Windows 95, Windows 98, or Windows NT 4.0 in the United States. In addition, you want to back up and restore data between servers with different sort orders and you want to use the sort order with the fastest processing method to maximize server performance. What should you specify for the Sort Order option during setup?

A. Binary order

B. Dictionary order, case-sensitive

C. Dictionary order, case-insensitive

D. Dictionary order, case-insensitive, accent-insensitive

## 70-028.02.01.001

You want to install SQL Server on an Intel-based computer running Windows NT Server with Service Pack 4 applied. All client computers in the network environment run Windows 95, Windows 98, or Windows NT. Which character set should you specify during setup?

▶ **Correct Answer: D**

A. **Incorrect:** Code page 437 is specified when you want to use United States English only, and it includes character-based applications that depend on extended characters for graphics. Code page 1252 provides greater compatibility with other languages and is recommended when using Windows 95, Windows 98, or Windows NT clients exclusively.

B. **Incorrect:** Code page 850 is specified for MS-DOS applications that use extended characters.

C. **Incorrect:** Code page 1251 is specified when you want to include all the characters used by the Cyrillic languages of Eastern Europe.

D. **Correct:** Code page 1252 is the default character set and is specified when using Windows 95, Windows 98, or Windows NT clients exclusively. Code page 1252 provides compatibility with United States English and some other languages and is also known as the ANSI character set.

## 70-028.02.01.002

You want to install SQL Server on an Intel-based computer running Windows NT Server with Service Pack 4 applied. All client computers in the network environment run Windows 95, Windows 98, or Windows NT 4.0 in the United States. In addition, you want to back up and restore data between servers with different sort orders and you want to use the sort order with the fastest processing method to maximize server performance. What should you specify for the Sort Order option during setup?

▶ **Correct Answer: A**

A. **Correct:** Binary order sorts characters by the value of the character in the installed character set. Since this is the simplest method of sorting and requires minimal processing, binary is the fastest sort order.

B. **Incorrect:** Dictionary order, case-sensitive sorts characters by the order in which they appear in the dictionary with uppercase characters sorted before lowercase, and uppercase characters with diacritical marks sorted before lowercase characters. Because of the amount of processing required, dictionary order, case-sensitive is the slowest sort order.

C. **Incorrect:** Dictionary order, case-insensitive sorts characters by the order in which they appear in the dictionary with upper or lowercase characters sorted in any order followed by upper or lowercase characters with diacritical marks. This method requires more processing than binary order.

D. **Incorrect:** Dictionary order, case-insensitive, accent-insensitive sorts characters by the order in which they appear in the dictionary with uppercase, lowercase, or characters with diacritical marks sorted in any order. This method requires more processing than binary order.

**70-028.02.01.003**

You want to deploy SQL Server on three Pentium II computers.

The required result is to automate the installation of SQL Server.

The first optional result is to specify the Local System account to run SQL Server services.

The second optional result is to specify a typical installation.

The proposed solution is to run an unattended installation using the SQL70INS.ISS file.

What does the proposed solution provide?

A. The required result and all optional results.

B. The required result and one of the optional results.

C. The required result but none of the optional results.

D. The proposed solution does not provide the required result.

## 70-028.02.01.003

You want to deploy SQL Server on three Pentium II computers.

The required result is to automate the installation of SQL Server.

The first optional result is to specify the Local System account to run SQL Server services.

The second optional result is to specify a typical installation.

The proposed solution is to run an unattended installation using the SQL70INS.ISS file.

What does the proposed solution provide?

▶ **Correct Answer: A**

A. **Correct:** Performing an unattended installation would automate the installation of SQL Server on the three Pentium II computers. The SQL70INS.ISS setup initialization file runs a typical installation and assigns SQL Server services to the local system account.

B. **Incorrect:** See the explanation for answer A.

C. **Incorrect:** See the explanation for answer A.

D. **Incorrect:** See the explanation for answer A.

## 70-028.02.01.004

Your company uses SQL Server 6.5 on a computer running Windows NT Server 4.0 Service Pack 3, and you want to upgrade to SQL Server 7.0.

The required result is to upgrade all databases.

The first optional result is to transfer replication settings.

The second optional result is to transfer SQL Executive settings.

The proposed solution is to install Windows NT Service Pack 4 on the computer, install SQL Server 7.0, and use the SQL Server Upgrade Wizard to upgrade the SQL Server 6.5 databases.

What does the proposed solution provide?

A. The required result and all optional results.

B. The required result and one of the optional results.

C. The required result but none of the optional results.

D. The proposed solution does not provide the required result.

## 70-028.02.01.004

Your company uses SQL Server 6.5 on a computer running Windows NT Server 4.0 Service Pack 3, and you want to upgrade to SQL Server 7.0.

The required result is to upgrade all databases.

The first optional result is to transfer replication settings.

The second optional result is to transfer SQL Executive settings.

The proposed solution is to install Windows NT Service Pack 4 on the computer, install SQL Server 7.0, and use the SQL Server Upgrade Wizard to upgrade the SQL Server 6.5 databases.

What does the proposed solution provide?

▶ **Correct Answer: A**

A. **Correct:** Installing Windows NT Service Pack 4 on the computer allows you to use the SQL Server Upgrade Wizard to upgrade SQL Server version 6.5 to SQL Server 7.0. The wizard upgrades databases you specify and transfers replication settings and SQL Executive settings.

B. **Incorrect:** See the explanation for answer A.

C. **Incorrect:** See the explanation for answer A.

D. **Incorrect:** See the explanation for answer A.

## 70-028.02.01.005

Your company uses SQL Server 6.5 on computers running Windows NT Server 4.0 Service Pack 3, and you want to upgrade to SQL Server 7.0.

The required result is to upgrade all databases.

The first optional result is to transfer replication settings.

The second optional result is to consolidate multiple SQL Server 6.5 databases from three SQL Server installations.

The proposed solution is to install Windows NT Service Pack 4 on the computers, install SQL Server 7.0, and use the SQL Server Upgrade Wizard to upgrade the SQL Server 6.5 databases.

What does the proposed solution provide?

A. The required result and all optional results.

B. The required result and one of the optional results.

C. The required result but none of the optional results.

D. The proposed solution does not provide the required result.

## 70-028.02.01.005

Your company uses SQL Server 6.5 on computers running Windows NT Server 4.0 Service Pack 3, and you want to upgrade to SQL Server 7.0.

The required result is to upgrade all databases.

The first optional result is to transfer replication settings.

The second optional result is to consolidate multiple SQL Server 6.5 databases from three SQL Server installations.

The proposed solution is to install Windows NT Service Pack 4 on the computers, install SQL Server 7.0, and use the SQL Server Upgrade Wizard to upgrade the SQL Server 6.5 databases.

What does the proposed solution provide?

▶ **Correct Answer: B**

A. **Incorrect:** See the explanation for answer B.

B. **Correct:** Installing Windows NT Service Pack 4 on the computers allows you to use the SQL Server Upgrade Wizard to upgrade SQL Server version 6.5 to SQL Server 7.0. The wizard upgrades databases you specify and transfers replication settings. However, the wizard is unable to consolidate multiple SQL Server 6.5 databases from multiple servers. To perform this function, consolidate the SQL Server 6.5 databases on one server and then use the wizard to upgrade the consolidated server.

C. **Incorrect:** See the explanation for answer B.

D. **Incorrect:** See the explanation for answer B.

# Further Reading

The *Microsoft SQL Server 7.0 System Administration Training* volume of the *Microsoft SQL Server 7.0 System Administration Training Kit,* Chapter 2, Lesson 1 provides details on choosing character sets and sort orders. Chapter 3, Lesson 2 covers the options encountered while using the SQL Server Upgrade Wizard.

Use Microsoft SQL Server Books Online (free download available at http://support.microsoft.com/download/support/mslfiles/sqlbol.exe) to search for "character set" and "1252" for information about character sets and details on code page 1252. Search for "sort order" and "sort order performance" for descriptions and performance of each sort order. Search for "unattended installation" and "creating a setup initialization file" for details on setting up an unattended installation. Search for "upgrading from an earlier version of SQL Server" for details on consolidating databases from multiple servers.

Download the white paper "Installing Microsoft Server 7.0" available under "support" at http://www.microsoft.com/sql for details on SQL Server setup and unattended installation.

Download the white paper "Converting Databases to Microsoft Server 7.0" available under "support" at http://www.microsoft.com/sql for information about using the SQL Server Upgrade Wizard.

O B J E C T I V E   2 . 2

# Configure SQL Server.

This objective examines two aspects of SQL Server configuration: configuring SQL Mail and configuring the default American National Standards Institute (ANSI) settings. You can configure SQL Server to send and receive e-mail by establishing a client connection with a mail server. The ANSI database options can be configured to determine ANSI default, null, and warning settings.

There are two services for handling mail in SQL Server 7.0. SQL Mail uses MSSQLServer service to process mail for all of the mail system stored procedures. The system stored procedures can manipulate data, process queries received by e-mail, and return the result set by creating a reply e-mail. SQL Mail establishes a simple Messaging Application Programming Interface (MAPI) connection with a mail host.

SQLAgentMail uses the SQLServerAgent service to process mail. You can configure SQLAgentMail to send an e-mail when an alert is triggered or when a scheduled task either succeeds or fails. SQLAgentMail establishes either a simple or extended MAPI connection with a mail host.

There are four main steps for configuring mail in SQL Server:

1. Create an e-mail account for SQL Server on the e-mail server and verify connection of the SQL Server to the e-mail server.

2. Configure SQL Server to log in to Windows NT with an e-mail account.

3. Install a mail client/profile on the SQL Server.

4. Configure SQL Mail. Configure SQLAgentMail if desired.

Database options determine the characteristics of each database. The ANSI database options are a means for assigning ANSI-compatible values to data types. Only the system administrator or database owner can modify database options, set by using the sp_dboption system stored procedure or, in some cases, SQL Server Enterprise Manager. After you set a database option, the modification takes effect immediately.

There are three ANSI database options. *ANSI null default* determines whether the default value for all data types is NULL. The default value is NOT NULL. For

ANSI compatibility, setting ANSI null default to TRUE changes the database default to NULL.

When ANSI null default is set to TRUE, all user-defined data types or columns that are not explicitly defined as NOT NULL during a CREATE TABLE or ALTER TABLE statement default to NULL values. Columns that are defined with constraints follow constraint rules regardless of this setting.

*ANSI nulls* handles comparisons of values to a NULL. The default value is FALSE. When ANSI nulls is set to TRUE, all comparisons of any value to a NULL value evaluate to NULL (unknown). When ANSI nulls is set to false, only comparisons of non-Unicode values to a NULL value evaluate to TRUE if both values are NULL.

*ANSI warnings* determines if errors or warnings are issued. The default value is FALSE. When ANSI warnings is TRUE, errors or warnings are issued when conditions such as "divide by zero" occur or null values appear in aggregate functions. When ANSI warnings is false, no warnings are raised when null values appear in aggregate functions, and null values are returned when conditions such as "divide by zero" occur.

Questions related to this objective are designed to determine if you have an awareness of these issues. To successfully answer the questions for this objective, you need a firm understanding of several key terms. For definitions of these terms, refer to the Glossary in this book.

## Key Terms

- American National Standards Institute (ANSI)
- Client Network utility
- Database option
- Filegroup
- Messaging Application Programming Interface (MAPI)
- Net-Library
- Remote server
- Server group
- Server Network utility
- SQLAgentMail
- SQL Mail
- SQL Server Enterprise Manager
- SQL Server Service Manager
- Startup option

## 70-028.02.02.001

You want to recover a damaged database by using single-user mode. What should you type at the command line to start SQL Server and prevent other users from logging in while you are committing these changes?

A. net start mssqlserver -m

B. net start mssqlserver -f

C. net start mssqlserver -o

D. net start mssqlserver -t

## 70-028.02.02.002

You run SQL Server Setup and verify that the MSSQLServer service starts. You want to use SQL Server Enterprise Manager to remotely administer another SQL server. What should you do?

A. Register the local server with the Cluster Administrator.

B. Register the other server with the Cluster Administrator.

C. Register the local server with SQL Server Enterprise Manager.

D. Register the other server with SQL Server Enterprise Manager.

## 70-028.02.02.001

You want to recover a damaged database by using single-user mode. What should you type at the command line to start SQL Server and prevent other users from logging in while you are committing these changes?

▶ **Correct Answer: A**

A. **Correct:** -m starts SQL Server in single-user mode, preventing other users from logging in. -m also enables the sp_configure Allow Updates option so you can change SQL Server configuration options.

B. **Incorrect:** -f starts SQL Server using the minimal configuration option. While -f enables the sp_configure Allow Updates option so you can change SQL Server configuration options, it does not prevent other users from logging in. Use this option to correct configuration problems that prevent the server from starting.

C. **Incorrect:** -o is not an available option for starting SQL Server.

D. **Incorrect:** -t starts SQL Server with a specified trace flag (*trace#*) in effect. Use trace flags to start servers with nonstandard behavior.

## 70-028.02.02.002

You run SQL Server Setup and verify that the MSSQLServer service starts. You want to use SQL Server Enterprise Manager to remotely administer another SQL server. What should you do?

▶ **Correct Answer: D**

A. **Incorrect:** The Cluster Administrator allows you to manage SQL Server on a cluster.

B. **Incorrect:** See the explanation for answer A.

C. **Incorrect:** There is no need to register the local server since it is registered with the SQL Server Enterprise Manager automatically when you install SQL Server.

D. **Correct:** To use SQL Server Enterprise Manager to remotely administer a server, you must manually register the other server with the Enterprise Manager. Registration information includes the server name, login authentication method, and server group.

## 70-028.02.02.003

You want to connect to a remote SQL Server system. How can you change the client network libraries used for the connection?

A.  Use the Client Network utility.

B.  Use the Server Network utility.

C.  Use SQL Server Service Manager.

D.  Use the Services icon in the Control Panel.

## 70-028.02.02.003

You want to connect to a remote SQL Server system. How can you change the client network libraries used for the connection?

▶ **Correct Answer: A**

   A. **Correct:** The Client Network utility is used to manage the client network libraries (Net-Libraries) and define server alias names.

   B. **Incorrect:** The Server Network utility is used to manage the server network libraries and specify the network protocol stacks on which the server will listen for client requests. The Server Network utility is not used to change the client network libraries.

   C. **Incorrect:** The SQL Server Service Manager is used to start, stop, and pause SQL Server Services. The Service Manager is not used to change the client network libraries.

   D. **Incorrect:** The Services icon in the Control Panel is used to start, stop, and pause Windows NT services and the services managed by SQL Server Service Manager. The Services icon is not used to change the client network libraries.

**70-028.02.02.004**

You want to use SQL Mail to process and respond to e-mail queries. Your mail server runs Microsoft Exchange Server 5.5 in your Windows NT domain.

The required result is to configure SQL Mail and SQLAgentMail to start mail sessions.

The first optional result is to determine the correct stored procedure to use for automating the processing of e-mail.

The second optional result is to minimize SQL Server administrative duties that require your time.

The proposed solution is to install Microsoft Outlook 98 on the SQL Server computer. Configure a domain user login account for the MSSQLServer and SQLServerAgent services. Configure a mail profile for SQL Mail. Use SQL Server Enterprise Manager to view the Support Services folder, access the properties of the SQL Mail icon, and specify the MAPI profile name. Create a regularly scheduled job that uses the sp_add_job system stored procedure.

What does the proposed solution provide?

A. The required result and all optional results.

B. The required result and one optional result.

C. The required result but none of the optional results.

D. The proposed solution does not provide the required result.

## 70-028.02.02.004

You want to use SQL Mail to process and respond to e-mail queries. Your mail server runs Microsoft Exchange Server 5.5 in your Windows NT domain.

The required result is to configure SQL Mail and SQLAgentMail to start mail sessions.

The first optional result is to determine the correct stored procedure to use for automating the processing of e-mail.

The second optional result is to minimize SQL Server administrative duties that require your time.

The proposed solution is to install Microsoft Outlook 98 on the SQL Server computer. Configure a domain user login account for the MSSQLServer and SQLServerAgent services. Configure a mail profile for SQL Mail. Use SQL Server Enterprise Manager to view the Support Services folder, access the properties of the SQL Mail icon, and specify the MAPI profile name. Create a regularly scheduled job that uses the sp_add_job system stored procedure.

What does the proposed solution provide?

▶ **Correct Answer: D**

A. **Incorrect:** See the explanation for answer D.

B. **Incorrect:** See the explanation for answer D.

C. **Incorrect:** See the explanation for answer D.

D. **Correct:** To meet the required result of configuring SQL Mail and SQLAgentMail to start mail sessions, a mail profile must be configured for both SQL Mail and SQLAgentMail. SQL Mail and SQLAgentMail can use the same profile but they must be configured separately. By configuring one domain user login account for both the MSSQLServer and SQLServerAgent services, you lessen the amount of account maintenance required and minimize administrative duties. However, creating a regularly scheduled job that uses the sp_add_job system stored procedure will not automate the processing of e-mail. The sp_processmail system stored procedure is used to automate mail processing.

**70-028.02.02.005**

You want to set the ANSI warnings database option. Which system stored procedure should you use?

A. sp_dsninfo

B. sp_dboption

C. sp_enumdsn

D. sp_dbcmptlevel

## 70-028.02.02.005

You want to set the ANSI warnings database option. Which system stored procedure should you use?

▶ **Correct Answer: B**

    A. **Incorrect:** The sp_dsninfo system stored procedure returns ODBC or OLE DB data source information from the Distributor associated with the current server.

    B. **Correct:** The sp_dboption system stored procedure is used to set all database options.

    C. **Incorrect:** The sp_enumdsn system stored procedure returns a list of all defined ODBC and OLE DB data source names for a server running under a specific Windows NT user account.

    D. **Incorrect:** The sp_dbcmptlevel system stored procedure sets certain database behaviors to be compatible with the specified earlier version of SQL Server.

# Further Reading

The *Microsoft SQL Server 7.0 System Administration Training* volume of the *Microsoft SQL Server 7.0 System Administration Training Kit,* Chapter 2, Lesson 2 provides information about startup options. Chapter 4, Lesson 1 provides details on the SQL Server Enterprise Manager, server groups, and network utilities. Chapter 5, Lesson 3 provides practice in setting database options.

Use Microsoft SQL Server Books Online (free download available at http://support.microsoft.com/download/support/mslfiles/sqlbol.exe) to search for "SQL Server startup options," "starting SQL Server manually," and "sqlserver application" for information about using startup options. Search for "configuring remote servers" and "registering servers" for details on administering remote servers. Search for "network libraries" and "network utilities" for information about network library and utility capabilities. Search for "database options" for details on configuring ANSI settings. Search for "SQL Mail" and "using SQL Mail" for information about using and configuring SQL Mail. Search for "using SQLagentmail" and "setting up SQLagentmail" for details on using and configuring SQLAgentMail.

*SQL Server System Administration.* New Riders, Indianapolis, IN, 1999. ISBN 1-56205-955-6. Chapter 5 contains a very detailed procedure for setting up SQL Mail.

*Using Microsoft SQL Server 7.0.* Que, Indianapolis, IN, 1999. ISBN 0-7897-1628-3. Chapter 9 contains information about setting up SQL Mail and SQLAgentMail.

O B J E C T I V E   2 . 3

# Implement full-text searching.

The Microsoft Search service is a full-text indexing and search engine that operates separately from SQL Server. The Search service allows SQL Server 7.0 to support more sophisticated searches on character string columns; earlier versions supported only basic character search capabilities. Microsoft Search service communicates with SQL Server to perform indexing and searching.

Full-text search service is installed when the Full-Text Search feature is selected during a custom installation. Microsoft Search service is not installed on Windows 95, Windows 98, or Windows NT Workstation clients; however, these clients can use the service when connected to a SQL Server Standard or Enterprise installation.

The Full-Text Indexing Wizard guides you through the process of defining full-text indexing on SQL Server databases, tables, or text-based columns with a new or existing full-text catalog. The wizard also creates or modifies population schedules that determine when the information stored in the full-text catalog is updated.

You can create and manage full-text catalogs and indexes using:

- SQL Server Enterprise Manager and wizards

- Applications that call the SQL Distributed Management Objects (SQL-DMO) full-text catalog and full-text index objects and methods

- Applications that use Transact-SQL and call system stored procedures for managing full-text catalogs and indexes

The basic steps to define, activate, and populate full-text indexes are:

1. Install the Microsoft Search service during SQL Server Setup.

2. Enable the database to support full-text indexes.

3. Create each full-text catalog.

4. Associate each table that will have a full-text index with a catalog and its index name.

5. Add each column that participates in a full-text index to the index definition.

6. Establish the full-text start-seed value for each table.

7. Populate all of the full-text indexes in a catalog at one time.

Full-text indexes are not updated automatically and must be periodically repopulated. Repopulation can be time-consuming and is usually run in the background. The data in full-text catalogs and indexes are not recovered by a system recovery and are not backed up or restored by the BACKUP and RESTORE statements. After a recovery or restore operation, the full-text catalogs and indexes must be resynchronized with the base tables.

Questions related to this objective are designed to determine if you have an awareness of these issues. To successfully answer the questions for this objective, you need a firm understanding of several key terms. For definitions of these terms, refer to the Glossary in this book.

## Key Terms

- Column

- Full-text catalog

- Full-text index

- Full-text service

- Table

## 70-028.02.03.001

You want to install SQL Server 7.0 on a Pentium II computer. To use the full-text search service, which installation option should you choose?

A. Custom

B. Typical

C. Minimum

## 70-028.02.03.002

You want to enable your database to support full-text indexes. Which system stored procedure should you use?

A. sp_fulltext_table

B. sp_fulltext_catalog

C. sp_fulltext_column

D. sp_fulltext_database

## 70-028.02.03.003

You want to associate tables that will have a full-text index with a catalog and its index. Which system stored procedure should you use?

A. sp_fulltext_table

B. sp_fulltext_column

C. sp_fulltext_catalog

D. sp_fulltext_database

## 70-028.02.03.001

You want to install SQL Server 7.0 on a Pentium II computer. To use the full-text search service, which installation option should you choose?

▶ **Correct Answer: A**

    A. **Correct:** The full-text search engine runs as the Microsoft Search Service on Windows NT and is installed when the full-text search feature is selected during custom installation.

    B. **Incorrect:** Full-text search cannot be installed using the typical SQL Server installation option.

    C. **Incorrect:** Full-text search cannot be installed using the minimum SQL Server installation option.

## 70-028.02.03.002

You want to enable your database to support full-text indexes. Which system stored procedure should you use?

▶ **Correct Answer: D**

    A. **Incorrect:** The sp_fulltext_table system stored procedure marks or unmarks a table for full-text indexing.

    B. **Incorrect:** The sp_fulltext_catalog system stored procedure creates or drops a full-text catalog and starts or stops the indexing action for a catalog.

    C. **Incorrect:** The sp_fulltext_column system stored procedure specifies whether a particular column of a table participates in full-text indexing.

    D. **Correct:** The sp_fulltext_database system stored procedure initializes full-text indexing or removes all full-text catalogs from the current database.

## 70-028.02.03.003

You want to associate tables that will have a full-text index with a catalog and its index. Which system stored procedure should you use?

▶ **Correct Answer: A**

    A. **Correct:** The sp_fulltext_table system stored procedure marks or unmarks a table for full-text indexing.

    B. **Incorrect:** The sp_fulltext_column system stored procedure specifies whether a particular column of a table participates in full-text indexing.

    C. **Incorrect:** The sp_fulltext_catalog system stored procedure creates or drops a full-text catalog and starts or stops the indexing action for a catalog.

    D. **Incorrect:** The sp_fulltext_database system stored procedure initializes full-text indexing or removes all full-text catalogs from the current database.

**70-028.02.03.004**

How can you enable a table for full-text indexing using SQL Server Enterprise Manager? (Choose two.)

A. Use the Tools menu.

B. Right-click the table.

C. Use the Action menu.

D. Access the table properties.


**70-028.02.03.005**

You want to deploy SQL Server 7.0 and implement full-text searching. On which operating system should you install SQL Server?

A. Windows 95

B. Windows 98

C. Windows NT Server 4.0

D. Windows NT Workstation 4.0

## 70-028.02.03.004

How can you enable a table for full-text indexing using SQL Server Enterprise Manager? (Choose two.)

▶ **Correct Answers: B and C**

A. **Incorrect:** The Tools menu is used to enable a database for full-text indexing. You need to enable a table for full-text indexing.

B. **Correct:** To enable a table for full-text indexing, use the SQL Server Enterprise Manager to view the database tables, right-click the table, select Full-Text Index Table, and then select Define Full-Text Indexing on a Table.

C. **Correct:** To enable a table for full-text indexing, use the SQL Server Enterprise Manager to view the database tables, select the desired table in the results pane, choose the Action menu, select Full-Text Index Table, and then select Define Full-Text Indexing on a Table. The Action menu contains the same menus you access by right-clicking the table.

D. **Incorrect:** Accessing table properties does not allow you to enable a table for full-text indexing.

## 70-028.02.03.005

You want to deploy SQL Server 7.0 and implement full-text searching. On which operating system should you install SQL Server?

▶ **Correct Answer: C**

A. **Incorrect:** Microsoft Search service is not installed on Windows 95 clients; however, these clients can use the service when connected to a SQL Server Standard or Enterprise installation.

B. **Incorrect:** Microsoft Search service is not installed on Windows 98 clients; however, these clients can use the service when connected to a SQL Server Standard or Enterprise installation.

C. **Correct:** The Microsoft Search service full-text engine runs using the Microsoft Search service installed on Windows NT Server 4.0. However, SQL Server 7.0 full-text search support cannot be used in a Windows NT Server 4.0, Enterprise Edition clustering environment.

D. **Incorrect:** Microsoft Search service is not installed on Windows NT Workstation clients; however, these clients can use the service when connected to a SQL Server Standard or Enterprise installation.

# Further Reading

The *Microsoft SQL Server 7.0 System Administration Training* volume of the *Microsoft SQL Server 7.0 System Administration Training Kit,* Chapter 2, Lesson 2 provides information about installing the full-text search service. Chapter 7, Lesson 2 contains detailed information about creating full-text indexes.

Use Microsoft SQL Server Books Online (free download available at http://support.microsoft.com/download/support/mslfiles/sqlbol.exe) to search for "Microsoft Search Service" for details on installing full-text search service. Search for "full-text indexes" and "creating and maintaining full-text indexes" for details on creating full-text indexes.

# Configuring and Managing Security

The Configuring and Managing Security domain examines the issues involved in the setup and maintenance of SQL Server security. These issues include:

- Determining SQL Server users and assigning user logins to groups or individuals

- Determining database users and assigning those users access to databases

- Listing administrative activities and users that are subject to security, and assigning the users to activities using server roles

- Listing database items, activities, and users that are subject to security, and assigning the users to items and activities using database roles

- Granting users or roles the permissions for database objects and statements

- Determining user and data access by auditing server and database activity

## Tested Skills and Suggested Practices

- **Assigning SQL Server access to Windows NT accounts, SQL Server login accounts, and built-in administrator accounts. Be able to assign server access to Windows NT accounts and SQL Server login accounts. Learn the built-in administrator accounts.**

  - Practice 1: Using the SQL Server Enterprise Manager and the sp_grantlogin system stored procedure, assign Windows NT users and group accounts access to SQL Server.

  - Practice 2: Using the SQL Server Enterprise Manager and the sp_addlogin system stored procedure, create a SQL Server login.

  - Practice 3: Read about the two types of built-in administrator accounts. Familiarize yourself with the uses of each type of account.

- **Assigning database access to Windows NT accounts, SQL Server login accounts, the guest user account, and the dbo (database owner) user account. Be able to assign database access to Windows NT accounts and SQL Server login accounts. Learn the function of the guest and dbo user accounts.**

  - Practice 1: Using the SQL Server Enterprise Manager and the sp_grantdbaccess system stored procedure, assign database access to a login.

  - Practice 2: Read about the guest and dbo accounts. Learn how permissions are set for guest accounts. Familiarize yourself with the uses of each type of account.

- **Creating and assigning SQL Server roles, including fixed server, fixed database, public, user-defined database, and application roles. Be able to create and assign server roles.**

  - Practice 1: Learn the purpose of fixed server roles. Use the SQL Server Enterprise Manager and the sp_addsrvrolemember system stored procedure to add members to fixed server roles.

  - Practice 2: Learn the purpose of fixed and user-defined database roles. Use the SQL Server Enterprise Manager or the sp_addrolemember system stored procedure to add members to fixed or user-defined database roles. Using SQL Server Enterprise Manager or the sp_addrole system stored procedure, create a user-defined database role.

  - Practice 3: Learn how public roles are created. Read how permissions set for the public role affect security.

  - Practice 4: Learn the purpose of application roles. Using SQL Server Enterprise Manager or the sp_addapprole system stored procedure, create a new application role.

- **Granting to database users and roles the appropriate permissions for database objects and statements.**

  - Practice 1: Learn the purpose of the three permission types: object, statement, and implied. Familiarize yourself with the various object and statement permissions. Learn the purpose of the three permission states: grant, revoke, and deny. Read how permission states assigned to individuals, groups, and roles can conflict.

  - Practice 2: Using SQL Server Enterprise Manager and the GRANT statement, assign object and statement permissions.

  - Practice 3: Familiarize yourself with the syntax for activating an application role. Using the sp_setapprole system stored procedure, activate an application role.

- **Auditing server and database activity. Plan for server and database activity audits. Be able to use various SQL Server tools to audit server and database activity.**

  - Practice 1: Learn the uses of the tools for auditing server and database activities, including: Windows NT Event Viewer; Windows NT Performance Monitor; Transact-SQL system stored procedures, functions, SET statements, DBCC statements, and trace flags; SQL Server Profiler; Index Tuning Wizard; SQL Server Query Analyzer; and Current Activity (in SQL Server Enterprise Manager). Use each tool to monitor server and database activity.

# Assign SQL Server access to Windows NT accounts, SQL Server login accounts, and built-in administrator accounts.

To use a SQL Server database, a user must first access the server using a login account. Three types of login accounts can be used:

- The user's Windows NT user account or the account of any Windows NT group of which the user is a member

- A SQL Server login account

- A default SQL Server login account

Users connecting to SQL Server using a Windows NT–authenticated login are represented by their Windows NT user accounts and the accounts of all Windows NT groups of which they are members. Use SQL Server Enterprise Manager or the sp_grantlogin system stored procedure to assign Windows NT users or group accounts access to SQL Server. Only system or security administrators can grant access to Windows NT users or groups.

Users connecting to SQL Server using a SQL Server–authenticated login must be assigned SQL Server login accounts. Use SQL Server Enterprise Manager or the sp_addlogin system stored procedure to create a SQL Server login. Only system or security administrators can create SQL Server logins.

SQL Server provides two default login accounts: System Administrator (sa) and BUILTIN\Administrators. The sa login is a special SQL Server login that has all rights on the SQL Server and in all databases. This login is assigned to the sysadmin fixed server role and cannot be changed. The login is provided for backward compatibility with earlier versions of SQL Server and should not be used routinely. Rather than using the sa login, system administrators should have their own logins and should be made members of the sysadmin fixed server role. The sa login should be used only in situations where there is no other way to log in to SQL Server.

The BUILTIN\Administrators login is a default Windows NT login account for all Windows NT administrators that has all rights on the SQL Server and in all databases. Members of the BUILTIN\Administrators group are automatically members of the sysadmin fixed server role.

Questions related to this objective are designed to determine if you have an awareness of these issues. To successfully answer the questions for this objective, you need a firm understanding of several key terms. For definitions of these terms, refer to the Glossary in this book.

## Key Terms

- Application role
- Database
- Default database
- Function
- Local group
- Login (account)
- Master database
- Model database
- Msdb database
- Pubs database
- SQL Server Enterprise Manager
- Stored procedure
- System databases
- System stored procedures
- Tempdb database
- Transact-SQL
- User (account)

**70-028.03.01.001**

You want to allow members of the STSNET local group to connect to SQL Server. Which system stored procedure should be used?

A.  sp_addlogin

B.  sp_grantlogin

C.  sp_grantdbaccess

D.  sp_change_users_login

**70-028.03.01.002**

You want to create a SQL Server login account. Which system stored procedure should you use?

A.  sp_addlogin

B.  sp_revokelogin

C.  sp_grantdbaccess

D.  sp_change_users_login

## 70-028.03.01.001

You want to allow members of the STSNET local group to connect to SQL Server. Which system stored procedure should be used?

▶ **Correct Answer: B**

A.  **Incorrect:** The sp_addlogin system stored procedure creates a new SQL Server login that allows a user to connect to a server running SQL Server using SQL Server Authentication.

B.  **Correct:** The sp_grantlogin system stored procedure allows a Windows NT user or group account to connect to SQL Server using Windows NT Authentication.

C.  **Incorrect:** The sp_grantdbaccess system stored procedure adds a security account in the current database for a SQL Server login or Windows NT user or group, and enables it to be granted permissions to perform activities in the database.

D.  **Incorrect:** The sp_change_users_login system stored procedure changes the relationship between a SQL Server login and a SQL Server user in the current database.

## 70-028.03.01.002

You want to create a SQL Server login account. Which system stored procedure should you use?

▶ **Correct Answer: A**

A.  **Correct:** The sp_addlogin system stored procedure creates a new SQL Server login that adds a record to the SYSLOGINS table of the master database, allowing a user to connect to a server running SQL Server using SQL Server Authentication.

B.  **Incorrect:** The sp_revokelogin system stored procedure removes the login entries from SQL Server for a Windows NT user or group created with sp_grantlogin or sp_denylogin.

C.  **Incorrect:** The sp_grantdbaccess system stored procedure adds a security account in the current database for a SQL Server login or Windows NT user or group, and enables it to be granted permissions to perform activities in the database.

D.  **Incorrect:** The sp_change_users_login system stored procedure changes the relationship between a SQL Server login and a SQL Server user in the current database.

## 70-028.03.01.003

You are behind schedule, and you quickly add a new login using SQL Server Enterprise Manager. However, you forget to specify the default database. By default, to which database do new SQL Server Login properties apply?

A. pubs

B. model

C. master

D. tempdb

## 70-028.03.01.004

You want to assign SQL Server access to some users in your Windows NT domain. All members of the SQLUsers Windows NT group require access. How should you assign access to the users?

A. Add a SQL Server login account for the Windows NT group account.

B. Add a SQL Server login account for each Windows NT user account.

C. Create an application role and assign access to the Windows NT group account.

D. Create an application role and assign access to each Windows NT user account.

## 70-028.03.01.003

You are behind schedule, and you quickly add a new login using SQL Server Enterprise Manager. However, you forget to specify the default database. By default, to which database do new SQL Server Login properties apply?

▶ **Correct Answer: C**

A. **Incorrect:** The pubs database is a sample database provided with SQL Server. If a default database is not specified when a SQL Server login is defined, pubs does not become the default database for the login.

B. **Incorrect:** The model database provides the template for new user databases. If a default database is not specified when a SQL Server login is defined, model does not become the default database for the login.

C. **Correct:** The master database controls user databases and the operation of SQL Server as a whole. When a SQL Server login is defined, the default database for the login can be specified. If a default database is not specified, master becomes the default database for the login.

D. **Incorrect:** The tempdb database provides a storage area for temporary tables, temporary stored procedures, and other temporary working storage needs. If a default database is not specified when a SQL Server login is defined, tempdb does not become the default database for the login.

## 70-028.03.01.004

You want to assign SQL Server access to some users in your Windows NT domain. All members of the SQLUsers Windows NT group require access. How should you assign access to the users?

▶ **Correct Answer: A**

A. **Correct:** Since the entire SQLUsers Windows NT group requires access to SQL Server, you can add a login account for the group.

B. **Incorrect:** Since the entire SQLUsers Windows NT group requires access to SQL Server, adding a login account for the group would be more efficient than adding a login account for each Windows NT user account.

C. **Incorrect:** Application roles are SQL Server roles created to support the security needs of an application and cannot be used to assign SQL Server login accounts.

D. **Incorrect:** Application roles are SQL Server roles created to support the security needs of an application and cannot be used to assign SQL Server login accounts.

**70-028.03.01.005**

Your environment includes a Windows NT domain and SQL Server 7.0. You need to find the name of a Windows NT group for a Windows NT group security identification number. Which function should you use?

A.  OBJECT_NAME

B.  SUSER_SNAME

C.  USER_NAME ()

D.  CURRENT_USER

## 70-028.03.01.005

Your environment includes a Windows NT domain and SQL Server 7.0. You need to find the name of a Windows NT group for a Windows NT group security identification number. Which function should you use?

▶ **Correct Answer: B**

A. **Incorrect:** The OBJECT_NAME function displays the database object name and cannot display the group name for a Windows NT group security identification number.

B. **Correct:** The SUSER_SNAME function can display a Windows NT account or group name for a specified Windows NT account or group security identification number. This function can also display the SQL Server login name for a specified SQL Server login security identifier.

C. **Incorrect:** The USER_NAME () function displays the current user, but not the group name for a Windows NT group security identification number.

D. **Incorrect:** The CURRENT_USER function displays the current user, but not the group name for a Windows NT group security identification number.

# Further Reading

The *Microsoft SQL Server 7.0 System Administration Training* volume of the *Microsoft SQL Server 7.0 System Administration Training Kit,* Chapter 11, Lesson 1 provides information about assigning SQL Server access to Windows NT accounts, assigning SQL Server login accounts, and default databases.

Use Microsoft SQL Server Books Online (free download available at http://support.microsoft.com/download/support/mslfiles/sqlbol.exe) to search for "login" or "sp_grantlogin" for information about assigning SQL Server access to Windows NT accounts. Search for "login" or "sp_addlogin" for information about assigning SQL Server login accounts. Search for "system databases" for information about default databases.

OBJECTIVE 3.2

# Assign database access to Windows NT accounts, SQL Server login accounts, the guest user account, and the dbo user account.

After a user is assigned access to SQL Server through a login account, the next step is to assign database access. Database access may be assigned to:

- The user's Windows NT user account or the account of any group of which the user is a member

- A SQL Server login account

- A guest account

- A dbo account

A login account must have an assigned database user account or use of the default database user accounts. A database user account can be assigned to Windows NT users, Windows NT groups, or SQL Server logins. You can assign a database user account to a login by using SQL Server Enterprise Manager, from either the Logins folder or the Database folder, or the sp_grantdbaccess system stored procedure. Only database owners and database access administrators can assign a database user account to a login.

When a database is created, special user accounts—called guest and dbo—are created inside the database. The guest account allows a user to log into a database without a user account. A user login assumes the identity of the guest user when a guest user account is created for the database, and the user login has access to SQL Server but does not have access to the database. Permissions can be applied to the guest account, and the guest user can be deleted and added to all databases except master and tempdb.

Only members of the sysadmin fixed server role, including the sa login account, are mapped to the dbo account. Objects created by members of the sysadmin fixed server role automatically belong to the dbo account rather than to the user's account. The dbo account cannot be removed from a database.

Questions related to this objective are designed to determine if you have an awareness of these issues. To successfully answer the questions for this objective, you need a firm understanding of several key terms. For definitions of these terms, refer to the Glossary in this book.

# Key Terms

- Database

- Database owner

- Dbo account

- Default database

- Group

- Guest account

- Heterogeneous data

- Login (account)

- Master database

- Permissions

- Public role

- Role

- Sa login

- SQL Server Enterprise Manager

- Sysadmin role

- System administrator

- System stored procedures

- Tempdb database

- User (account)

## 70-028.03.02.001

You want to add a user account to a database. Which system stored procedure should you use?

A. sp_addrole

B. sp_addlogin

C. sp_grantlogin

D. sp_grantdbaccess

## 70-028.03.02.002

You want to grant database access to a Windows NT group account using SQL Server Enterprise Manager. You expand your SQL Server in Enterprise Manager. Which folder is used to create new SQL Server logins and grant the logins database access?

A. Security

B. Databases

C. Management

D. Support Services

E. Data Transformation

## 70-028.03.02.001

You want to add a user account to a database. Which system stored procedure should you use?

▶ **Correct Answer: D**

    A. **Incorrect:** The sp_addrole system stored procedure creates a new SQL Server role in the current database.

    B. **Incorrect:** The sp_addlogin system stored procedure creates a new SQL Server login that allows a user to connect to a server running SQL Server using SQL Server Authentication.

    C. **Incorrect:** The sp_grantlogin system stored procedure allows a Windows NT user or group account to connect to SQL Server using Windows NT Authentication.

    D. **Correct.** The sp_grantdbaccess system stored procedure adds a security account in the current database for a SQL Server login or Windows NT user or group, and enables it to be granted permissions to perform activities in the database.

## 70-028.03.02.002

You want to grant database access to a Windows NT group account using SQL Server Enterprise Manager. You expand your SQL Server in Enterprise Manager. Which folder is used to create new SQL Server logins and grant the logins database access?

▶ **Correct Answer: A**

    A. **Correct:** The Security folder contains the Logins object, which allows you to assign SQL Server logins and specify the databases that can be accessed by the login.

    B. **Incorrect:** The Databases folder in the SQL Server Enterprise Manager allows you to select a particular database and view its contents and properties; however, you cannot assign SQL Server logins using the Databases folder.

    C. **Incorrect:** The Management folder contains management functions for SQL Server, including SQL Server Agent, SQL Server Logs, and the Current Activity window.

    D. **Incorrect:** The Support Services folder allows you to administer support services, including full-text search and SQL Mail.

    E. **Incorrect:** The Data Transformation folder provides access to Data Transformation Services, which enable you to import and export data between multiple heterogeneous sources.

## 70-028.03.02.003

Because all permissions assigned to the public role are applied to the _____ user account, you should use caution when assigning permissions to the public role.

A. Guest

B. Administrator

C. SQLAgentCmdExec

D. IUSR_<*computername*>

## 70-028.03.02.004

Under which two conditions do logins assume the identity of the guest user account? (Choose two.)

A. The database contains a guest user account.

B. The Windows NT domain contains a guest user account.

C. The login has access to SQL Server but does not have access to the database through its own user account.

D. The login does not have access to SQL Server and does not have access to the database through its own user account.

**70-028.03.02.003**

Because all permissions assigned to the public role are applied to the _____ user account, you should use caution when assigning permissions to the public role.

▶ **Correct Answer: A**

A. **Correct:** There are two default user accounts: dbo and guest. The guest user account is not given any permissions, but is by default a member of the public role. To ensure database security, drop the guest user account if necessary.

B. **Incorrect:** Permissions assigned to the public role are not applied to the administrator account. An administrator account is for users whose job function requires full permissions.

C. **Incorrect:** The SQLAgentCmdExec is an account assigned to non-sysadmin users, allowing them to execute CmdExec and ActiveScripting job steps. Since the SQLAgentCmdExec account is used on the SQL Server Agent service and not on the SQL Server service, permissions assigned to the public role are not applied to the SQLAgentCmdExec account.

D. **Incorrect:** IUSR_*<computername>* is the account used by Microsoft Internet Information Server for anonymous connections to the server. IUSR_*<computername>* is not used by SQL Server.


**70-028.03.02.004**

Under which two conditions do logins assume the identity of the guest user account? (Choose two.)

▶ **Correct Answers: A and C**

A. **Correct:** One of the conditions for a user login assuming the identity of the guest user is that a guest user account must first be created for the database.

B. **Incorrect:** The Windows NT domain does not need to contain a guest user account for the user login to assume the identity of a guest user account in SQL Server.

C. **Correct:** One of the conditions for a user login assuming the identity of the guest user is when the user login can connect to SQL Server but does not already have access to the database.

D. **Incorrect:** One of the conditions for a user login assuming the identity of the guest user is when the user login *does* have access to SQL Server but does not already have access to the database.

## 70-028.03.02.005

You want to grant database access to some logins. To which of the following can user accounts be assigned? (Choose three.)

A. Windows NT users

B. Windows NT groups

C. SQL Server logins

D. SQL Server groups

**70-028.03.02.005**

You want to grant database access to some logins. To which of the following can user accounts be assigned? (Choose three.)

▶ **Correct Answers: A, B, and C**

A. **Correct:** SQL Server user accounts may be assigned to Windows NT users.

B. **Correct:** SQL Server user accounts may be assigned to Windows NT groups.

C. **Correct:** SQL Server user accounts may be assigned to SQL server logins.

D. **Incorrect:** SQL Server 7.0 does not use groups. Instead, roles are used to assign permissions to multiple users.

# Further Reading

The *Microsoft SQL Server 7.0 System Administration Training* volume of the *Microsoft SQL Server 7.0 System Administration Training Kit,* Chapter 11, Lesson 3 provides details on assigning database access to Windows NT users, Windows NT groups, or SQL Server logins. This lesson also contains definitions of the guest and dbo accounts.

Use Microsoft SQL Server Books Online (free download available at http: // support.microsoft.com/download/support/mslfiles/sqlbol.exe) to search for "sp_grantdbaccess" for information about assigning database access to Windows NT users, Windows NT groups, or SQL Server logins. Search for "guest" for information about the guest account. Search for "dbo" for information about the dbo account.

OBJECTIVE 3.3

# Create and assign SQL Server roles.

After assigning SQL Server access and database access, the next level of security is provided by creating and assigning SQL Server roles. Roles are administrative units within SQL Server that allow you to organize users into a unit to which you can apply permissions. There are four SQL Server role types:

- Fixed server roles

- Fixed database roles

- User-defined database roles

- Application roles

Fixed server roles provide administrative tasks on SQL Server. Server roles can contain Windows NT users, Windows NT groups, or SQL Server logins. Server roles for SQL Server are fixed and no new server roles may be added. Fixed server roles and their abilities are listed below.

- **sysadmin:** Has permission to perform any activity in SQL Server

- **serveradmin:** Has permission to configure serverwide settings

- **setupadmin:** Has permission to install replication and manage extended procedures

- **securityadmin:** Has permission to manage server logins

- **processadmin:** Has permission to manage processes running in SQL Server

- **dbcreator:** Has permission to create and alter databases

- **diskadmin:** Has permission to manage disk files

Use SQL Server Enterprise Manager or the sp_addsrvrolemember system stored procedure to add members to fixed server roles. Members of a fixed server role can execute sp_addsrvrolemember to add members only to the same fixed server role.

Fixed database roles provide database permissions for one database only. Database roles can contain Windows NT users, Windows NT groups, SQL Server logins, and other database roles. Fixed database roles and their abilities are listed below.

- **db_owner:** Has permission to perform the activities of all database roles, in addition to other maintenance and configuration activities in the database

- **db_accessadmin:** Has permission to add or remove Windows NT groups, Windows NT users, and SQL Server users to/from the database

- **db_datareader:** Has permission to view data in all user tables in the database

- **db_datawriter:** Has permission to add, change, or delete data to/from all user tables in the database

- **db_ddladmin:** Has permission to add, modify, or drop objects in the database

- **db_securityadmin:** Has permission to manage SQL Server database roles and to manage statement and object permissions in the database

- **db_backupoperator:** Has permission to back up the database

- **db_denydatareader:** Has permission to make schema changes in the database but cannot see any data

- **db_denydatawriter:** Has permission to view data in the database but cannot change any data

Use SQL Server Enterprise Manager or the sp_addrolemember system stored procedure to add members to fixed database roles. Only members of the db_owner or db_securityadmin fixed database roles can execute the sp_addrolemember system stored procedure. In addition, role owners can execute sp_addrolemember to add members to any SQL Server roles they own.

In addition to the fixed server and fixed database roles, a special role called the public role is added to every database by default, and every database user automatically belongs to the public role. Users cannot be added or removed from the public role. Permissions may be assigned to the public role. Use caution when assigning public role permissions, since the permissions assigned to the public role are assigned to all database users. The public role may be compared to the Everyone group in Windows NT.

When there is no applicable Windows NT group, or if you do not have permissions to manage Windows NT user accounts, user-defined database roles allow you to create your own group of database users with a set of common permissions. User-defined database roles can contain Windows NT users, Windows NT groups, SQL Server logins, and other database roles.

Use SQL Server Enterprise Manager or the sp_addrole system stored procedure to create a new user-defined database role. Only members of the db_owner, db_securityadmin, and sysadmin roles can execute the sp_addrole system stored procedure. Use SQL Server Enterprise Manager or the sp_addrolemember system stored procedure to add members to user-defined database roles. Only members of the db_owner or db_securityadmin fixed database roles can execute the sp_addrolemember system stored procedure. In addition, role owners can execute sp_addrolemember to add members to any SQL Server roles they own.

Application roles allow you to set up security for a particular application, ensuring that users gain access to data through specific applications only. Application roles differ from other roles in that they have no members. When a user signs on to an application, the application role is activated, controlling all database access for the user's connection.

Application roles also require a password (usually incorporated within the application) to be activated. An activated application role temporarily overrides the user's other permissions in the database.

You can use SQL Server Enterprise Manager or the sp_addapprole system stored procedure to create a new application role. Only members of the db_owner, db_securityadmin, and sysadmin roles can execute the sp_addapprole system stored procedure.

Questions related to this objective are designed to determine if you have an awareness of these issues. To successfully answer the questions for this objective, you need a firm understanding of several key terms. For definitions of these terms, refer to the Glossary in this book.

# Key Terms

- Application role

- Database

- Everyone group

- Fixed database role

- Fixed server role

- Object

- Permissions

- Public role

- Role

- Schema

- SQL Server Enterprise Manager

- System stored procedures

- Table

- User (account)

- User-defined database role

## 70-028.03.03.001

You want to drop a security account from the db_backupoperator fixed database role. Which system stored procedure should you use?

A. sp_droprole

B. sp_dropapprole

C. sp_droprolemember

D. sp_dropsrvrolemember

## 70-028.03.03.002

You are the SQL Server administrator, and you need to implement security for a database.

The required result is to allow a group of 10 users to access five tables in the SALES database.

The first optional result is to permit users access when they use a custom data input application.

The second optional result is to configure SQL Server to ignore all existing permissions in the SALES database for the 10 user accounts and any roles to which they belong.

The proposed solution is to define an application role for the custom application. Assign the appropriate permissions to access the five tables in the SALES database. Provide users with the password information needed so that the application can use the sp_setapprole system stored procedure to activate the application role.

What does the proposed solution provide?

A. The required result and all optional results.

B. The required result and one of the optional results.

C. The required result but none of the optional results.

D. The proposed solution does not provide the required result.

## 70-028.03.03.001

You want to drop a security account from the db_backupoperator fixed database role. Which system stored procedure should you use?

▶ **Correct Answer: C**

    A. **Incorrect:** The sp_droprole system stored procedure removes a SQL Server role from the current database.

    B. **Incorrect:** The sp_dropapprole system stored procedure removes an application role from the current database.

    C. **Correct:** The sp_droprolemember system stored procedure removes an account from a SQL Server role in the current database.

    D. **Incorrect:** The sp_dropsrvrolemember system stored procedure removes a SQL Server login or a Windows NT user or group from a fixed server role.

## 70-028.03.03.002

You are the SQL Server administrator, and you need to implement security for a database.

The required result is to allow a group of 10 users to access five tables in the SALES database.

The first optional result is to permit users access when they use a custom data input application.

The second optional result is to configure SQL Server to ignore all existing permissions in the SALES database for the 10 user accounts and any roles to which they belong.

The proposed solution is to define an application role for the custom application. Assign the appropriate permissions to access the five tables in the SALES database. Provide users with the password information needed so that the application can use the sp_setapprole system stored procedure to activate the application role.

What does the proposed solution provide?

▶ **Correct Answer: A**

    A. **Correct:** Defining an application role, assigning the role appropriate permissions, and allowing the application to activate the role allows users to access the five tables in the SALES database only when using the custom data input application. An activated application role temporarily ignores the users' other permissions in the database.

    B. **Incorrect:** See the explanation for answer A.

    C. **Incorrect:** See the explanation for answer A.

    D. **Incorrect:** See the explanation for answer A.

**70-028.03.03.003**

Which term replaces the SQL Server 6.5 concepts of aliases and groups?

A. Jobs

B. Roles

C. Rules

D. Constraints

**70-028.03.03.004**

You want to grant JohnK permission to add, modify, and drop objects in your database. To which fixed database role should you grant JohnK membership?

A. db_ddladmin

B. db_datareader

C. db_datawriter

D. db_securityadmin

## 70-028.03.03.003

Which term replaces the SQL Server 6.5 concepts of aliases and groups?

▶ **Correct Answer: B**

    A. **Incorrect:** In SQL Server 6.5, aliases and groups allowed users to access databases. A job is an implementation of an administrative action that contains one or more steps. The term *job* replaces the SQL Server 6.5 term *task.*

    B. **Correct:** In SQL Server 6.5, aliases and groups allowed users to access databases. In SQL Server 7.0, roles provide a means of assembling users into a single unit to which permissions can be applied. Aliases and groups from earlier versions of SQL Server have been replaced with roles and permissions, which are more powerful.

    C. **Incorrect:** In SQL Server 6.5, aliases and groups allowed users to access databases. A *rule* is a database object bound to a column or user-defined data type that specifies what data can be entered in that column.

    D. **Incorrect:** In SQL Server 6.5, aliases and groups allowed users to access databases. A *constraint* is a property that can be placed on a column or set of columns in a table.

## 70-028.03.03.004

You want to grant JohnK permission to add, modify, and drop objects in your database. To which fixed database role should you grant JohnK membership?

▶ **Correct Answer: A**

    A. **Correct:** Members of the db_ddladmin fixed database role have permission, within a database, to add, modify, and drop objects in the database.

    B. **Incorrect:** Members of the db_datareader role have permission to view data from all user tables within a database.

    C. **Incorrect:** Members of the db_datawriter role have permission to add, change, and delete data from all user tables within a database.

    D. **Incorrect:** Members of the db_securityadmin role have permission to modify role membership and user permissions in the database.

**70-028.03.03.005**

Because your enterprise is expanding rapidly, you hire TonyV to manage SQL Server logins. To which fixed server role should you grant TonyV membership?

A.  sysadmin

B.  setupadmin

C.  serveradmin

D.  securityadmin

## 70-028.03.03.005

Because your enterprise is expanding rapidly, you hire TonyV to manage SQL Server logins. To which fixed server role should you grant TonyV membership?

▶ **Correct Answer: D**

A. **Incorrect:** Members of the sysadmin role have complete access to SQL Server. The sysadmin role is not the best choice in this situation, since managing logins does not require complete access. Only the minimum level of access required for a user job should be granted.

B. **Incorrect:** Members of the setupadmin fixed server role have permission to install and configure replication, and can install extended stored procedures.

C. **Incorrect:** Members of the serveradmin fixed server role have permission to configure serverwide settings.

D. **Correct:** Members of the securityadmin fixed server role have permission to create, modify, and drop server logins.

# Further Reading

The *Microsoft SQL Server 7.0 System Administration Training* volume of the *Microsoft SQL Server 7.0 System Administration Training Kit,* Chapter 11, Lesson 3 provides details on managing security with database roles, including fixed server, fixed database, public, and user-defined database roles. Chapter 12, Lesson 4 contains information about managing security with application roles.

Use Microsoft SQL Server Books Online (free download available at http://support.microsoft.com/download/support/mslfiles/sqlbol.exe) to search for "roles," "application security and application roles," and "creating security roles" and related areas for information about database roles. Search for "application roles" for information about application roles.

OBJECTIVE 3.4

# Grant to database users and roles the appropriate permissions on database objects and statements.

After assigning SQL Server access, assigning database access, and creating and assigning SQL Server roles, the final layer of security is granting the appropriate permissions to database users and roles. Before granting permissions, you must determine the type of permission and the permission state to assign to the users or application roles.

Permission types classify the permissions by function. There are three types of permissions. *Object permissions* allow users to work with objects—to manipulate data or execute procedures using tables, views, or system stored procedures against a database object. Object permissions give users the right to use the corresponding specific Transact-SQL statements.

*Statement permissions* allow users to create databases or database objects and to back up databases and their transaction logs. Since these administrative tasks are performed only infrequently and by a select group of staff members, statement permissions should be assigned with caution. Statement permissions give users the right to use the corresponding specific Transact-SQL statements.

*Implied permissions* are assigned only to members of predefined system roles (sysadmin) or owners of database objects (dbcreator) and cannot be changed. Implied permissions cannot be assigned to other users. Members of the sysadmin fixed server role automatically receive full permission to do or see anything in a SQL Server installation. Members of the dbcreator fixed server role also have implied permissions allowing them to perform all activities with the objects they own.

Permission states identify the status of a permission type. There are three permission states. GRANT allows a user in the current database to work with data and objects in the current database (object permissions) or to execute specific Transact-SQL statements (statement permissions). A granted permission also removes denied or revoked permissions only at the level granted (user, group, or role). If a permission is denied at another level, it still applies, although it does not prevent the user from accessing the object.

REVOKE removes a previously granted or denied permission from a user to work with data and objects in the current database only at the level revoked (user, group, or role). If a permission is granted or denied at another level, it still applies, although it does not prevent the user from accessing the object.

DENY nullifies a permission to work with data and objects in the current database from a security account in the current database and it prevents the security account from inheriting the permission through its group or role memberships. Denied permissions take precedence.

*Application roles* are SQL Server roles created to support the security needs of an application. Since application roles contain no members, the permissions of the application role are granted when the application role is activated for the user's connection when using the specific application. The client application activates the application role by running the sp_setapprole system stored procedure with the user-supplied password. Although application roles allow the application to handle user authentication, SQL Server must still authenticate the application when it accesses databases. Therefore, a password must be provided by the application to authenticate the application.

When an application role is activated, all permissions applied to the login, user account, groups, or database roles in all databases are ignored for the duration of the connection. The connection uses only the permissions associated with the application role for the database in which the application role exists. The application role permissions remain in effect until the connection logs out of SQL Server.

Questions related to this objective are designed to determine if you have an awareness of these issues. To successfully answer the questions for this objective, you need a firm understanding of several key terms. For definitions of these terms, refer to the Glossary in this book.

# Key Terms

- Application role
- Column
- Deny
- Encryption
- Grant
- Implied permission
- Object
- Object permission
- Permission state
- Permission type
- Permissions
- Revoke
- Statement permission
- System stored procedures
- Table
- Transact-SQL
- Unicode
- User (account)
- View

**70-028.03.04.001**

You want to execute a stored procedure on a database. Which type of SQL Server permission is required?

A. Object

B. Statement

C. Predefined

**70-028.03.04.002**

How can you grant permission to the AppDev application role to select from the "tests" table?

A. ON tests
   GRANT SELECT
   TO AppDev

B. TO AppDev
   GRANT SELECT
   ON tests

C. GRANT SELECT
   TO AppDev
   ON tests

D. GRANT SELECT
   ON tests
   TO AppDev

## 70-028.03.04.001

You want to execute a stored procedure on a database. Which type of SQL Server permission is required?

▶ **Correct Answer: A**

A. **Correct:** Object permissions allow you to work with data or execute a stored procedure.

B. **Incorrect:** Statement permissions only allow you to create a database or an item in a database, not execute a stored procedure.

C. **Incorrect:** There is no predefined permission type. However, the implied permission type is a permission users receive just by belonging to a predefined server or database group. Implied permissions may not always allow you to execute a stored procedure.

## 70-028.03.04.002

How can you grant permission to the AppDev application role to select from the "tests" table?

▶ **Correct Answer: D**

A. **Incorrect:** See the explanation for answer D.

B. **Incorrect:** See the explanation for answer D.

C. **Incorrect:** See the explanation for answer D.

D. **Correct:** To grant permission, you must use the GRANT statement, which allows a user (in this case, the AppDev application role) permission to view, change, or perform database actions (in this case, the SELECT statement on the *tests* table). The SELECT statement is an object permission. The GRANT statement uses the following syntax for object permissions:

```
GRANT {ALL [PRIVILEGES] | permission[,…n]}
    {
        [(column[,…n])] ON {table | view}
        | ON {table | view}[(column[,…n])]
        | ON {stored_procedure | extended_procedure}
    }
TO security_account[,…n]
[WITH GRANT OPTION]
[AS {group | role}]
```

### 70-028.03.04.003

You want to activate the AppDev application role with a password of mt_7296RN. You want to encrypt the password. Which syntax should you use?

A.  EXEC sp_setapprole 'AppDev', {'mt_7296RN'}'ODBC'

B.  EXEC sp_setapprole 'AppDev', {ENCRYPT N'mt_7296RN'}

C.  EXEC sp_setapprole 'AppDev', {ENCRYPT 'mt_7296RN'}'ODBC'

D.  EXEC sp_setapprole 'AppDev', {ENCRYPT N'mt_7296RN'}'ODBC'

### 70-028.03.04.004

You want to achieve these results:

- Grant a user permissions to only two columns of a table

- Optimize SQL Server performance

- Minimize the complexity of your security model

- Simplify SQL Server administration

The proposed solution is to assign column permissions for the two columns of the table to the user and grant the rights to create objects to individual user accounts.

What does the proposed solution provide?

A.  SQL Server administration is simplified.

B.  SQL Server will perform optimally.

C.  The complexity of your security model is minimized.

D.  The user can only access the two columns of the table.

## 70-028.03.04.003

You want to activate the AppDev application role with a password of mt_7296RN. You want to encrypt the password. Which syntax should you use?

▶ **Correct Answer: D**

A. **Incorrect:** See the explanation for answer D.

B. **Incorrect:** See the explanation for answer D.

C. **Incorrect:** See the explanation for answer D.

D. **Correct:** To activate the application role, you must use the EXEC statement with the sp_setapprole system stored procedure. To encrypt the password, convert the password to a Unicode string (ENCRYPT N), specify the password ('mt_7296RN'), and set the encryption style ('ODBC'). The syntax for activating application roles is:

```
EXEC sp_setapprole [@rolename =] 'name' ,
[@password =] {Encrypt N 'password'} | 'password'
[,[@encrypt =] 'encrypt_style']
```

## 70-028.03.04.004

You want to achieve these results:

- Grant a user permissions to only two columns of a table

- Optimize SQL Server performance

- Minimize the complexity of your security model

- Simplify SQL Server administration

The proposed solution is to assign column permissions for the two columns of the table to the user and grant the rights to create objects to individual user accounts.

What does the proposed solution provide?

▶ **Correct Answer: D**

A. **Incorrect:** SQL Server administration becomes more complex when individual user accounts are granted the rights to create objects.

B. **Incorrect:** For best SQL Server performance, Microsoft recommends using views rather than column permissions.

C. **Incorrect:** The security model becomes more complex when individual user accounts are granted the rights to create objects.

D. **Correct:** By assigning column permissions for the two columns of the table to the user, the user can only access the two columns of the table. None of the other desired results is achieved.

**70-028.03.04.005**

You want to prevent a user from deleting data in a table. There must be no chance of a role membership overriding the permission state. Which permission state should you use?

A. DENY

B. GRANT

C. REVOKE

## 70-028.03.04.005

You want to prevent a user from deleting data in a table. There must be no chance of a role membership overriding the permission state. Which permission state should you use?

▶ **Correct Answer: A**

A. **Correct:** The DENY permission state does not allow deleting data in a table and it overrides every other permission type, including role memberships.

B. **Incorrect:** The GRANT permission state allows deleting data in a table and can be overridden by role memberships.

C. **Incorrect:** The REVOKE permission state does not allow deleting data in a table but it can be overridden by role memberships.

# Further Reading

The *Microsoft SQL Server 7.0 System Administration Training* volume of the *Microsoft SQL Server 7.0 System Administration Training Kit,* Chapter 12, Lesson 1 provides information about permission types. Lesson 2 contains details on granting, revoking, and denying permissions and permission conflicts. Lesson 4 provides steps for activating application roles and information about using views to simplify security.

Use Microsoft SQL Server Books Online (free download available at http://support.microsoft.com/download/support/mslfiles/sqlbol.exe) to search for "managing permissions" for information about permission types. Search for "permission conflicts and states" for information about permission states. Search for "GRANT" and "how to allow access by granting permissions" for details on granting permissions. Search for "sp_setapprole" for details on activating the permissions associated with an application role in the current database. Search for "scenarios for using views" for details on the appropriate uses of views.

OBJECTIVE 3.5

# Audit server and database activity.

Once you've set up server access, database access, roles, and permissions, it's important to devise a plan that monitors server and database access to determine who is accessing databases and what is happening to the data. SQL Server provides a number of tools for auditing server and database activity.

The Windows NT Event Viewer provides information about errors, warnings, and the successes or failures of tasks. You can set up the built-in auditing capability of Windows NT Server to write audits to the Event Viewer security log, which can then be used to view the audited user activities.

The Windows NT Performance Monitor is a Windows NT component that provides status information about system performance. SQL Server adds counters to Windows NT Performance Monitor to provide additional information about SQL Server performance. Use Performance Monitor to monitor overall performance of SQL Server.

Transact-SQL is the standard language for communicating directly with SQL Server. There are five Transact-SQL items that allow you to audit server and database activities: system stored procedures, functions, SET statements, database consistency checker (DBCC) statements, and trace flags.

The SQL Server Profiler is a tool that captures a continuous record of server activity in real time. The Profiler is the best tool for monitoring user activity, including user access methods, user activity, object access, application use, and performance bottlenecks.

The Index Tuning Wizard allows you to select and create an optimal set of indexes and statistics for a SQL Server database without requiring an expert understanding of the structure of the database, the workload, or the internals of SQL Server.

SQL Server Query Analyzer is a utility that allows you to enter Transact-SQL statements and stored procedures in a graphical user interface. SQL Server Query Analyzer also provides the capability for graphically analyzing the execution of queries.

Current Activity (in SQL Server Enterprise Manager) provides a graphic snapshot of the currently running SQL Server processes, including user activity, blocked processes, and locks.

Questions related to this objective are designed to determine if you have an awareness of these issues. To successfully answer the questions for this objective, you need a firm understanding of several key terms. For definitions of these terms, refer to the Glossary in this book.

## Key Terms

- Database consistency checker (DBCC)

- Fragmentation

- Function

- Index

- Index Tuning Wizard

- Performance Monitor

- Query

- SQL Server Profiler

- SQL Server Query Analyzer

- SQL Server Service Manager

- System stored procedures

- Trace file

- Transact-SQL

## 70-028.03.05.001

You need to view information about SQL Server users. Which system stored procedure should you use?

A. sp_who

B. sp_lock

C. sp_monitor

D. sp_statistics

## 70-028.03.05.002

You want SQL Server to automatically track the last 100 events. Which system stored procedure should you use?

A. xp_logevent

B. sp_logdevice

C. sp_addmessage

D. xp_trace_setqueryhistory

## 70-028.03.05.001

You need to view information about SQL Server users. Which system stored procedure should you use?

▶ **Correct Answer: A**

A. **Correct:** The sp_who system stored procedure provides information about current SQL Server users and processes. This information can be filtered to show only those processes that are not idle.

B. **Incorrect:** The sp_lock system stored procedure provides information about locks.

C. **Incorrect:** The sp_monitor system stored procedure provides statistics about SQL Server performance.

D. **Incorrect:** The sp_statistics system stored procedure provides a list of all indexes on a specified table.

## 70-028.03.05.002

You want SQL Server to automatically track the last 100 events. Which system stored procedure should you use?

▶ **Correct Answer: D**

A. **Incorrect:** The xp_logevent extended stored procedure logs a user-defined message in the SQL Server log file and in the Windows NT Event Viewer.

B. **Incorrect:** The sp_logdevice system stored procedure was used in SQL Server versions prior to 7.0 to ensure the proper device layout for database restores.

C. **Incorrect:** The sp_addmessage system stored procedure adds a new error message to the sysmessages table.

D. **Correct:** The xp_trace_setqueryhistory profiler extended stored procedure starts a trace consisting of the last 100 queries, including any server exceptions. The query history may be used to recover from a server failure.

**70-028.03.05.003**

You want to investigate a few queries to check their performance. Which three tools are best suited for measuring the CPU time per query, index usage, and actual input/output? (Choose three.)

A. SQL Server Profiler

B. Index Tuning Wizard

C. SQL Server Query Analyzer

D. SQL Server Service Manager

E. SQL Server Enterprise Manager

F. Windows NT Performance Monitor

## 70-028.03.05.003

You want to investigate a few queries to check their performance. Which three tools are best suited for measuring the CPU time per query, index usage, and actual input/output? (Choose three.)

▶ **Correct Answers: A, B, and C**

    A. **Correct:** SQL Server Profiler is a tool that captures a continuous record of server activity in real time, including CPU time per query. Use SQL Server Profiler to help identify slow queries.

    B. **Correct:** The Index Tuning Wizard can be used to analyze your queries, including index usage, and suggest the indexes that should be created. The wizard allows you to select and create an optimal set of indexes and statistics for a SQL Server database without requiring an expert understanding of the structure of the database, the workload, or the internals of SQL Server.

    C. **Correct:** SQL Server Query Analyzer is a SQL Server utility that allows you to write queries, execute multiple queries simultaneously, view results (output), analyze the query plan (input), and receive assistance to improve the query performance.

    D. **Incorrect:** SQL Server Service Manager is a SQL Server utility that provides a graphical way to start, pause, and stop the MSDTC, MSSQLServer, and SQLServerAgent services. The performance of SQL Server objects is not measured by the SQL Server Service Manager.

    E. **Incorrect:** SQL Server Enterprise Manager is a graphical application that allows for easy, enterprise-wide configuration and management of SQL Server and SQL Server objects. SQL Server Enterprise Manager does not measure the performance of SQL Server.

    F. **Incorrect:** The Windows NT Performance Monitor is a dynamic, real-time display used for measuring the performance of network and SQL Server components rather than queries.

**70-028.03.05.004**

You want to use Transact-SQL to monitor SQL Server. Which DBCC statement should you use to monitor fragmentation of data and indexes?

A. SQLPERF

B. CHECKALLOC

C. SHOWCONTIG

D. SHOW_STATISTICS

**70-028.03.05.005**

You want to display the time in which SQL Server performed input and output operations since it was last started. Which function should you use?

A. @@IDLE

B. @@IO_BUSY

C. @@CPU_BUSY

D. @@CONNECTIONS

## 70-028.03.05.004

You want to use Transact-SQL to monitor SQL Server. Which DBCC statement should you use to monitor fragmentation of data and indexes?

▶ **Correct Answer: C**

    A. **Incorrect:** The DBCC statement SQLPERF provides statistics about the use of transaction-log space in all databases.

    B. **Incorrect:** The DBCC statement CHECKALLOC checks the allocation and use of all pages in the specified database.

    C. **Correct:** The DBCC statement SHOWCONTIG displays fragmentation information for the data and indexes of the specified table.

    D. **Incorrect:** The DBCC statement SHOW_STATISTICS displays the current distribution statistics for the specified target on the specified table.

## 70-028.03.05.005

You want to display the time in which SQL Server performed input and output operations since it was last started. Which function should you use?

▶ **Correct Answer: B**

    A. **Incorrect:** The @@IDLE function displays the time in milliseconds (based on the resolution of the system timer) that SQL Server has been idle since it was last started.

    B. **Correct:** The @@IO_BUSY function displays the time in milliseconds (based on the resolution of the system timer) that SQL Server has spent performing input and output operations since it was last started.

    C. **Incorrect:** The @@CPU_BUSY function displays the time in milliseconds (based on the resolution of the system timer) that the CPU has spent doing work since SQL Server was last started.

    D. **Incorrect:** The @@CONNECTIONS function displays the number of connections or attempted connections since SQL Server was last started.

# Further Reading

The *Microsoft SQL Server 7.0 System Administration Training* volume of the *Microsoft SQL Server 7.0 System Administration Training Kit,* Chapter 14, Lesson 1 provides basic information about server and database monitoring tasks and tools. Lesson 2 provides details on using monitoring tools, including Windows NT Event Viewer, SQL Server Performance Monitor, Transact-SQL, SQL Server Profiler, Index Tuning Wizard, Query History, SQL Server Query Analyzer, and Current Activity (in SQL Server Enterprise Manager).

Use Microsoft SQL Server Books Online (free download available at http://support.microsoft.com/download/support/mslfiles/sqlbol.exe) to search for "choosing a tool to monitor server performance and activity" and "query tuning" for information about server and query monitoring tools. Search for "how to set a trace filter" for information about retrieving information, including query history. Search for "dbcc" for information about the Database Consistency Checker (DBCC).

# Managing and Maintaining Data

The Managing and Maintaining Data domain examines the procedures for managing and maintaining data in the SQL Server environment. These procedures include:

- Creating and managing databases

- Loading data

- Backing up databases

- Restoring databases

- Managing replication

- Automating administrative tasks

- Accessing remote data

## Tested Skills and Suggested Practices

- **Creating and managing databases. Be able to create data files, filegroups, and transaction log files and specify growth characteristics.**

    - Practice 1: Using the Database Creation Wizard, SQL Server Enterprise Manager, or the CREATE DATABASE statement, create a database and transaction log. Learn about the various database options. Using the sp_dboption system stored procedure or the SQL Server Enterprise Manager, set database options for a database.

    - Practice 2: Learn ways to configure the data and log files to grow automatically, increase the current or maximum size of existing data and log files, add secondary data files or log files, and expand the transaction log.

    - Practice 3: Using SQL Server Enterprise Manager, the ALTER DATABASE statement, or the CREATE DATABASE statement, create a filegroup within a database.

- **Loading data using various methods. Be able to load data using the INSERT, SELECT INTO, and BULK INSERT Transact-SQL statements. Be able to load data using the bcp (bulk copy program) utility and Data Transformation Services (DTS).**

  - Practice 1: Learn the purpose of the INSERT, SELECT INTO, and BULK INSERT Transact-SQL statements. Use each statement to load data.

  - Practice 2: Learn the purpose of the bcp utility. Use the bcp utility to load data.

  - Practice 3: Learn the purpose of the DTS Import and Export Wizards. Use the wizards to import and export data.

  - Practice 4: Learn the purpose of DTS Designer. Use the designer to import, export, and transform data.

- **Backing up system databases and user databases. Be able to back up system databases by performing a complete database backup, a transaction log backup, a differential database backup, and a filegroup backup.**

  - Practice 1: Learn the purpose of backup devices. Create a named backup device using SQL Server Enterprise Manager or the sp_addumpdevice system stored procedure.

  - Practice 2: Learn the purpose of a complete database backup. Perform a complete database backup using the Create Backup Wizard, SQL Server Enterprise Manager, or the BACKUP DATABASE Transact-SQL statement.

  - Practice 3: Learn the purpose of a transaction log backup. Perform a transaction log backup using SQL Server Enterprise Manager or the BACKUP LOG Transact-SQL statement.

  - Practice 4: Learn the purpose of a differential database backup. Perform a differential database backup using SQL Server Enterprise Manager or the BACKUP DATABASE Transact-SQL statement with the Differential option.

  - Practice 5: Learn the purpose of a filegroup backup. Perform a filegroup backup using SQL Server Enterprise Manager or the BACKUP DATABASE Transact-SQL statement with the filegroup name.

- **Restoring system databases and user databases. Learn how to prepare for a restore operation. Be able to restore system databases from a complete database backup, a transaction log backup, a differential database backup, and a filegroup backup.**

  - Practice 1: Learn the steps necessary to prepare for a restore operation, including validating backups, restricting access to the database, backing up the transaction log, and switching to the master database.

- Practice 2: Learn the purpose of restoring from a complete database backup. Restore a complete database backup using the SQL Server Enterprise Manager or the RESTORE DATABASE Transact-SQL statement. Learn how to use the RECOVERY option for a complete database backup.

- Practice 3: Learn the purpose of restoring from a transaction log backup. Restore a transaction log backup using SQL Server Enterprise Manager or the RESTORE LOG Transact-SQL statement. Learn how to use the RECOVERY option for a transaction log backup. Learn how the Stopat option is used to restore to a specific point in time.

- Practice 4: Learn the purpose of restoring from a differential database backup. Restore a differential database backup using SQL Server Enterprise Manager or the RESTORE DATABASE Transact-SQL statement. Learn how to use the RECOVERY option for a differential database backup.

- Practice 5: Learn the purpose of restoring from a filegroup backup. Restore a filegroup backup using SQL Server Enterprise Manager or the RESTORE DATABASE Transact-SQL statement with the filegroup name. Learn how to use the NORECOVERY option for a filegroup backup.

- **Managing replication. Be able to configure replication servers, create publications, and set up and manage subscriptions.**

  - Practice 1: Learn the purpose of the Distributor, Publisher, and Subscriber. Configure a Distributor and Publisher using the Configure Publishing and Distribution Wizard. Enable a Subscriber using the Publisher and Distributor Properties dialog box.

  - Practice 2: Familiarize yourself with the three publication types and know the reasons for using each type. Use the Create Publication Wizard to create a new publication.

  - Practice 3: Learn about push and pull subscriptions and the reasons for using each. Use the Push Subscription Wizard and the Pull Subscription Wizard to create subscriptions.

- **Automating administrative tasks. Learn about the tasks that can be automated using SQL Server Agent. Be able to define jobs, alerts, and operators. Be able to set up SQLAgentMail for job notification and alerts.**

  - Practice 1: Learn how jobs are used to automate activities for a system administrator. Define a job.

  - Practice 2: Learn how alerts are used to automate activities for a system administrator. Define an alert.

■ Practice 3: Learn how operators must be defined to receive notification from an alert or job. Define an operator.

■ Practice 4: Learn how SQLAgentMail is used to notify operators of alerts or job actions. Set up SQLAgentMail.

■ **Enabling access to remote data. Be able to set up linked servers and security for linked databases. Be able to view metadata for linked servers.**

■ Practice 1: Set up linked servers using the sp_addlinkedserver, the sp_dropserver, and the sp_serveroption system stored procedures or SQL Server Enterprise Manager.

■ Practice 2: Set up security for linked databases using the sp_addlinkedsrvlogin and sp_droplinkedsrvlogin system stored procedures or SQL Server Enterprise Manager.

■ Practice 3: Use various system stored procedures to view metadata for linked servers.

# Create and manage databases.

The appropriate setup and management of databases allows for growth and ensures data availability. When creating a database and transaction log, you must select the appropriate file size and growth settings. Creating filegroups improves database performance by allowing a database to be created across multiple disks, multiple disk controllers, or RAID systems.

Recall that SQL Server creates databases by storing data and objects in the following database system file types:

- *Primary data file:* Contains the startup information for the database and is used to store data. Each database has only one primary data file.

- *Secondary data files:* Hold data and objects that do not fit in the primary data file. There can be one or multiple secondary data files located across multiple physical disks.

- *Transaction log files:* Hold the log information used to recover the database. Each database must have at least one transaction log file.

To create a database, use the Database Creation Wizard, SQL Server Enterprise Manager, or the CREATE DATABASE statement. You must first specify the database name, and you may then change the defaults (taken from the model database) for the database location, filegroup, initial size, and file properties. When a database is created, a transaction log for that database is also created. You may change the defaults for initial size and file properties.

*Database options* determine the characteristics of each database. Only the system administrator or database owner can modify database options using the sp_dboption system stored procedure or SQL Server Enterprise Manager. A few options can be set only by using the sp_dboption system stored procedure. After you set a database option, the modification takes effect immediately.

After a database is created, data needs may change and you may need to expand the size of the data or log files. There are three ways to control the size of a database.

You can configure the data and log files to grow automatically; you can manually increase the current or maximum size of existing data and log files; or you can manually add secondary data or log files.

Use the ALTER DATABASE statement or SQL Server Enterprise Manager to expand database files automatically by an amount you specify. The automatic Filegrowth option reduces the administrative tasks involved in database size management, and it also reduces the possibility of a database running out of space unexpectedly.

If an existing file is not configured to grow automatically, you can still increase its size using the ALTER DATABASE statement or SQL Server Enterprise Manager. If you increase the size setting beyond the file's current maximum size without increasing the MAXSIZE statement, the maximum size will be set equal to the new size.

You can also expand the size of a database by creating secondary data files using the ALTER DATABASE statement or SQL Server Enterprise Manager. Using secondary data files or log files to make use of separate physical disks is a good performance improvement strategy when you do not use the disk-striping capabilities of RAID systems.

When a transaction log runs out of space, SQL Server cannot record transactions and does not allow changes to the database. You can expand the transaction log using the ALTER DATABASE statement or SQL Server Enterprise Manager.

Filegroups assemble database files together for administrative and data allocation purposes. Filegroups can improve system performance by assisting in the placement of data and indexes onto specific disk drives. The system administrator can create filegroups for each disk drive, then assign specific tables, indexes, or data from a table to specific filegroups. Queries for data from the table will be spread across the disks, improving performance.

There are three types of filegroups:

- *Primary:* Contains the primary data file and any other files not put into another filegroup. All pages for the system tables are allocated in the primary filegroup.

- *User-defined:* Created by the user when first creating or later altering the database.

- *Default:* Contains the pages for all tables and indexes that do not have a filegroup specified when created.

Use SQL Server Enterprise Manager, the ALTER DATABASE statement, or the CREATE DATABASE statement to create a filegroup within a database.

Questions related to this objective are designed to determine if you have an awareness of these issues. To successfully answer the questions for this objective, you need a firm understanding of several key terms. For definitions of these terms, refer to the Glossary in this book.

# Key Terms

- Database

- Database options

- Default filegroup

- File

- Filegroup

- Master database

- Model database

- Nonlogged operations

- Primary data file

- Primary filegroup

- RAID (redundant array of independent disks)

- Sa (system administrator) login

- Secondary data files

- SQL Server Enterprise Manager

- System tables

- Transaction log

## 70-028.04.01.001

Why should you back up the master database after you create a new database?

A. To prevent the loss of any jobs, alerts, or operators

B. To secure the default configuration used to create new databases

C. To allow the new database to be easily recovered if the master database becomes damaged

D. To allow the new database to be recovered because the CREATE DATABASE command is a nonlogged operation

**70-028.04.01.001**

Why should you back up the master database after you create a new database?

▶ **Correct Answer: C**

    A. **Incorrect:** Backing up the master database after creating a new database does not prevent the loss of jobs, alerts, or operators. These items are not backed up in the master database.

    B. **Incorrect:** Backing up the master database does back up changes to server-wide configuration options. However, the backup of configuration options becomes no more or less urgent after creating a new database.

    C. **Correct:** When a new database is created, modified, or dropped, you should back up the master database to allow for easy recovery. The SYSDATABASES table in the master database is updated when a new database is created, modified, or dropped.

    D. **Incorrect:** The CREATE DATABASE command is a logged operation. However, since the SYSDATABASES table in the master database is updated when a new database is created, the master database must be backed up to recover the new database.

**70-028.04.01.002**

You are preparing to create a new database.

The required result is to create the testdb database as a duplicate of the model database with a primary filegroup.

The first optional result is to specify the initial file size as 10 MB.

The second optional result is to specify that the growth increment is 10 percent.

The proposed solution is to issue this CREATE DATABASE command:

CREATE DATABASE testdb
ON
    PRIMARY (NAME=testdb_data,
    FILENAME = 'c:\mssql7\data\testdb.mdf', SIZE=10MB, MAXSIZE=15MB, FILEGROWTH=10)
LOG ON
    (NAME=order_log,
    FILENAME = 'c:\mssql7\data\order.ldf', SIZE=2MB, MAXSIZE=5MB, FILEGROWTH=0)

What does the proposed solution provide?

A. The required result and all optional results.

B. The required result and one optional result.

C. The required result but none of the optional results.

D. The proposed solution does not provide the required result.

## 70-028.04.01.002

You are preparing to create a new database.

The required result is to create the testdb database as a duplicate of the model database with a primary filegroup.

The first optional result is to specify the initial file size as 10 MB.

The second optional result is to specify that the growth increment is 10 percent.

The proposed solution is to issue this CREATE DATABASE command:

CREATE DATABASE testdb
ON
    PRIMARY (NAME=testdb_data,
    FILENAME = 'c:\mssql7\data\testdb.mdf', SIZE=10MB, MAXSIZE=15MB, FILEGROWTH=10)
LOG ON
    (NAME=order_log,
    FILENAME = 'c:\mssql7\data\order.ldf', SIZE=2MB, MAXSIZE=5MB, FILEGROWTH=0)

What does the proposed solution provide?

▶ **Correct Answer: B**

A. **Incorrect:** See the explanation for answer B.

B. **Correct:** By issuing the CREATE DATABASE command and specifying a primary filegroup, a duplicate of the model database with a primary file group is created. The Size option specifies initial filegroup size of 10 MB. The Filegrowth option specifies the filegroup growth increment of 10. However, since percent was not specified, the default measurement for Filegrowth is megabytes.

C. **Incorrect:** See the explanation for answer B.

D. **Incorrect:** See the explanation for answer B.

## 70-028.04.01.003

You create the testdb database using SQL Server Enterprise Manager as the sa user. You need to change the database options.

The required result is to allow the testdb database to accept nonlogged operations.

The first optional result is to allow only the sa user to access the database.

The second optional result is to force all database columns to be NOT NULL.

The proposed solution is to use the Options tab in the testdb Properties window to disable the ANSI NULL default option and to enable the DBO Use Only and Truncate Log On Checkpoint options.

What does the proposed solution provide?

A. The required result and all optional results.

B. The required result and one optional result.

C. The required result but none of the optional results.

D. The proposed solution does not provide the required result.

## 70-028.04.01.003

You create the testdb database using SQL Server Enterprise Manager as the sa user. You need to change the database options.

The required result is to allow the testdb database to accept nonlogged operations.

The first optional result is to allow only the sa user to access the database.

The second optional result is to force all database columns to be NOT NULL.

The proposed solution is to use the Options tab in the testdb Properties window to disable the ANSI NULL default option and to enable the DBO Use Only and Truncate Log On Checkpoint options.

What does the proposed solution provide?

▶ **Correct Answer: D**

A. **Incorrect:** See the explanation for answer D.

B. **Incorrect:** See the explanation for answer D.

C. **Incorrect:** See the explanation for answer D.

D. **Correct:** When a database is created, it is a duplicate of the model database. Some database options can be changed using SQL Server Enterprise Manager. All database options can be changed using the sp_dboption system stored procedure. The Select Into/Bulk Copy database option must be selected to accept nonlogged operations. Disabling the ANSI NULL default option reverts the ANSI NULL default option to NOT NULL, forcing all database columns to be NOT NULL. In addition, enabling the DBO User Only option allows only database owners to access the database, not only the sa user. Finally, enabling the Truncate Log On Checkpoint option truncates the transaction log at every checkpoint.

**70-028.04.01.004**

When using Query Analyzer, what is required to add a second data file to the testdb database using the ALTER DATABASE command?

A. The testdb database must be shut down.

B. You must be connected using the sa login.

C. You must be connected to the master database.

D. The size of the second data file must be equal to or greater than the first data file.

**70-028.04.01.005**

What would happen if the primary filegroup ran out of space?

A. No new information could be added to the system tables.

B. No existing database files could be extended.

C. A new default filegroup could not be created.

D. Information in the system tables could not be queried.

## 70-028.04.01.004

When using Query Analyzer, what is required to add a second data file to the testdb database using the ALTER DATABASE command?

▶ **Correct Answer: C**

A. **Incorrect:** It is not necessary for the testdb database to be shut down when adding a data file.

B. **Incorrect:** Since ALTER DATABASE permissions default to members of the db_owner and db_ddladmin fixed database roles, and to members of the sysadmin and dbcreator fixed server roles, it is not necessary to be connected using the sa user name.

C. **Correct:** The ALTER DATABASE command allows you to add a database file to the testdb database if you are connected to the master database and have permission to use the command.

D. **Incorrect:** The minimum size of the added database file is 512 KB, and is the initial size for the file. If a maximum size is not specified, the file will grow until the disk is full.

## 70-028.04.01.005

What would happen if the primary filegroup ran out of space?

▶ **Correct Answer: A**

A. **Correct:** If the primary filegroup runs out of space, no new information can be added to the system tables.

B. **Incorrect:** Existing database files can be extended by selecting the option to automatically grow files or by specifying a larger file size.

C. **Incorrect:** A new default filegroup can be created to ease competition for data space using the ALTER DATABASE command.

D. **Incorrect:** Information in the system tables can be queried even if the primary filegroup runs out of space.

# Further Reading

The *Microsoft SQL Server 7.0 System Administration Training* volume of the *Microsoft SQL Server 7.0 System Administration Training Kit,* Chapter 5, Lesson 2 provides information about creating databases. Lesson 3 describes the database options and managing file growth. Lesson 4 discusses strategies for using filegroups.

Use Microsoft SQL Server Books Online (free download available at http://support.microsoft.com/download/support/mslfiles/sqlbol.exe) to search for "creating a database" for information about creating databases. Search for "CREATE DATABASE" for the CREATE DATABASE command syntax. Search for "setting database options" for details on database options. Search for "ALTER DATABASE" for the ALTER DATABASE command syntax. Search for "default filegroups" for information about using filegroups.

OBJECTIVE 4.2

# Load data using various methods.

As a system administrator, you must understand how to manage and transfer data between applications and environments. In many businesses, SQL Server is often used along with other data sources, including other relational database systems, mainframes, and e-mail servers. Some type of data transfer between data sources is often required, including the movement, copying, archiving, and migration of data. In addition, data transfer may require the transformation of data, including changes to format, structure, mapping, consistency, and validation.

The transfer method you choose for importing or exporting data depends on several factors, including whether data will be imported or exported; source and destination data format; source and destination data location; whether the import or export is a one-time occurrence or a scheduled task; whether a command-prompt utility, Transact-SQL statement, or graphical interface is preferred (for ease of use); and whether data transformation is required.

SQL Server provides the following tools for transferring data:

- **SELECT INTO statement:** Creates a new table and selects data to import to the new table from an existing SQL Server table.

- **INSERT statement with the SELECT statement:** Selects data to import to an existing table from an existing SQL Server table.

- **BULK INSERT statement:** Imports a data file into a database table or view in a user-specified format.

- **bcp utility:** A command-prompt utility that imports and exports native SQL Server data files or ASCII text files.

- **DTS Import Wizard and DTS Export Wizard:** Allow users to interactively import, export, or transform data between heterogeneous data sources or to import/export all of the objects in a SQL Server 7.0 database to another SQL Server 7.0 database.

- **DTS Designer:** Allows experienced database administrators to import, export, and transform homogeneous and heterogeneous data from multiple sources and to define complex data workflows.

Questions related to this objective are designed to determine if you have an awareness of these issues. To successfully answer the questions for this objective, you need a firm understanding of several key terms. For definitions of these terms, refer to the Glossary in this book.

## Key Terms

- Bcp (bulk copy program) utility

- Bulk copy

- Data migration

- Data transfer

- Data transformation

- Data Transformation Services (DTS)

- DTS Designer

- DTS Export Wizard

- DTS Import Wizard

- Heterogeneous data

- Homogeneous data

- Nonlogged operations

- Online analytical processing (OLAP)

- Owner password

- Package

- Query

- Schema

- SQL statement

- Table

- User password

**70-028.04.02.001**

You need to move a schema from SQL Server 7.0 on an Intel platform to SQL Server 7.0 on a DEC Alpha platform. Which tool should you use to transfer the data?

A. The bcp utility

B. DTS Export Wizard

C. SQL Server Transfer Manager

D. DTS Designer

**70-028.04.02.002**

What is true about a DTS package that is not secured with an owner password?

A. It could be protected by a user password.

B. It could be accessed by any database user.

C. It could be accessed by any user with access to the storage file.

D. All the components of the package are encrypted except the package name, description, ID, version, and creation date.

## 70-028.04.02.001

You need to move a schema from SQL Server 7.0 on an Intel platform to SQL Server 7.0 on a DEC Alpha platform. Which tool should you use to transfer the data?

► **Correct Answer: B**

A. **Incorrect:** The bcp utility copies data between SQL Server and a data file in a user-specified format and is not used to move schema.

B. **Correct:** The DTS Export Wizard allows you to move a schema from SQL Server 7.0 on an Intel platform to SQL Server 7.0 on a DEC Alpha platform using DTS packages. The DTS Import Wizard also allows you to move the schema.

C. **Incorrect:** The SQL Server Transfer Manager found in previous versions of SQL Server is no longer available. DTS provides all of the functionality formerly provided by SQL Server Transfer Manager.

D. **Incorrect:** DTS Designer allows experienced users to create complex DTS packages that import, export, and transform heterogeneous data using graphics tools on a designer work surface.

## 70-028.04.02.002

What is true about a DTS package that is not secured with an owner password?

► **Correct Answer: C**

A. **Incorrect:** If a DTS package is not secured with an owner password, the package cannot be protected by a user password. An owner password is required to specify a user password.

B. **Incorrect:** If a DTS package is not secured with an owner password, the package may be accessed by database users, but only those users who have access to the storage file.

C. **Correct:** If a DTS package is not secured with an owner password, the package may be accessed by any user with access to the storage file.

D. **Incorrect:** If a DTS package is not secured with an owner password, no components of the package are encrypted.

## 70-028.04.02.003

You are preparing to create a DTS package to import from one database on your local SQL Server to another using the DTS Import Wizard.

The required result is to copy all the data from table 1 in database 1 to table 2 in database 2 using a SQL statement query.

The first optional result is to drop and recreate table 2 if it exists.

The second optional result is to save the DTS package on SQL Server.

The proposed solution is to use the Data Transformation Services Import Wizard. Specify the local server and select database 1 as the data source. Specify the local server and select database 2 as the destination. Select Copy Table(s) from the Source Database option and select only Table 1 and Table 2 as the source and destination tables. Select the Run Immediately option, and select Save DTS Package with the SQL Server option.

What does the proposed solution provide?

A.  The required result and all optional results.

B.  The required result and one optional result.

C.  The required result but none of the optional results.

D.  The proposed solution does not provide the required result.

## 70-028.04.02.003

You are preparing to create a DTS package to import from one database on your local SQL Server to another using the DTS Import Wizard.

The required result is to copy all the data from table 1 in database 1 to table 2 in database 2 using a SQL statement query.

The first optional result is to drop and recreate table 2 if it exists.

The second optional result is to save the DTS package on SQL Server.

The proposed solution is to use the Data Transformation Services Import Wizard. Specify the local server and select database 1 as the data source. Specify the local server and select database 2 as the destination. Select Copy Table(s) from the Source Database option and select only Table 1 and Table 2 as the source and destination tables. Select the Run Immediately option, and select Save DTS Package with the SQL Server option.

What does the proposed solution provide?

▶ **Correct Answer: D**

A. **Incorrect:** See the explanation for answer D.

B. **Incorrect:** See the explanation for answer D.

C. **Incorrect:** See the explanation for answer D.

D. **Correct:** In selecting Copy Table(s) from the Source Database option rather than the Use A Query To Specify The Data To Transfer option, you have not copied the data using a SQL statement query. Selecting the Use a Query option also allows you to select the Drop And Recreate Destination Table If It Exists option. Selecting Save DTS Package with the SQL Server option saves the DTS package on the SQL Server.

**70-028.04.02.004**

You are preparing to load data using the bcp utility. How should you configure the orders database for bulk copy?

A. Select the Select Into/Bulk Copy check box on the Options tab on the orders database Properties window.

B. Deselect the Select Into/Bulk Copy check box on the Options tab on the orders database Properties window.

C. Select the Select Into/Bulk Copy check box on the Options tab on the orders database server Properties window.

D. Deselect the Select Into/Bulk Copy check box on the Options tab on the orders database server Properties window.

## 70-028.04.02.004

You are preparing to load data using the bcp utility. How should you configure the orders database for bulk copy?

▶ **Correct Answer: A**

A. **Correct:** Selecting the Select Into/Bulk Copy check box on the Options tab on the orders database Properties window performs a nonlogged bulk copy. Configuring a nonlogged bulk copy is recommended to increase copy speed and to keep the transaction log from filling up.

B. **Incorrect:** The Select Into/Bulk Copy check box on the Options tab on the orders database Properties window must be *selected* to perform a nonlogged bulk copy. Configuring a nonlogged bulk copy is recommended to increase copy speed and to keep the transaction log from filling up.

C. **Incorrect:** The Select Into/Bulk Copy check box on the Options tab on the orders *database* Properties window must be *selected* to perform a nonlogged bulk copy. Configuring a nonlogged bulk copy is recommended to increase copy speed and to keep the transaction log from filling up.

D. **Incorrect:** See the explanation for answer C.

# Further Reading

The *Microsoft SQL Server 7.0 System Administration Training* volume of the *Microsoft SQL Server 7.0 System Administration Training Kit,* Chapter 6, Lesson 1 provides information about the various methods used for transferring data, including the INSERT and SELECT INTO statements, the bcp utility, Data Transformation Services (DTS), and the BULK INSERT statement. Lesson 2 provides an introduction to Data Transformation Services. Lesson 3 contains detailed information about using Data Transformation Services.

Use Microsoft SQL Server Books Online (free download available at http://support.microsoft.com/download/support/mslfiles/sqlbol.exe) to search for "dts" and related topics for information about using Data Transformation Services to transfer data. Search for "bulkcopy" for details on using the bcp utility. Search for "insert," "select," and "bulk insert" for information about the INSERT, SELECT INTO, and BULK INSERT statements. Search for "choosing a tool to import or export data" for information about the various methods of loading data.

*SQL Server System Administration.* New Riders, Indianapolis, IN, 1999. ISBN 1-56205-955-6. Chapter 8 contains detailed procedures for various methods of transferring data, including bulk copy, the INSERT and SELECT INTO statements, and Data Transformation Services.

OBJECTIVE 4.3

# Back up system and user databases by performing a complete database backup, a transaction log backup, a differential database backup, and a filegroup backup.

As a system administrator, it is important to routinely implement your backup plan so data can remain accessible and reliable. A backup plan includes the backup of databases, transaction logs, and data files to backup devices.

Before attempting a backup operation, you must choose the backup device you will use—disk, tape, or named pipe. All backup devices have a physical name used by the operating system to access the device. To make the backup process easier, you may decide to provide backup devices with a logical name stored in the system tables by creating the named backup device before using it. In backup and restore operations, you may then reference the device by its logical name only. You can create named backup devices with SQL Server Enterprise Manager or by executing the sp_addumpdevice system stored procedure.

There are four ways to back up data: the complete database backup, the transaction log backup, the differential backup, and the file/filegroup backup. The criticality of the data in the databases in a SQL Server environment should determine which backup methods are used.

A *complete database backup* records all pages in a database, including the transaction log. Only the data in the database is copied to the backup file; unused space is not copied. Therefore, a complete database backup may be smaller than the actual database. You should plan the frequency of complete database backups so production work is not affected yet the loss of significant amounts of data is prevented. Databases containing critical or volatile data may need to be backed up more frequently, while databases containing noncritical data may be backed up less frequently. Read-only databases may need to be backed up only after data changes. You should have more than one backup of the database, rotating media so there are two or more versions of the database available for a restore. When files are added or removed from a database, you should create a database backup immediately.

You can perform a complete database backup while the database is online and in use. However, the following operations are not allowed during a database backup: creating or deleting database files, creating indexes, performing nonlogged operations, or shrinking either the database (automatically or manually) or the database files. If a complete database backup is started when one of these operations is in progress, the backup terminates. If a complete database backup is in progress and one of these operations is attempted, the operation fails and the backup continues.

The transaction log is not truncated when performing a complete database backup. Truncating the transaction log prevents the transaction log from becoming full and requiring manual truncation. Therefore, during a complete database backup, it is recommended that you set the transaction log to truncate automatically when a checkpoint occurs in the database. Enable automatic truncation by setting the Truncate Log On Checkpoint database option to TRUE using the sp_dboption system stored procedure or SQL Server Enterprise Manager.

You can perform a complete database backup using the Create Backup Wizard, SQL Server Enterprise Manager, or the BACKUP DATABASE Transact-SQL statement.

A *transaction log backup* records only the transactions that have modified a database since the last complete database, differential database, or transaction log backup. Although the transaction log records database modifications and transaction operations in order to recover transactions, only regular transaction log backups provide the ability to recover from disasters such as media failure. Using complete database and transaction log backups together, you can restore a database to the exact point of failure, minimizing the loss of data due to the failure.

Since transaction log backups use fewer resources than do database backups and can be created more frequently than database backups, the period of time in which a failure could occur and the amount of data that could be lost are reduced. In addition, transaction log backups can recover a database to a specific point in time. Although transaction log backups increase recoverability, using complete database and transaction log backups requires a backup plan. You should perform a complete database backup regularly (for example, every night) and back up the transaction log frequently (hourly or based on system activity).

You can perform a transaction log backup using SQL Server Enterprise Manager or the BACKUP LOG Transact-SQL statement. The BACKUP LOG statement should not be executed while the Truncate Log On Checkpoint database option is enabled, nor can it be executed if Select Into/Bulk Copy is enabled or if nonlogged changes have been made to the database. If any of these conditions exist, use the BACKUP DATABASE statement to create a database or differential database backup instead.

A *differential database backup* records only the changes made to the database since the last complete database backup and requires less time to complete than a complete database backup. Using complete database and differential database backups together, the risk of data loss is reduced.

Since differential database backups do not allow a database to be restored to the exact point of failure, maximum protection from data loss can be achieved by creating transaction log backups after each differential database backup is created. Restoring a database using a combination of complete database, differential database, and transaction log backups requires a backup plan. You should perform a complete database backup regularly (for example, every night) and perform a differential database backup periodically (every four hours or based on system activity). You might also want to perform transaction log backups between differential database backups (for example, every 30 minutes).

You can perform a differential database backup using SQL Server Enterprise Manager or by using the BACKUP DATABASE Transact-SQL statement and selecting the Differential option. The syntax is identical to the complete database backup.

A *file or filegroup backup* records all pages in a specified file or filegroup, allowing a database to be backed up in smaller units. Since file and filegroup backups do not back up the transaction log, you must create transaction log backups after a file or filegroup backup is created to prevent data loss.

If tables or indexes span multiple filegroups, all filegroups affected by the creation of the table or index must be backed up together, and then a transaction log backup must be made. Otherwise, only parts of a table or index will be backed up, preventing the table or index from being recovered if later restored. An error is generated if filegroups that the table and index span are missing when a filegroup backup is created. You should consider these requirements when designing databases with tables and indexes arranged on multiple filegroups.

You can perform a file or filegroup backup using SQL Server Enterprise Manager or by using the BACKUP DATABASE Transact-SQL statement and specifying a file or filegroup name.

Questions related to this objective are designed to determine if you have an awareness of these issues. To successfully answer the questions for this objective, you need a firm understanding of several key terms. For definitions of these terms, refer to the Glossary in this book.

# Key Terms

- Automatic recovery

- Backup

- Backup device

- Backup file

- Backup media

- Database backup (also known as *full* or *complete database backup*)

- Database file

- Differential database backup

- Filegroup

- File or filegroup backup

- Index

- Logical name

- Media header

- Physical name

- Role

- Table

- Transaction log

- Transaction log backup

## 70-028.04.03.001

Which three roles have the privileges required to perform a complete database backup? (Choose three.)

A. sysadmin

B. db_owner

C. diskadmin

D. dbcreator

E. serveradmin

F. db_backupoperator

## 70-028.04.03.001

Which three roles have the privileges required to perform a complete database backup? (Choose three.)

▶ **Correct Answers: A, B, and F**

A. **Correct:** The sysadmin fixed server role can perform any activity within SQL Server, including a complete database backup.

B. **Correct:** The db_owner fixed database role has all permissions to the database, including a complete database backup.

C. **Incorrect:** The diskadmin fixed server role can manage disk files but cannot perform a complete database backup.

D. **Incorrect:** The dbcreator fixed server role can create and alter databases but cannot perform a complete database backup.

E. **Incorrect:** The serveradmin fixed server role can set serverwide configuration options and shut down the server but cannot perform a complete database backup.

F. **Correct:** The db_backupoperator fixed database role can issue DBCC, CHECKPOINT, and BACKUP statements.

## 70-028.04.03.002

You are preparing to back up the orders database using the BACKUP DATABASE command.

The required result is to append the backup to an existing file on tape.

The first optional result is to retain the media header information of the backup volume.

The second optional result is to restart the backup operation from the point of failure.

The proposed solution is to issue this command:

BACKUP DATABASE orders
   TO TAPE = 'c:\mssql\backup\orderbac.bak'
   WITH NOINIT, RESTART

What does the proposed solution provide?

A. The required result and all optional results.

B. The required result and one optional result.

C. The required result but none of the optional results.

D. The proposed solution does not provide the required result.

## 70-028.04.03.002

You are preparing to back up the orders database using the BACKUP DATABASE command.

The required result is to append the backup to an existing file on tape.

The first optional result is to retain the media header information of the backup volume.

The second optional result is to restart the backup operation from the point of failure.

The proposed solution is to issue this command:

```
BACKUP DATABASE orders
    TO TAPE = 'c:\mssql\backup\orderbac.bak'
    WITH NOINIT, RESTART
```

What does the proposed solution provide?

▶ **Correct Answer: A**

A. **Correct:** Using the BACKUP DATABASE command with the Noinit option appends the database backup to the existing file on tape and retains the media header information of the existing volume. Using the Restart option restarts a stalled backup operation from the point of failure for tape back-ups only.

B. **Incorrect:** See the explanation for answer A.

C. **Incorrect:** See the explanation for answer A.

D. **Incorrect:** See the explanation for answer A.

## 70-028.04.03.003

Evaluate this command:

USE master
EXEC sp_addumpdevice 'disk', 'testbac'
    'c:\backupdir\testbac.bak'
BACKUP DATABASE testdb TO testbac

Which two tasks will the command accomplish? (Choose two.)

A. Create the testbac backup file.

B. Create a temporary backup file.

C. Perform a complete database backup.

D. Append a complete backup to testbac.

E. Overwrite any previous backups to testbac.

## 70-028.04.03.004

You perform a differential backup and a transaction log backup for the testdb database. A row in the testdb database has changed six times since the last complete database backup. How will the differential backup differ from the transaction log backup?

A. The differential backup will store the last value for the row; the transaction log backup will store six transactions for the row.

B. The differential backup will store six values for the row; the transaction log backup will store only the last transaction for the row.

C. The differential backup will store six values for the row; the transaction log backup will store only the first transaction for the row.

D. The differential backup will store the last value for the row; the transaction log backup will store only the last transaction for the row.

## 70-028.04.03.003

Evaluate this command:

USE master
EXEC sp_addumpdevice 'disk', 'testbac'
   'c:\backupdir\testbac.bak'
BACKUP DATABASE testdb TO testbac

Which two tasks will the command accomplish? (Choose two.)

▶ **Correct Answers: A and C**

   A. **Correct:** The sp_addumpdevice system stored procedure creates a backup device (the hard disk file testbac.bak).

   B. **Incorrect:** Since the sp_addumpdevice system stored procedure creates a named backup device with the logical name testbac.bak, a temporary backup file is not created.

   C. **Correct:** The BACKUP DATABASE testdb TO testbac command creates a complete database backup.

   D. **Incorrect:** To append a complete backup to the testbac.bak hard disk file, the Noinit option must be specified.

   E. **Incorrect:** To overwrite any previous backups to the testbac.bak hard disk file, the Init option must be specified.

## 70-028.04.03.004

You perform a differential backup and a transaction log backup for the testdb database. A row in the testdb database has changed six times since the last complete database backup. How will the differential backup differ from the transaction log backup?

▶ **Correct Answer: A**

   A. **Correct:** A differential database backup records only the data changes made to the database after the last complete database backup and stores only the last set of values for a row. A transaction log backup stores all changes to the row, but does not store the row data.

   B. **Incorrect:** A differential database backup stores only the *last* set of values for a row. A transaction log backup stores *all* changes to the row, but does not store the row data.

   C. **Incorrect:** A differential database backup stores only the *last* set of values for a row. However, a transaction log backup stores *all* changes to the row, but does not store the row data.

   D. **Incorrect:** See the explanation for answer C.

**70-028.04.03.005**

Evaluate this command:

BACKUP LOG WITH TRUNCATE_ONLY

Which two tasks will the command accomplish? (Choose two.)

A. Removes the active part of the log without making a backup copy

B. Backs up the log without truncating it

C. Backs up the log if the database becomes damaged

D. Truncates the log

E. Backs up the log if the database has not been recovered

## 70-028.04.03.005

Evaluate this command:

BACKUP LOG WITH TRUNCATE_ONLY

Which two tasks will the command accomplish? (Choose two.)

▶ **Correct Answers: A and D**

A. **Correct:** The BACKUP LOG command with the Truncate_Only option removes the active part of the log without making a backup copy.

B. **Incorrect:** The BACKUP LOG command with the No_Truncate option backs up the log without truncating it.

C. **Incorrect:** The BACKUP LOG command with the No_Truncate option backs up the log if the database becomes damaged.

D. **Correct:** The BACKUP LOG command with the Truncate_Only option truncates the log.

E. **Incorrect:** The BACKUP LOG command with the No_Truncate option backs up the log if the database has not been recovered.

# Further Reading

The *Microsoft SQL Server 7.0 System Administration Training* volume of the *Microsoft SQL Server 7.0 System Administration Training Kit,* Chapter 9, Lesson 1 provides an overview of backup devices. Lesson 2 provides details on performing complete database, differential database, transaction log, and filegroup backups.

Use Microsoft SQL Server Books Online (free download available at http://support.microsoft.com/download/support/mslfiles/sqlbol.exe) to search for "BACKUP" and related topics for information about using the BACKUP command and creating complete database, transaction log, differential database, and filegroup backups. Search for "sp_addumpdevice" for details on creating a backup device. Search for "truncating the transaction log" for details on using the Truncate_Only and No_Log options to truncate the transaction log.

*SQL Server System Administration.* New Riders, Indianapolis, IN, 1999. ISBN 1-56205-955-6. Chapter 6 contains detailed information about backup devices, the BACKUP statement, and performing backups.

# Restore system and user databases from a complete database backup, a transaction log backup, a differential database backup, and a filegroup backup.

The restore operation allows you to return a database to the state it was in when a backup was created. You may need to restore data as a result of hardware or software failures or mishaps, or to move or copy a database from one server to another. Before you perform a restore operation, you must:

- Verify the backups

- Restrict access to the database

- Back up the transaction log

- Switch to the master database

To verify backup devices, use the SQL Server Enterprise Manager database property sheet or the following Transact-SQL statements to view information for each backup to ensure that the backup device is valid and contains the expected backup sets:

- RESTORE HEADERONLY

- RESTORE FILELISTONLY

- RESTORE LABELONLY

- RESTORE VERIFYONLY

Next, database access must be restricted so users cannot interfere with the restore operation. A member of the sysadmin or db_owner role must set the DBO Use Only database option to TRUE before restoring the database. Set the DBO Use Only database option using the database property sheet in SQL Server Enterprise Manager or the sp_dboption system stored procedure.

Third, back up the transaction log before performing restore operations so changes that occurred between the last transaction log backup and the time the database was taken offline can be restored. The transaction log backup is used to recover the database as the last step in the restore process.

Finally, to ensure that you are not using the database that you are trying to restore, switch to the master database before restoring the database. Execute the USE master command before beginning to restore the database.

Data can be restored from a complete database backup, a transaction log backup, a differential backup, or a file or filegroup backup.

Restoring a complete database backup returns the database to the state it was in when the backup was created. All readable and complete transactions in the database backup are recovered or "rolled forward." Any incomplete transactions in the database backup are removed or "rolled back" to ensure the database remains consistent. You should restore from a complete database backup when:

- The physical disk containing the database is damaged.

- The database is damaged, corrupted, or deleted.

- The database must be copied or moved to a different SQL Server, such as a standby SQL Server.

A complete database restore can be performed using the SQL Server Enterprise Manager or the RESTORE DATABASE Transact-SQL statement.

In a complete database restore, the RECOVERY option instructs the restore operation to roll back any uncommitted transactions, returning a database to a consistent state. When the RECOVERY option is specified, the database is ready for use. It is important not to specify the RECOVERY option until the last backup is restored. If you use a complete database backup and do not have transaction log or differential backups, specify the RECOVERY option. If transaction log or differential backups exist, specify the NORECOVERY option to postpone the recovery process until the last backup is restored.

Restoring a transaction log reapplies all completed transactions in the log to the database. When applying a transaction log backup to a database, all transactions on the transaction log are rolled forward until the exact state of the database at the time the backup operation started is recreated. Then all transactions that were incomplete when the backup operation started are rolled back.

Transaction logs are usually restored to apply changes made to the database since the last complete database or differential backup. In addition, you can use a database backup and a sequence of transaction log backups to recover a database up to any point in time included within the transaction logs. When you restore transaction logs, use the Stopat option if you want to specify a point in time to which you want the database restored. A transaction log restore can be performed using SQL Server Enterprise Manager or the RESTORE LOG Transact-SQL statement.

In a transaction log restore, it is important not to specify the RECOVERY option until the last backup is restored. Restore a complete database backup, specifying the NORECOVERY option, before restoring a transaction log. If you have multiple transaction logs to restore, specify the NORECOVERY option for all transaction logs except the last one, which suspends the recovery process until the last transaction log is restored. The Stopat option recovers a database to the state it was in at a date and time you specify. SQL Server restores all transaction log records written to the database up to the specified date and time.

When you perform a differential database backup, only the parts of the database that have changed since the last complete database backup are restored. This action returns the database to the exact condition it was in when the differential backup was performed. Restoring a differential database backup may take less time than restoring a series of transaction logs representing the same database activity. A differential database restore can be performed using SQL Server Enterprise Manager or the RESTORE DATABASE Transact-SQL statement.

In a differential database restore, it is important not to specify the RECOVERY option until the last backup is restored. Restore a complete database backup, specifying the NORECOVERY option, before restoring a differential backup. If there are transaction logs to be restored, specify the NORECOVERY option when restoring a differential database backup. Otherwise, specify the RECOVERY option.

Restoring from a file or filegroup backup reduces restore time by restoring only part of a database. Restore from a file or filegroup when a specific file is deleted or damaged. SQL Server requires you to restore the filegroup backups as a unit if a table and its associated indexes exist on two different filegroups. A file or filegroup restore can be performed using SQL Server Enterprise Manager or the RESTORE DATABASE Transact-SQL statement and selecting the File and/or Filegroup options.

After restoring a file or filegroup, you must apply all transaction logs created since the time of the backup from which the file or filegroup was restored. Therefore, the RECOVERY option is not an option when restoring a file or filegroup. If you have not performed a transaction log backup since the time of the last file or filegroup backup, the file or filegroup restore operation will terminate with an error. If the primary data file and the transaction log file are intact, you can still make a transaction log backup using the No_Truncate option before attempting to restore the file or filegroup. The log must not be truncated because the start of the transaction log backup must contain the start of the oldest transaction outstanding at the time the earliest file or filegroup backup was created.

Questions related to this objective are designed to determine if you have an awareness of these issues. To successfully answer the questions for this objective, you need a firm understanding of several key terms. For definitions of these terms, refer to the Glossary in this book.

## Key Terms

- Backup

- Backup device

- Backup file

- Backup media

- Backup set

- Database backup (also known as *full* or *complete database backup*)

- Differential database backup

- Filegroup

- File or filegroup backup

- Index

- Master database

- Media failure

- Recovery

- Restore

- Roll back

- Roll forward

- Table

- Transaction

- Transaction log

- Transaction log backup

## 70-028.04.04.001

You are preparing to restore a backup. Which Transact-SQL statement should you execute to display the logical and physical names of the database and transaction logs included in a backup set?

A. RESTORE LABELONLY

B. RESTORE HEADERONLY

C. RESTORE VERIFYONLY

D. RESTORE FILELISTONLY

## 70-028.04.04.002

With which backup file(s) should you use the NORECOVERY option to restore the transaction logs?

A. All

B. Only the last

C. Only the first

D. All but the last

## 70-028.04.04.001

You are preparing to restore a backup. Which Transact-SQL statement should you execute to display the logical and physical names of the database and transaction logs included in a backup set?

▶ **Correct Answer: D**

A. **Incorrect:** The RESTORE LABELONLY statement displays information about the backup media identified by the given backup device.

B. **Incorrect:** The RESTORE HEADERONLY statement retrieves all the backup header information for all backup sets on a particular backup device, including the name, type of media, backup method, date and time the backup was performed, backup size, and backup sequence number.

C. **Incorrect:** The RESTORE VERIFYONLY statement checks to see that the backup set is complete and that all volumes are readable, but it does not attempt to verify the structure of the data contained in the backup volumes.

D. **Correct:** The RESTORE FILELISTONLY statement displays a list of the database and transaction log files contained in a backup set, including the logical and physical names of the files, type of file, filegroup membership, size of the backup set, and maximum allowed size of the backup set.


## 70-028.04.04.002

With which backup file(s) should you use the NORECOVERY option to restore the transaction logs?

▶ **Correct Answer: D**

A. **Incorrect:** See the explanation for answer D.

B. **Incorrect:** See the explanation for answer D.

C. **Incorrect:** See the explanation for answer D.

D. **Correct:** The RESTORE statement NORECOVERY option instructs the restore operation to not roll back any uncommitted (incomplete) transactions. SQL Server requires the use of the NORECOVERY option on *all but the final* RESTORE statement when restoring a database backup and multiple transaction logs. The database remains unavailable until the RECOVERY option is used on the final transaction log backup.

## 70-028.04.04.003

The dbtest database exists on the DBTEST, DBTEST2, and DBTEST3 database files. The file DBTEST3 contains a single table and was backed up to the DBTEST3BAC backup file. Since DBTEST was last backed up, one transaction log backup named DBTESTBACLOG was performed. A media failure has occurred and DBTEST3 needs to be restored.

Which two steps are required to maintain database consistency? (Choose two.)

A. Restore the transaction log backup using the WITH RECOVERY clause.

B. Restore the transaction log backup using the WITH NORECOVERY clause.

C. Restore the dbtest database with the DBTEST3BAC backup file using the WITH RECOVERY clause.

D. Restore the dbtest database with the DBTEST3BAC backup file using the WITH NORECOVERY clause.

E. Restore the dbtest database with the DBTEST1BAC, DBTEST2BAC, and DBTEST3BAC backup files using the WITH NORECOVERY clause.

## 70-028.04.04.003

The dbtest database exists on the DBTEST, DBTEST2, and DBTEST3 database files. The file DBTEST3 contains a single table and was backed up to the DBTEST3BAC backup file. Since DBTEST was last backed up, one transaction log backup named DBTESTBACLOG was performed. A media failure has occurred and DBTEST3 needs to be restored.

Which two steps are required to maintain database consistency? (Choose two.)

▶ **Correct Answers: A and D**

A. **Correct:** The second step in maintaining database consistency is to restore the transaction log backup using the RECOVERY clause. Since there is only one transaction log backup, the RECOVERY clause is used to instruct the restore operation to roll back any uncommitted (incomplete) transactions and make the database ready for use. Use these commands to restore and recover the transaction log:

```
USE master
RESTORE LOG dbtest
FROM dbtestbaclog
WITH RECOVERY
```

B. **Incorrect:** Since there is only one transaction log backup, use the RECOVERY clause to instruct the restore operation to roll back any uncommitted transactions and make the database ready for use.

C. **Incorrect:** Since you must apply the transaction logs that were created since the backup to bring the restored file into a state that is consistent with the rest of the database, the RECOVERY clause is not allowed when restoring a file.

D. **Correct:** The first step in maintaining database consistency is to restore the dbtest database with the DBTEST3BAC backup file using the NORECOVERY clause. Since you must apply the transaction logs that were created since the backup to bring the restored file into a state that is consistent with the rest of the database, the RECOVERY clause is not allowed when restoring a file. Use these commands to restore DBTEST3:

```
USE master
RESTORE DATABASE dbtest
    FILE = dbtestbac3
FROM dbtestbac
WITH NORECOVERY
```

E. **Incorrect:** Since only DBTEST3 needs to be restored, there is no reason to restore the DBTEST1 and DBTEST2 databases.

## 70-028.04.04.004

What is the purpose of the Stopat option in restore and recovery operations?

A. To recover a standby SQL Server

B. To check the progress of log restores

C. To recover the transaction logs to the exact moment before an accidental UPDATE was performed

D. To restore and recover the database files to the exact moment before the database was accidentally deleted

## 70-028.04.04.005

Evaluate this command:

```
USE master
RESTORE LOG dbtest
FROM dbtestbaclog
WITH FILE=1
STATS, NORECOVERY
```

Which task will this command accomplish?

A. It will roll back any uncommitted transactions.

B. It will roll forward any uncommitted transactions.

C. It will restore the first transaction log without recovering the database.

D. It will restore a complete database backup from file 1 and recover using the transaction logs.

## 70-028.04.04.004

What is the purpose of the Stopat option in restore and recovery operations?

▶ **Correct Answer: C**

   A. **Incorrect:** The RESTORE LOG statement Standby option is used for consecutive restores of the same database, such as the recovery of a standby server.

   B. **Incorrect:** The RESTORE LOG statement Stats option is used when you need to display the progress of the restore operation.

   C. **Correct:** The RESTORE LOG statement Stopat option specifies that the transaction log be restored to the state it was in as of the specified date and time.

   D. **Incorrect:** The RESTORE LOG statement Stopat option can be specified only when restoring transaction log backups and cannot be used to restore entire database files.

## 70-028.04.04.005

Evaluate this command:

```
USE master
RESTORE LOG dbtest
FROM dbtestbaclog
WITH FILE=1
STATS, NORECOVERY
```

Which task will this command accomplish?

▶ **Correct Answer: C**

   A. **Incorrect:** The command restores the first transaction log without recovering the database. NORECOVERY instructs the restore operation to not roll back any uncommitted (incomplete) transactions.

   B. **Incorrect:** The command restores the first transaction log without recovering the database. NORECOVERY instructs the restore operation to not roll back any uncommitted (incomplete) transactions. Uncommitted transactions cannot be rolled forward.

   C. **Correct:** The command restores the first transaction log without recovering the database. RESTORE LOG DBTEST FROM DBTESTBACLOG restores the transaction log DBTEST from the DBTESTBACLOG backup log file. WITH FILE=1 identifies the backup set to be restored, transaction log file 1. STATS allows SQL Server to display a message after every 10 percent of the backup completed. NORECOVERY instructs the restore operation to not roll back any uncommitted (incomplete) transactions.

   D. **Incorrect:** The command restores the first transaction log without recovering the database.

# Further Reading

The *Microsoft SQL Server 7.0 System Administration Training* volume of the *Microsoft SQL Server 7.0 System Administration Training Kit,* Chapter 10, Lesson 1 provides an overview of the recovery and restore processes. Lesson 2 contains details on using the RESTORE statement. Lesson 3 provides information about performing a database restore from a complete database backup, a differential database backup, a transaction log backup, and a file or filegroup backup.

Use Microsoft SQL Server Books Online (free download available at http://support.microsoft.com/download/support/mslfiles/sqlbol.exe) to search for "restore" and related topics for information about using the RESTORE statement to restore from a complete database backup, a differential database backup, a transaction log backup, and a file or filegroup backup.

*SQL Server System Administration.* New Riders, Indianapolis, IN, 1999. ISBN 1-56205-955-6. Chapter 6 contains detailed information about the RESTORE statement and recovering databases.

O B J E C T I V E   4 . 5

# Manage replication.

Replication allows you to distribute data from one SQL Server to others in varying locations. Using a Publisher and a Distributor, you can automate the distribution of data to Subscribers. A *Publisher* is a server that makes data available to Subscribers. A *Distributor* is a server that receives a copy of all changes to the published data, stores the changes, and then makes them available to the appropriate Subscribers. A *Subscriber* is a server that receives copies of published data. A Publisher and Distributor may be located on the same server.

Managing replication involves three main tasks for the system administrator:

- Configuring servers, including the Distributor, Publisher, and Subscriber

- Creating publications

- Setting up and managing subscriptions

Using system administrator permissions, you must configure the Distributor before you create dependent Publishers. Use the Configure Publishing and Distribution Wizard in SQL Server Enterprise Manager to configure a Distributor. If the Distributor and Publisher are using the same server, the wizard provides an option to configure both the Publisher and the Distributor. The distribution database is installed automatically when you configure a Distributor.

Use the Configure Publishing and Distribution Wizard in SQL Server Enterprise Manager to configure a Publisher. If the Distributor and Publisher are using the same server, the wizard allows you to configure them simultaneously.

After you have configured the Distributor and Publisher, you are ready to configure Subscribers. There are two types of Subscribers: registered and anonymous.

For a *registered* Subscriber, information about the Subscriber is stored at the Publisher and performance information about the Subscriber is kept at the Distributor. A registered Subscriber must be enabled at the Publisher and either a push or a pull subscription must be created.

Enable registered Subscribers by adding Subscribers to the list of Subscribers on the Publisher and Distributor Properties dialog box, by configuring the security settings and default agent schedules for the Subscriber, and by verifying that you have a valid account to access the Distributor and the Distribution working folder.

For an *anonymous* Subscriber, no information about the Subscriber is stored at the Publisher or the Distributor. Anonymous Subscribers do not have to be enabled at the Publisher, and they can only be pulled from the Subscriber.

After you have configured your servers, you can create publications. A *publication* is a group of articles available for replication as a unit. Publications may be created only after the Distributor, Publisher, and Subscriber servers are configured. Use the Create Publication Wizard to create new publications.

A *subscription* allows Subscribers to receive copies of published data. Each publication type supports a push or a pull subscription. Use the Push Subscription Wizard and the Pull Subscription Wizard to create subscriptions. In a push subscription, the Publisher maintains a subscription by sending—or pushing—the appropriate data changes to one or more Subscribers. For snapshot and transactional replication, the Distribution Agent is maintained at the Distributor; for merge replication, the Merge Agent is maintained at the Distributor. In a pull subscription, the Subscriber maintains a subscription by requesting—or pulling—data changes from a Publisher. For snapshot and transactional replication, the Distribution Agent is maintained at the Subscriber; for merge replication, the Merge Agent is maintained at the Subscriber.

Questions related to this objective are designed to determine if you have an awareness of these issues. To successfully answer the questions for this objective, you need a firm understanding of several key terms. For definitions of these terms, refer to the Glossary in this book.

# Key Terms

- Anonymous subscription

- Article

- Distribute

- Distribution Agent

- Distribution database

- Distributor

- Filtering

- Horizontal filtering

- Latency

- Log Reader Agent

- Merge Agent

- Merge replication

- Publication

- Publication database

- Publish

- Publisher

- Pull subscription

- Push subscription

- Replication
- Replication agents
- Replication types
- Snapshot Agent
- Snapshot replication
- Subscribe
- Subscriber
- Subscription database
- Synchronization
- Transactional replication
- Vertical filtering

## 70-028.04.05.001

The Trust Insurance Company has multiple sites running SQL Server 7.0, each making changes to customer data independent of the others. Periodically, each site updates a Publisher server. Conflicts in the data are resolved and changes are applied to all the Subscribers.

Which type of replication is used by the Trust Insurance Company?

A. Merge replication

B. Snapshot replication

C. Transactional replication

## 70-028.04.05.002

The human resources department of the Acme Sporting Goods chain maintains a database of company policies. Each store has a read-only copy of the database. The policies rarely change and periodically each store receives a new version of the data.

Which type of replication is used by Acme Sporting Goods?

A. Merge replication

B. Snapshot replication

C. Transactional replication

## 70-028.04.05.001

The Trust Insurance Company has multiple sites running SQL Server 7.0, each making changes to customer data independent of the others. Periodically, each site updates a Publisher server. Conflicts in the data are resolved and changes are applied to all the Subscribers.

Which type of replication is used by the Trust Insurance Company?

▶ **Correct Answer: A**

A. **Correct:** Merge replication allows sites to make autonomous changes to replicated data and, at a later time, merges the changes made at all sites. Since the sites need to update customer data independently of each other, merge replication is the best choice. Merge replication offers the highest degree of autonomy; however, it does not guarantee transactional integrity.

B. **Incorrect:** Snapshot replication takes a picture of the published data in the database at a moment in time and sends it to the Subscribers. Sites cannot update data independently from each other, as data moves from the Publisher server to the Subscribers only.

C. **Incorrect:** Transactional replication applies changes made at the source to the destination in the order in which the changes were made. Sites cannot update data independently from each other, as data moves from the Publisher server to the Subscribers only.

## 70-028.04.05.002

The human resources department of the Acme Sporting Goods chain maintains a database of company policies. Each store has a read-only copy of the database. The policies rarely change and periodically each store receives a new version of the data.

Which type of replication is used by Acme Sporting Goods?

▶ **Correct Answer: B**

A. **Incorrect:** Merge replication allows sites to make autonomous changes to replicated data and, at a later time, merges the changes made at all sites. Since the stores have read-only copies of the database and do not need to update data, merge replication is not the best choice.

B. **Correct:** Snapshot replication takes a picture of the published data in the database at a moment in time and sends it to the Subscribers. Data moves from the Publisher server to the Subscribers only. Since the stores have read-only copies of the database and do not need to update data, snapshot replication is the best choice.

C. **Incorrect:** Transactional replication applies changes made at the source to the destination in the order in which the changes were made. Data moves from the Publisher server to the Subscribers only. Since the company polices rarely change, latency is not an issue, so transactional replication is not the best choice.

**70-028.04.05.003**

What should you consider when determining the amount of memory needed for the distribution database?

A. The amount of data and the number of Subscribers

B. The maximum retention time for the transaction history

C. The number of transactions and the number of Publishers

D. The average transaction size and the estimated transaction rate

**70-028.04.05.004**

You create a new publication for the sample table in the testdb database. You need to create a push subscription to the publication. Which two roles can create a push subscription? (Choose two.)

A. sysadmin

B. db_owner

C. dbcreator

D. serveradmin

E. db_accessdomain

F. db_securityadmin

## 70-028.04.05.003

What should you consider when determining the amount of memory needed for the distribution database?

▶ **Correct Answer: A**

    A. **Correct:** When determining the amount of memory needed for the distribution database, you should consider the amount of data and the number of Subscribers.

    B. **Incorrect:** When determining the amount of *space* (not memory) needed for the distribution database and the distribution working folder for snapshot or merge replication, you should consider the maximum retention time for the transaction history.

    C. **Incorrect:** When determining the amount of *space* (not memory) needed for the distribution database and the distribution working folder for transactional replication, you should consider the average transaction size and the estimated transaction rate.

    D. **Incorrect:** See the explanation for answer C.

## 70-028.04.05.004

You create a new publication for the sample table in the testdb database. You need to create a push subscription to the publication. Which two roles can create a push subscription? (Choose two.)

▶ **Correct Answers: A and B**

    A. **Correct:** Only users who are members of the sysadmin or db_owner roles can create a push subscription. However, for a member of the db_owner role to create a push subscription, the Subscribers must be registered by a member of the sysadmin role.

    B. **Correct:** See the explanation for answer A.

    C. **Incorrect:** Only users who are members of the sysadmin or db_owner roles can create a push subscription.

    D. **Incorrect:** See the explanation for answer C.

    E. **Incorrect:** See the explanation for answer C.

    F. **Incorrect:** See the explanation for answer C.

**70-028.04.05.005**

You are setting up merge replication. Why might you decide to use a pull subscription?

A. To run the Merge Agent at the Distributor

B. To administer all the subscriptions centrally

C. To allow the Subscriber to decide when to subscribe

D. To use the Distributor resources for the subscribe operations

## 70-028.04.05.005

You are setting up merge replication. Why might you decide to use a pull subscription?

▶ **Correct Answer: C**

A. **Incorrect:** A feature of pull subscriptions is that the Merge Agent for merge publications runs at the Subscriber, which can reduce the amount of processing overhead on the Distributor.

B. **Incorrect:** A *push* subscription allows you to administer all the subscriptions centrally.

C. **Correct:** A pull subscription allows members of the sysadmin or db_owner roles at the Subscriber to decide when to receive updates.

D. **Incorrect:** See the explanation for answer A.

# Further Reading

The *Microsoft SQL Server 7.0 System Administration Training* volume of the *Microsoft SQL Server 7.0 System Administration Training Kit,* Chapter 15, Lesson 3 defines SQL Server replication types. Chapter 16, Lesson 3 provides details on publishing tasks. Lesson 4 contains procedures for creating subscriptions.

Use Microsoft SQL Server Books Online (free download available at http://support.microsoft.com/download/support/mslfiles/sqlbol.exe) to search for "overview of replication" and related topics for basic information about managing replication. Search for "enhancing performance" for details on enhancing replication performance. Search for "using the push and pull subscription wizards," "adding a push subscription," and "adding a pull subscription" for details on push and pull subscriptions.

*SQL Server System Administration.* New Riders, Indianapolis, IN, 1999. ISBN 1-56205-955-6. Chapter 9 contains detailed information about replication.

OBJECTIVE 4.6

# Automate administrative tasks.

SQL Server Agent is designed to be an assistant to the system administrator, allowing the automation of repetitive administrative tasks. SQL Server Agent is a service that runs on Windows NT server, independent of SQL Server. However, SQL Server Agent uses SQL Server to store information needed to perform operations, and SQL Server must be running for operations to be completed. You can use SQL Server Agent to automate jobs, alerts, and SQLAgentMail. To automate these tasks, you must be able to define jobs, define alerts, define operators, and set up SQLAgentMail for notification and alerts.

You can create jobs to implement administrative tasks such as backing up databases, replicating data, or creating databases. The following steps define a job:

1. Specify the job name, category, owner, and description. Use the General tab in the Job Properties dialog box, the Create Job Wizard, or the sp_add_job system stored procedure. The job definition is stored in the MSDB..SYSJOBS system table.

2. Create job steps. Job steps are the actions performed by the job. You must name each step, select the step type, and enter the command for the action. Use the General tab in the Job Step dialog box, the Create Job Wizard, or the sp_add_jobstep system stored procedure. The job step definitions are stored in the MSDB..SYSJOBSTEPS system table.

3. Sequence job steps. If your job has more than one job step, set the order in which the job steps are executed. You can add or delete steps or change the order at any time. Use the Steps tab in the Job Properties dialog box, the Create Job Wizard, or the sp_add_jobstep system stored procedure.

4. Specify job step actions. Specify the output file for Transact-SQL job steps. Specify actions to be taken when a job step succeeds or fails. You can also define the number of and interval between retry attempts for failed job steps. Use the Advanced tab in the Job Step dialog box, the Create Job Wizard, or the sp_add_jobstep system stored procedure.

5. Schedule the job. Indicate how the job will run. Use the Schedules tab in the Job Properties dialog box, the Create Job Wizard, or the sp_add_jobschedule system stored procedure. The job schedules are stored in the MSDB..SYSJOBSCHEDULES system table.

6. Specify job notifications. Specify the actions to perform when a job is completed successfully or unsuccessfully, or when it is completed regardless of status. Use the Notifications tab in the Job Properties dialog box, the Create Job Wizard, or the sp_add_job system stored procedure.

You can define alerts to automatically notify you when a specific event occurs. When events such as errors and messages are generated by SQL Server and entered into the Windows NT application log, SQL Server Agent checks the events in the application log and compares them to alerts that you have defined. When a match is found, an alert is fired. The alert definition is stored in the MSDB..SYSALERTS system table. The following SQL Server events are logged in the Windows NT application log by default:

- SYSMESSAGES errors with a severity of 19 or higher

- RAISERROR statements invoked by using the WITH LOG syntax

- Applications logged using the xp_logevent extended stored procedure

Use the SQL Server Enterprise Manager, the Create Alert Wizard, or the sp_add_alert system stored procedure to define alert conditions. Use the SQL Server Enterprise Manager, the Create Alert Wizard, or the sp_add_notification system stored procedure to define alert responses.

You can specify operators to be automatically notified about specified events. When a job completes or an alert is fired, you may elect to notify an operator by pager, e-mail, or a NET SEND command. Operators must be defined before you can send notification from an alert or job. The operator definitions are stored in the MSDB..SYSOPERATORS system table. Use the General tab in the Operator Properties dialog box or the sp_add_operator system stored procedure to define an operator.

*Fail-safe operators* are those who are notified when the operators assigned to the alert cannot be paged or when the SQL Server Agent cannot access the system tables in MSDB. A fail-safe operator is defined only on the Alert System tab in the SQL Server Agent Properties dialog box.

You can set up SQLAgentMail to be sent automatically to operators for notification and alerts. SQLAgentMail uses the SQLServerAgent service to process mail. You can configure SQLAgentMail to send an e-mail when an alert is triggered or when a scheduled task either succeeds or fails. SQLAgentMail establishes either a simple or an extended MAPI connection with a mail host. Follow these steps to set up SQLAgentMail:

1. Create an e-mail account for SQL Server on the e-mail server.

2. Configure SQL Server to log in to Windows NT with an e-mail account.

3. Install a mail client/profile on the SQL Server.

4. On the General tab in the SQL Server Agent Properties dialog box, click This Account, and enter the Windows NT account name and password used to create the mail profile for SQLAgentMail.

5. Select the SQLMail button. In Mail profile, select the mail profile you created for SQLAgentMail.

6. Click Test to confirm SQLAgentMail operation. The message "SQLAgentMail has started successfully and stopped a mail session with this profile" indicates that the profile is correct.

Questions related to this objective are designed to determine if you have an awareness of these issues. To successfully answer the questions for this objective, you need a firm understanding of several key terms. For definitions of these terms, refer to the Glossary in this book.

# Key Terms

- Alert

- Application log

- Event log

- Fail-safe operator

- Job

- Job step

- MAPI (Messaging Application Programming Interface)

- Master database

- NET SEND

- Operator

- Severity level number

- SNMP (Simple Network Management Protocol)

- SQLAgentMail

- SQL Server Agent

- System tables

- User-defined error message

## 70-028.04.06.001

You are using the Create Job Wizard to create a job that backs up the transaction log for the orders database every three hours. Which schedule option should you choose?

A. One Time

B. Recurring

C. Start Whenever The CPU(s) Become Idle

D. Start Automatically When SQL Server Agent Starts

## 70-028.04.06.002

You created a fail-safe operator to be paged when none of the operators to be paged are on duty, and you configured an alert for the "unexpected stop" error. What happens if the SQL Server Agent stops unexpectedly before the fail-safe operator is notified of the error?

A. The operator is notified because the fail-safe operator information is cached.

B. The operator is never notified because the information would be lost.

C. The operator is notified that the SQL Server Agent stopped when the SQL Server Agent is restarted.

D. The operator is not notified because the SQL Server Agent must be running to notify an operator.

## 70-028.04.06.001

You are using the Create Job Wizard to create a job that backs up the transaction log for the orders database every three hours. Which schedule option should you choose?

▶ **Correct Answer: B**

A. **Incorrect:** The One Time schedule option schedules the job only once, on a date and at a time you specify.

B. **Correct:** The Recurring schedule option schedules the job multiple times, based on a schedule you specify.

C. **Incorrect:** The Start Whenever The CPU(s) Become Idle schedule option executes the job during periods of low CPU activity.

D. **Incorrect:** The Start Automatically When SQL Server Agent Starts schedule option executes the job when the SQL Server Agent is started.

## 70-028.04.06.002

You created a fail-safe operator to be paged when none of the operators to be paged are on duty, and you configured an alert for the "unexpected stop" error. What happens if the SQL Server Agent stops unexpectedly before the fail-safe operator is notified of the error?

▶ **Correct Answer: C**

A. **Incorrect:** Although the fail-safe operator information is cached, no notification will occur if SQL Server Agent stops unexpectedly unless it is restarted.

B. **Incorrect:** Since the fail-safe operator information is cached, the fail-safe operator can still be notified if SQL Server Agent stops unexpectedly.

C. **Correct:** When SQL Server Agent stops unexpectedly, it attempts to restart. When it restarts successfully, the operator is notified.

D. **Incorrect:** See the explanation for answer C.

**70-028.04.06.003**

In which system table in the master database are user-defined error messages stored?

A. sysmessages

B. sysprocesses

C. sysdatabases

D. sysconfigures

**70-028.04.06.004**

At your company, the human resources manager should be notified by e-mail when an employee is deleted from the database. In case further action needs to be taken, the human resources manager needs to know the name of the end user who deleted the employee. Which two msdb database tables will the SQL Server Agent review when the delete employee stored procedure is executed? (Choose two.)

A. sysjobs

B. syspermissions

C. sysjobsteps

D. sysoperators

E. sysnotifications

## 70-028.04.06.003

In which system table in the master database are user-defined error messages stored?

▶ **Correct Answer: A**

A. **Correct:** User-defined error messages can be added to the sysmessages table in the master database using the sp_addmessage system stored procedure. The sysmessages table contains the severity level, a description, and the system message group ID for user-defined error messages.

B. **Incorrect:** The sysprocesses table in the master database holds information about client or system processes running on SQL Server. A user-defined error is not a process.

C. **Incorrect:** The sysdatabases table in the master database contains one row for each database on SQL Server. A user-defined error is not part of a database.

D. **Incorrect:** The sysconfigures table in the master database contains the configuration options defined before the most recent SQL Server startup, plus any dynamic configuration options set since then. A user-defined error is not a configuration option.

## 70-028.04.06.004

At your company, the human resources manager should be notified by e-mail when an employee is deleted from the database. In case further action needs to be taken, the human resources manager needs to know the name of the end user who deleted the employee. Which two msdb database tables will the SQL Server Agent review when the delete employee stored procedure is executed? (Choose two.)

▶ **Correct Answers: D and E**

A. **Incorrect:** The sysjobs msdb database table stores the information for each scheduled job to be executed by SQL Server Agent.

B. **Incorrect:** The syspermissions database table describes permissions that have been granted or denied.

C. **Incorrect:** The sysjobsteps msdb database table contains the information for each step in a job to be executed by SQL Server Agent.

D. **Correct:** The sysoperators msdb database table provides the operator ID and the name of the end user who executed the delete employee stored procedure.

E. **Correct:** The sysnotifications msdb database table provides the information in the sysoperators msdb database table to the operator to be notified—in this case, the human resources manager.

**70-028.04.06.005**

What would cause an event to be written to the EventLog service?

A. Any sysmessages error

B. Execution of the RAISERROR statement with any option

C. Execution of the RAISERROR statement using the With Log option

D. A SQL Server error with severity level between 11 and 18

## 70-028.04.06.005

What would cause an event to be written to the EventLog service?

▶ **Correct Answer: C**

A. **Incorrect:** Only SYSMESSAGES errors of severity 19 or higher are written to the EventLog service. You must use sp_altermessage to designate specific SYSMESSAGES errors as Always Logged to log error messages with a severity lower than 19.

B. **Incorrect:** RAISERROR statements must be invoked using the WITH LOG syntax to be written to the EventLog service. RAISERROR WITH LOG is the method recommended for writing to the Windows NT application log from SQL Server.

C. **Correct:** RAISERROR WITH LOG is the method recommended for writing to the Windows NT application log from SQL Server.

D. **Incorrect:** Only SQL Server errors of severity 19 or higher are written to the EventLog service. You must use sp_altermessage to designate specific SYSMESSAGES errors as Always Logged to log errors with a severity lower than 19.

# Further Reading

The *Microsoft SQL Server 7.0 System Administration Training* volume of the *Microsoft SQL Server 7.0 System Administration Training Kit,* Chapter 13, Lesson 2 contains procedures for defining operators and jobs. Lesson 3 contains procedures for defining alerts, user-defined errors, and fail-safe operators.

Use Microsoft SQL Server Books Online (free download available at http://support.microsoft.com/download/support/mslfiles/sqlbol.exe) to search for "jobs" and related topics for details on defining jobs. Search for "alerts" and related topics for details on defining alerts. Search for "operators" for details on defining operators. Search for "SQLAgentMail" and "notification" for information about setting up SQLAgentMail for job notification and alerts.

*SQL Server System Administration.* New Riders, Indianapolis, IN, 1999. ISBN 1-56205-955-6. Chapter 5 provides details on configuring jobs, alerts, and operators.

*Using Microsoft SQL Server 7.0.* Que, Indianapolis, IN, 1999. ISBN 0-7897-1628-3. Chapter 9 contains information about defining jobs, alerts, and operators as well as procedures for setting up SQLAgentMail.

O B J E C T I V E   4 . 7

# Enable access to remote data.

Linked servers allow queries, updates, commands, and transactions on OLE DB data sources across the enterprise. To enable access to these data sources, you must know how to set up linked servers and set up security for linked databases.

To set up a linked server, you must first register the connection information and data source information with SQL Server. When registration is completed, the data source can be referred to with a single logical name.

You can create or delete a linked server definition using the sp_addlinkedserver or sp_dropserver system stored procedures or SQL Server Enterprise Manager. The sp_serveroption system stored procedure allows you to define a linked server. This procedure sets server options for linked servers and provides options for distributed queries that can be enabled or disabled on a per-linked-server basis.

Servers may link when a login mapping is created at the source server, allowing the source to provide a login name and password to connect to the receiving server on its behalf. The default mapping for a linked server configuration is to pass the current security credentials of the login to the receiving server. Distributed queries are subject to the permissions set up for the data source at the receiving server. The provider detects permission violations when the query is executed.

You can create or delete login mappings for linked databases using the sp_addlinkedsrvlogin or sp_droplinkedsrvlogin system stored procedures or SQL Server Enterprise Manager.

After a linked server has been defined, the following system stored procedures allow you to view metadata for linked servers:

- **sp_linkedservers:** Displays information about the linked servers defined in a given SQL Server.

- **sp_catalogs:** Displays the list of catalogs in the specified linked server, which is equivalent to databases in SQL Server.

- **sp_column_privileges_ex:** Displays column privileges for the specified table from the specified linked server.

- **sp_columns_ex:** Displays the column information, one row per column, for the specified table from the specified linked server.

- **sp_foreignkeys:** Displays the foreign keys that reference primary keys for the specified table from the specified linked server.

- **sp_primarykeys:** Returns the primary key columns, one row per key column, for the specified remote table.

- **sp_indexes:** Returns index information for the specified remote table.

- **sp_table_privileges_ex:** Displays privilege information for the specified table from the specified linked server.

- **sp_tables_ex:** Displays table information for the specified tables from the specified linked server.

Questions related to this objective are designed to determine if you have an awareness of these issues. To successfully answer the questions for this objective, you need a firm understanding of several key terms. For definitions of these terms, refer to the Glossary in this book.

# Key Terms

- Argument
- Character set
- Data source
- Data source name (DSN)
- Distributed query
- Index
- Linked server
- Local server
- Login (account)
- Metadata
- OLE DB
- OLE DB provider
- Remote procedure call (RPC)
- Remote server
- Table

## 70-028.04.07.001

Evaluate this command:

USE master
EXEC sp_serveroption 'HRServer',
'data access', true

What will this command do?

A. Allow distributed queries on HRServer

B. Enable remote procedure calls to HRServer

C. Enable remote procedure calls from the local server

D. Map login accounts from the local server to HRServer

E. Ensure that the HRServer uses the same character set as the local server

## 70-028.04.07.001

Evaluate this command:

USE master
EXEC sp_serveroption 'HRServer',
'data access', true

What will this command do?

▶ **Correct Answer: A**

A. **Correct:** The sp_serveroption system stored procedure performed on HRServer with the Data Access option set to TRUE enables the linked server for distributed query access. The syntax for sp_serveroption is:

```
sp_serveroption [[@server =] 'server']
[,[@optname =] 'option_name']
[,[@optvalue =] 'option_value']
```

B. **Incorrect:** The sp_serveroption system stored procedure performed on HRServer with the RPC Out option set to TRUE enables remote procedure calls to HRServer.

C. **Incorrect:** The sp_serveroption system stored procedure performed on the local server with the RPC option set to TRUE enables remote procedure calls from the local server.

D. **Incorrect:** The sp_addlinkedsrvlogin system stored procedure maps login accounts from the local server to HRServer.

E. **Incorrect:** The sp_serveroption system stored procedure performed on HRServer with the Collation Compatible option set to FALSE verifies whether HRServer uses the same character set as the local server.

**70-028.04.07.002**

Evaluate this command:

USE master
EXEC sp_indexes 'HRDept', 'comm_rates', 'dbo', 'payroll', NULL, 0

What will this command do?

A. Create an index on the HRDEPT table of the comm_rates database on the PAYROLL server.

B. Create an index on the COMM_RATES table of the payroll database on the HRDEPT server.

C. Return all the index information from the COMM_RATES table of the payroll database on the HRDEPT server.

D. Return all the index information from the HRDEPT table of the comm_rates database on the PAYROLL server.

## 70-028.04.07.002

Evaluate this command:

USE master
EXEC sp_indexes 'HRDept', 'comm_rates', 'dbo', 'payroll', NULL, 0

What will this command do?

▶ **Correct Answer: C**

A. **Incorrect:** The CREATE INDEX statement is used to create an index on a given table. The Create Index Wizard and SQL Server Enterprise Manager can also be used to create an index.

B. **Incorrect:** The CREATE INDEX statement is used to create an index on a given table. The Create Index Wizard and SQL Server Enterprise Manager can also be used to create an index.

C. **Correct:** The sp_indexes system stored procedure with the HRDept, Comm_Rates, DBO, Payroll, NULL, and 0 options returns all index information from the COMM_RATES table of the payroll database of the HRDEPT server. The correct syntax for sp_indexes is:

```
sp_indexes {'table_server'} [,'table_name'] [,'table_schema'] [,'table_catalog']
[,'index'] [,'is_unique']
```

D. **Incorrect:** See the explanation for answer C.

## 70-028.04.07.003

You are preparing to set up security between a local and a linked SQL Server.

The required result is to allow the HRManager user to log in to the local server and access the data on the remote HRServer.

The first optional result is to give the HRManager the access to the HRServer with credentials of the rmtHRManager login account.

The second optional result is to associate a password with the rmtHRManager login account.

The proposed solution is to execute this system stored procedure:

```
EXEC sp_addlinkedsrvlogin
@rmtsrvname = 'HRServer',
@useself = 'false',
@locallogin = 'HRManager',
@rmtuser = 'rmtHRManager',
@rmtpassword = 'employee'
```

What does the proposed solution provide?

A. The required result and all optional results.

B. The required result and one optional result.

C. The required result but none of the optional results.

D. The proposed solution does not provide the required result.

## 70-028.04.07.003

You are preparing to set up security between a local and a linked SQL Server.

The required result is to allow the HRManager user to log in to the local server and access the data on the remote HRServer.

The first optional result is to give the HRManager the access to the HRServer with credentials of the rmtHRManager login account.

The second optional result is to associate a password with the rmtHRManager login account.

The proposed solution is to execute this system stored procedure:

EXEC sp_addlinkedsrvlogin
@rmtsrvname = 'HRServer',
@useself = 'false',
@locallogin = 'HRManager',
@rmtuser = 'rmtHRManager',
@rmtpassword = 'employee'

What does the proposed solution provide?

► **Correct Answer: A**

A. **Correct:** The sp_addlinkedsrvlogin system stored procedure creates or updates a mapping between logins on the local server running SQL Server and remote logins on the linked server. The RMTSRVNAME argument is HRServer, the name of the linked server to which the login mapping applies. The USESELF argument is FALSE, specifying that the RMTUSER and RMTPASSWORD arguments will be used to connect to RMTSRVNAME for the specified LOCALLOGIN. The LOCALLOGIN argument is HRManager, the login on the local server. The RMTUSER argument is rmtHRManager, the username used to connect to RMTSRVNAME because USESELF is false. The RMTPASSWORD is *employee*, the password associated with RMTUSER. The syntax for sp_addlinkedsrvlogin is:

```
sp_addlinkedsrvlogin [@rmtsrvname =] 'rmtsrvname'
[,[@useself =] 'useself']
[,[@locallogin =] 'locallogin']
[,[@rmtuser =] 'rmtuser']
[,[@rmtpassword =] 'rmtpassword']
```

B. **Incorrect:** See the explanation for answer A.

C. **Incorrect:** See the explanation for answer A.

D. **Incorrect:** See the explanation for answer A.

## 70-028.04.07.004

You are preparing to connect to an OLE DB data source.

The required result is to add the Oracle OraHR server as a linked server to the local server running SQL Server.

The first optional result is to specify MSDAORA as the OLE DB provider for this data source.

The second optional result is to specify the SQL*Net alias DB3 as the data source.

The proposed solution is to execute this system stored procedure:

EXEC sp_addlinkedserver 'OraHR', 'Oracle', 'MSDAORA', 'DB3'

What does the proposed solution provide?

A. The required result and all optional results.

B. The required result and one optional result.

C. The required result but none of the optional results.

D. The proposed solution does not provide the required result.

## 70-028.04.07.004

You are preparing to connect to an OLE DB data source.

The required result is to add the Oracle OraHR server as a linked server to the local server running SQL Server.

The first optional result is to specify MSDAORA as the OLE DB provider for this data source.

The second optional result is to specify the SQL*Net alias DB3 as the data source.

The proposed solution is to execute this system stored procedure:

EXEC sp_addlinkedserver 'OraHR', 'Oracle', 'MSDAORA', 'DB3'

What does the proposed solution provide?

▶ **Correct Answer: A**

A. **Correct:** The sp_addlinkedserver system stored procedure creates a link between the local server and the Oracle OraHR server. The server argument OraHR specifies the name of the linked server. The PRODUCT_NAME argument ORACLE specifies the product name of the OLE DB data source to add as a linked server. The PROVIDER_NAME argument MSDAORA is the unique programmatic identifier (PROGID) of the OLE DB provider corresponding to this data source. The DATA_SOURCE argument DB3 specifies the name of the data source as interpreted by the OLE DB provider. The syntax for sp_addlinkedserver is:

```
sp_addlinkedserver [@server =] 'server' [, [@srvproduct =] 'product_name']
[, [@provider =] 'provider_name'] [, [@datasrc =] 'data_source']
[, [@location =] 'location'] [, [@provstr =] 'provider_string']
[, [@catalog =] 'catalog']
```

B. **Incorrect:** See the explanation for answer A.

C. **Incorrect:** See the explanation for answer A.

D. **Incorrect:** See the explanation for answer A.

## 70-028.04.07.005

You are preparing to link to a remote SQL Server.

The required result is to create a link between the local SQL Server and the remote HRServer.

The first optional result is to specify SQL Server as the OLE DB provider.

The second optional result is to specify the data source used by the OLE DB provider.

The proposed solution is to execute this procedure:

EXEC sp_addlinkedserver 'HRServer'

What does the proposed solution provide?

A.  The required result and all optional results.

B.  The required result and one optional result.

C.  The required result but none of the optional results.

D.  The proposed solution does not provide the required result.

## 70-028.04.07.005

You are preparing to link to a remote SQL Server.

The required result is to create a link between the local SQL Server and the remote HRServer.

The first optional result is to specify SQL Server as the OLE DB provider.

The second optional result is to specify the data source used by the OLE DB provider.

The proposed solution is to execute this procedure:

EXEC sp_addlinkedserver 'HRServer'

What does the proposed solution provide?

▶ **Correct Answer: D**

A. **Incorrect:** See the explanation for answer D.

B. **Incorrect:** See the explanation for answer D.

C. **Incorrect:** See the explanation for answer D.

D. **Correct:** The sp_addlinkedserver system stored procedure creates a link between the local server and the remote HRServer. The server argument HRServer specifies the name of the linked server. However, the PRODUCT_NAME argument, SQL Server, is not specified so this solution does not provide the required result. If the PRODUCT_NAME SQL Server is specified, PROVIDER_NAME, DATA_SOURCE, LOCATION, PROVIDER_STRING, and CATALOG do not need to be specified. The syntax for sp_addlinkedserver is:

```
sp_addlinkedserver [@server =] 'server' [, [@srvproduct =] 'product_name']
[, [@provider =] 'provider_name'] [, [@datasrc =] 'data_source']
[, [@location =] 'location'] [, [@provstr =] 'provider_string']
[, [@catalog =] 'catalog']
```

# Further Reading

The *Microsoft SQL Server 7.0 System Administration Training* volume of the *Microsoft SQL Server 7.0 System Administration Training Kit,* Chapter 6, Lesson 4 provides information about setting up linked servers.

Use Microsoft SQL Server Books Online (free download available at http://support.microsoft.com/download/support/mslfiles/sqlbol.exe) to search for "configuring linked servers," "sp_serveroption," "sp_addlinkedserver," and related topics for details on setting up linked servers. Search for "sp_addlinkedsrvlogin" for details on setting up security for linked databases.

# Monitoring and Optimization

The Monitoring and Optimization domain examines how you can monitor system performance and optimize system resources for SQL Server. You can use SQL Server Profiler and Windows NT Performance Monitor to monitor system performance and determine whether performance problems exist. If they do, you can resolve them by tuning and optimizing SQL Server or by limiting resources used by queries.

## Tested Skills and Suggested Practices

- **Monitoring SQL Server performance. Be able to use SQL Server Profiler and the counters SQL Server adds to Windows NT Performance Monitor to monitor SQL Server components.**

  - Practice 1: Learn the purpose of SQL Server Profiler. Use SQL Server Profiler to monitor performance by setting up traces to collect information. Learn how the Index Tuning Wizard uses a workload file captured by SQL Server Profiler to analyze trace results.

  - Practice 2: Learn the purpose of the counters SQL Server adds to Performance Monitor. Use Performance Monitor to monitor performance. Learn the purpose of SQL Server objects, object instances, and counters. View the results of the counters on the Performance Monitor chart.

- **Tuning and optimizing SQL Server. Be able to tune and optimize SQL Server memory and CPU usage.**

  - Practice 1: Familiarize yourself with the counters used in Windows NT Performance Monitor to indicate SQL Server memory and CPU usage.

  - Practice 2: Familiarize yourself with the configuration options used to tune SQL Server memory and CPU usage.

- **Limiting resources used by queries. Be able to use the query cost value to control resources used by queries.**

  - Practice 1: Set the query cost value for the local server. Set the query cost value for the current session.

O B J E C T I V E   5 . 1

# Monitor SQL Server performance.

SQL Server monitoring tools allow you to determine the location of performance problems. As a system administrator, you must be able to use these tools to analyze data and determine query response time, transaction handling speed, and system usage efficiency.

The following tools are available for monitoring SQL Server performance:

- **SQL Server Profiler:** Captures a continuous record of server activity in real time by creating a *trace*—a file where server activity and events are captured for later use—of events you specify. Profiler is the best tool for collecting data about server resource and database activity events.

- **Performance Monitor:** Provides counts of system performance events. SQL Server counters provide additional information about SQL Server performance. Use Performance Monitor to monitor the overall performance of SQL Server.

- **Current Activity window:** Provides a graphic snapshot of the currently running SQL Server processes, including user activity, blocked processes, and locks.

- **Database Consistency Checker (DBCC) commands:** Provide the ability to check the logical and physical consistency of a database, check performance statistics, and perform basic maintenance functions.

- **sp_lock:** Provides a snapshot of information about locks, or restrictions on access to a resource.

- **sp_monitor:** Provides a snapshot of server statistics, including CPU usage, I/O usage, and amount of time idle since it was last executed.

- **sp_spaceused:** Provides an estimate of the amount of disk space currently used by a table or database.

- **sp_who:** Provides a snapshot of information about current SQL Server users and processes, including the currently executing statement and whether or not the statement is blocked.

SQL Server Profiler and Performance Monitor are the most important tools for monitoring SQL Server performance.

SQL Server Profiler allows you to collect data and monitor server and database activity. You must specify the data to collect in a trace, using SQL Server Profiler, SQL Server extended stored procedures, or the Create Trace Wizard.

To assess SQL Server performance, you should trace the locks, system stored procedures, and transactions events. The data from a SQL Server Profiler trace can be captured to a workload file and used by the Index Tuning Wizard to analyze the effectiveness of indexes and make recommendations for improvement.

Performance Monitor is a dynamic, real-time display for measuring the performance of objects in the system. The following is a list of SQL Server objects measured by Performance Monitor:

- **Access Methods:** Provides information about allocation of database objects

- **Backup Device:** Provides information about backup devices used by backup and restore operations

- **Buffer Manager:** Provides information about memory buffers used by SQL Server

- **Cache Manager:** Provides information about the SQL Server cache

- **Databases:** Provides information about SQL Server databases

- **General Statistics:** Provides information about general server-wide activity

- **Latches:** Provides information about *latches*—short-term objects primarily used to protect a row while it is read for connection—on internal resources used in SQL Server

- **Locks:** Provides information about individual lock requests made by SQL Server

- **Memory Manager:** Provides information about SQL Server memory usage

- **Replication Agents:** Provides information about currently running SQL Server replication agents

- **Replication Dist.:** Provides the number of commands and transactions read from the distribution database and delivered to the subscriber databases by the Distribution Agent

- **Replication Logreader:** Provides the number of commands and transactions read from the published databases and delivered to the distribution database by the Log Reader Agent

- **Replication Merge:** Provides information about SQL Server merge replication

- **Replication Snapshot:** Provides information about SQL Server snapshot replication

- **SQL Server Statistics:** Provides information about SQL queries

- **User Settable:** For custom stored procedures or any Transact-SQL statement that returns a value to be monitored

Object *instances* are specific examples of an object. Object instances are measured by *counters*, which provide information used to measure system traffic. Many counters are available for each object. The following SQL Server objects and counters associated with them are provided for Performance Monitor by default:

- SQL Server: Buffer Manager: Buffer Cache Hit Ratio

- SQL Server: General Statistics: User Connections

- SQL Server: Memory Manager: Total Server Memory (KB)

- SQL Server: SQL Statistics: SQL Compilations/sec

- SQL Server: Buffer Manager: Page Reads/sec

- SQL Server: Buffer Manager: Page Writes/sec

To add items to the Performance Monitor graph, use the Add To Chart dialog box to specify the object, counter, and instance for display.

Questions related to this objective are designed to determine if you have an awareness of these issues. To successfully answer the questions for this objective, you need a firm understanding of several key terms. For definitions of these terms, refer to the Glossary in this book.

# Key Terms

- Bottleneck

- Contention

- Create Trace Wizard

- Current Activity window

- Data column

- Deadlock

- Event

- Event categories

- Event class

- Filter

- Index

- Index Tuning Wizard

- Latches

- Lock

- Object

- Performance Monitor

- Query

- SQL Server Profiler

- Trace event criteria

- Trace file

- Transact-SQL

- Workload file

**70-028.05.01.001**

Which tool should you use to determine the number of deadlocks/sec occurring in a SQL Server database running on Windows NT?

A. Transact-SQL

B. SQL Server Profiler

C. Microsoft Event Viewer

D. Windows NT Performance Monitor

E. SQL Server Current Activity window

## 70-028.05.01.001

Which tool should you use to determine the number of deadlocks/sec occurring in a SQL Server database running on Windows NT?

▶ **Correct Answer: D**

A. **Incorrect:** The five Transact-SQL items that allow you to audit server and database activities (system stored procedures, functions, set statements, DBCC statements, and trace flags) do not provide the number of deadlocks/sec occurring in a SQL Server database running on Windows NT.

B. **Incorrect:** The SQL Server Profiler is a tool that captures a continuous record of server activity in real time. The Profiler is the best tool for monitoring database activity, including user access methods, user activity, object access, application use, and performance bottlenecks. While SQL Server Profiler may provide information about deadlock events, including the users and objects involved in the deadlock, the SQL Server Profiler does not provide the number of deadlocks/sec occurring in a SQL Server database running on Windows NT.

C. **Incorrect:** The Windows NT Event Viewer provides information about errors, warnings, and the successes or failures of tasks. Windows NT Event Viewer does not provide the number of deadlocks/sec occurring in a SQL Server database running on Windows NT.

D. **Correct:** Windows NT Performance Monitor is a Windows NT component that provides status information about system performance. SQL Server adds counters to Windows NT Performance Monitor to provide additional information about SQL Server performance. Use Performance Monitor to monitor overall performance of SQL Server, including the number of deadlocks/sec occurring in a SQL Server database running on Windows NT.

E. **Incorrect:** The Current Activity window provides a graphic snapshot of the currently running SQL Server processes, including user activity, blocked processes, and locks, but it does not provide the number of deadlocks/sec occurring in a SQL Server database running on Windows NT.

## 70-028.05.01.002

You suspect that unauthorized users are attempting to log in to your SQL Server. Which tool should you use to monitor unauthorized login attempts?

A. SQL Server Profiler

B. Microsoft Event Viewer

C. sp_who system stored procedure

D. Windows NT Performance Monitor

E. SQL Server Current Activity window

## 70-028.05.01.002

You suspect that unauthorized users are attempting to log in to your SQL Server. Which tool should you use to monitor unauthorized login attempts?

▶ **Correct Answer: A**

A. **Correct:** The SQL Server Profiler captures a continuous record of server activity in real time. Monitor the LoginFailed event class to assess security and audit login activity. Monitor the Event Sub Class event class and the SQL User Name or NT User Name data columns to determine the users who are failing to connect to SQL Server and the reasons why.

B. **Incorrect:** The Windows NT Event Viewer provides information about errors, warnings, and the successes or failures of tasks. Windows NT Event Viewer does not provide information about unauthorized login attempts.

C. **Incorrect:** The sp_who system stored procedure provides information about current SQL Server users and processes. This information can be filtered to show only those processes that are not idle. Sp_who does not provide information about unauthorized login attempts.

D. **Incorrect:** Windows NT Performance Monitor is a Windows NT component that provides status information about system performance. Performance Monitor does not provide information about unauthorized login attempts.

E. **Incorrect:** The Current Activity window provides a graphic snapshot of the currently running SQL Server processes, including user activity, blocked processes, and locks, but it does not provide information about unauthorized login attempts.

## 70-028.05.01.003

You are tuning the prod database on the local server.

The required result is to identify the cause of a deadlock in the prod database.

The first optional result is to identify the object on which the deadlock occurred.

The second optional result is to identify the chain of events leading up to the deadlock.

The proposed solution is to use the SQL Server Profiler Create Trace Wizard. Select the local server, the prod database, and the Identify The Cause Of A Deadlock option to create the deadlock contention trace.

What does the proposed solution provide?

A. The required result and all optional results.

B. The required result and one optional result.

C. The required result but none of the optional results.

D. The proposed solution does not provide the required results.

## 70-028.05.01.004

You plan to use the Index Tuning Wizard to build an optimal set of indexes for the prod database. Which tool should you use to create the workload file for the Index Tuning Wizard?

A. SQL Server Profiler

B. Microsoft Event Viewer

C. Windows NT Performance Monitor

D. SQL Server Current Activity window

## 70-028.05.01.003

You are tuning the prod database on the local server.

The required result is to identify the cause of a deadlock in the prod database.

The first optional result is to identify the object on which the deadlock occurred.

The second optional result is to identify the chain of events leading up to the deadlock.

The proposed solution is to use the SQL Server Profiler Create Trace Wizard. Select the local server, the prod database, and the Identify The Cause Of A Deadlock option to create the deadlock contention trace.

What does the proposed solution provide?

▶ **Correct Answer: A**

A. **Correct:** SQL Server Profiler is the best tool for monitoring database activity, including the cause of a deadlock in the prod database. Using the Create Trace Wizard and selecting the Identify The Cause Of A Deadlock option identifies the object on which the deadlock occurred and the chain of events leading up to the deadlock.

B. **Incorrect:** See the explanation for answer A.

C. **Incorrect:** See the explanation for answer A.

D. **Incorrect:** See the explanation for answer A.

## 70-028.05.01.004

You plan to use the Index Tuning Wizard to build an optimal set of indexes for the prod database. Which tool should you use to create the workload file for the Index Tuning Wizard?

▶ **Correct Answer: A**

A. **Correct:** Use SQL Server Profiler to create a trace containing a sample of normal database activity that is saved to a file or table. The stored trace is the workload file analyzed by the Index Tuning Wizard to recommend an optimal index configuration.

B. **Incorrect:** Windows NT Event Viewer provides information about errors, warnings, and the successes or failures of tasks. Windows NT Event Viewer cannot be used to create workload files.

C. **Incorrect:** Windows NT Performance Monitor is a Windows NT component that provides status information about system performance. Performance Monitor cannot be used to create workload files.

D. **Incorrect:** The Current Activity window provides a graphic snapshot of the currently running SQL Server processes, including user activity, blocked processes, and locks, but it cannot be used to create workload files.

**70-028.05.01.005**

You create a trace using the Create Trace Wizard to determine the worst performing queries. You choose to trace all of the databases and applications on the local server. Using SQL Server Profiler, how could you prevent the trace from monitoring SQL Query Analyzer?

A. Modify the Filters tab on the Trace Properties window.

B. Modify the General tab on the Trace Properties window.

C. Remove SQL Query Analyzer from the selected events you want to trace.

D. Remove the Application Name column from the data columns you want to capture.

## 70-028.05.01.005

You create a trace using the Create Trace Wizard to determine the worst performing queries. You choose to trace all of the databases and applications on the local server. Using SQL Server Profiler, how could you prevent the trace from monitoring SQL Query Analyzer?

► **Correct Answer: A**

    A. **Correct:** The Filters tab on the Trace Properties window allows you to include or exclude SQL Server Query Analyzer—a trace event criteria—from the trace.

    B. **Incorrect:** The General tab on the Trace Properties window allows you only to enter a name for the trace and select a trace type, a source for the trace to run against, and, optionally, a destination for the trace results. You cannot include or exclude SQL Server Query Analyzer—a trace event criteria—from the trace on the General tab.

    C. **Incorrect:** You cannot remove the SQL Query Analyzer from the events you want to trace on the Events tab on the Trace Properties window. SQL Server Query Analyzer is a trace event *criteria*, not an event, and it cannot be removed from the selected events you want to trace without removing other, desirable event criteria.

    D. **Incorrect:** You cannot remove the Application Name column from the data columns you want to capture on the Data Columns tab on the Trace Properties window. Removing the Application Name column removes all application names from the data you want to capture, not just SQL Server Query Analyzer.

# Further Reading

The *Microsoft SQL Server 7.0 System Administration Training* volume of the *Microsoft SQL Server 7.0 System Administration Training Kit,* Chapter 14, Lesson 1 discusses the reasons for monitoring SQL Server and the factors that affect SQL Server performance. Lesson 2 discusses the tools used for monitoring SQL Server, including Windows NT Performance Monitor, Transact-SQL statements, SQL Server Profiler, SQL Query Analyzer, and the SQL Server Enterprise Manager Current Activity screen.

Use Microsoft SQL Server Books Online (free download available at http://support.microsoft.com/download/support/mslfiles/sqlbol.exe) to search for "choosing a tool to monitor server performance and activity" and "comparing tool features and functions" for information about the tools used for monitoring SQL Server.

O B J E C T I V E   5 . 2

# Tune and optimize SQL Server.

After monitoring your SQL Server, you may find the need to tune and optimize SQL Server memory and CPU usage. SQL Server 7.0 is designed to tune many server configuration options automatically, requiring little tuning by a system administrator. It is recommended that configuration options be left at their default values, which allows SQL Server to auto-tune based on run-time conditions.

You must periodically monitor and analyze the computer running SQL Server to confirm that memory usage is within normal ranges. Analyze the following Performance Monitor counters to determine memory usage:

- **Memory: Available Bytes:** Number of bytes of memory currently available for use by processes. Low values may indicate an overall shortage of memory or that an application is not releasing memory.

- **Memory: Pages/sec:** Number of pages that were retrieved from disk due to hard page faults or written to disk to free space in the working set due to page faults. A high rate may indicate excessive paging.

- **Memory: Page Faults/sec:** Number of page faults caused by hard page faults when pages must be retrieved from disk or by writes to disk to free space in the working set. May indicate if disk activity is caused by paging.

- **Process: Page Faults/sec:** Number of page faults for the SQL Server process instance. May indicate if SQL Server rather than another process is causing excessive paging.

- **Process: Working Set:** Memory used by a process. May indicate that SQL Server is configured for too much memory if consistently below memory configuration amount. May indicate that a change is necessary in working set size.

- **SQL Server: Buffer Manager: Buffer Cache Hit Ratio:** Percentage of pages found in the buffer cache without having to read from disk. A rate of 90 percent or higher is desirable and indicates that more than 90 percent of all requests for data were satisfied from the data cache.

- **SQL Server: Buffer Manager: Free Buffers:** Number of free buffers available. Low values may indicate that more memory is required.

- **SQL Server: Memory Manager: Total Server Memory (KB):** Total amount of dynamic memory that the server is currently using. High values (compared with the amount of physical memory) may indicate that more memory is required.

You can also manage and optimize memory resources through configuration options using SQL Server Enterprise Manager or the sp_configure system stored procedure. Although it is recommended that configuration options be left at their default values, the following options can be configured to optimize server performance in response to SQL Server memory usage issues:

- **Min Server Memory:** Specifies the minimum amount of memory (in MB) SQL Server can use.

- **Max Server Memory:** Specifies the maximum amount of memory (in MB) SQL Server can use.

- **Max Worker Threads:** Specifies the total number of threads available to SQL Server. Generally, this configuration value should be set to the number of concurrent connections, but it cannot exceed 1,024.

- **Index Create Memory:** Specifies the maximum amount of memory (in KB) SQL Server can use when creating indexes.

- **Min Memory Per Query:** Specifies the minimum amount of memory (in KB) SQL Server can use for the execution of a query.

You should periodically monitor and analyze the computer running SQL Server to determine if CPU utilization rates are within normal ranges. Analyze the following Performance Monitor counters to determine CPU usage:

- **Processor: % Processor Time:** Amount of time the CPU spends processing a non-idle thread. A consistent state of 80 to 90 percent may indicate the need for a CPU upgrade or the addition of more processors.

- **System: % Total Processor Time:** Average amount of time that all CPUs in the system spend processing non-idle threads. A consistent state of 80 to 90 percent may indicate the need for CPU upgrades or the addition of more processors.

- **Processor: % Privileged Time:** Percentage of time the CPU spends executing Windows NT kernel commands. If consistently high in conjunction with the Physical Disk counters, SQL Server could be I/O-bound. Consider upgrading the disk subsystem.

- **Processor: % User Time:** Percentage of time the CPU spends executing user processes such as SQL Server. If consistently high, may indicate the need for a CPU upgrade or the addition of more processors.

- **System: Processor Queue Length:** Number of threads waiting for processor time. If more than a few program processes are contending for most of the processor's time, may indicate the need for a CPU upgrade or the addition of more processors.

You can also manage and optimize CPU resources through configuration options using SQL Server Enterprise Manager or the sp_configure system stored procedure. Although it is recommended that configuration options be left at their default values, the following options can be configured to optimize server performance in response to SQL Server CPU usage issues:

- **Affinity Mask:** Specifies processors on which SQL Server threads can run.

- **Cost Threshold for Parallelism:** Specifies the cost threshold for creating parallel queries.

- **Max Async IO:** Specifies the maximum number of asynchronous I/O requests that the server can issue against a file. Generally, leave the Max Async IO server configuration option at the default value of 32. For very sophisticated I/O subsystems with many disks and controllers, the value can be increased to 64 or possibly higher.

- **Max Degree of Parallelism:** Specifies the maximum number of threads used to execute parallel queries.

- **Max Worker Threads:** Specifies the total number of threads available to SQL Server processes.

- **Priority Boost:** Allows SQL Server to run at a higher priority than other processes running under Windows NT.

Questions related to this objective are designed to determine if you have an awareness of these issues. To successfully answer the questions for this objective, you need a firm understanding of several key terms. For definitions of these terms, refer to the Glossary in this book.

# Key Terms

- Cache

- Configuration options

- Input/output (I/O)

- Optimize

- Page faults

- Paging file

- Performance Monitor

- Thread

- Tuning

- Working set

## 70-028.05.02.001

You are using Performance Monitor to monitor the memory usage of the computer running SQL Server. You find that the Available Bytes counter value is very low. Which condition could be indicated by this value?

A. The Max Server Memory option is set too low.

B. There is a surplus of memory for SQL Server.

C. The system is experiencing an overall memory shortage.

D. SQL Server is consuming too much of the system's available memory.

**70-028.05.02.001**

You are using Performance Monitor to monitor the memory usage of the computer running SQL Server. You find that the Available Bytes counter value is very low. Which condition could be indicated by this value?

▶ **Correct Answer: C**

A. **Incorrect:** The low setting of the Max Server Memory option does not cause the Available Bytes counter to be low.

B. **Incorrect:** The Available Bytes counter indicates the number of bytes of memory currently available for use by system processes. A low number of available bytes does not indicate a surplus of memory for SQL Server.

C. **Correct:** The Available Bytes counter indicates the number of bytes of memory currently available for use by system processes. A low number of available bytes may indicate an overall shortage of memory or that an application is not releasing memory.

D. **Incorrect:** A low number of available bytes does not necessarily indicate that SQL Server is consuming too much of the system's available memory. To monitor the amount of memory being used by SQL Server, examine the following performance counters: Process: Working Set, SQL Server: Buffer Manager: Buffer Cache Hit Ratio, SQL Server: Buffer Manager: Free Buffers, SQL Server: Memory Manager: Total Server Memory (KB).

**70-028.05.02.002**

You are using Performance Monitor to monitor the memory usage of the computer running SQL Server. What should you do if the Buffer Cache Hit Ratio value is 60 percent?

A. Reduce the size of the working set.

B. Decrease the Max Server Memory option.

C. Add more memory until the value is 90 percent or higher.

D. Determine which applications are not releasing memory.

E. Monitor the Available Bytes counter, and increase memory if its value is too high.

## 70-028.05.02.002

You are using Performance Monitor to monitor the memory usage of the computer running SQL Server. What should you do if the Buffer Cache Hit Ratio value is 60 percent?

▶ **Correct Answer: C**

A. **Incorrect:** Reducing the size of the working set reduces the physical memory space available for SQL Server. The buffer cache hit ratio is the percentage of pages found in the buffer cache without having to read from disk and it cannot be set by reducing the size of the working set.

B. **Incorrect:** Decreasing the Max Server Memory option decreases the maximum amount of memory (in MB) in the buffer pool that SQL Server uses (not the amount of memory used by the entire process). The buffer cache hit ratio is the percentage of pages found in the buffer cache without having to read from disk and it cannot be set by decreasing the Max Server Memory option.

C. **Correct:** The buffer cache hit ratio is the percentage of pages found in the buffer cache without having to read from disk. A value of 90 percent or higher is desirable. If the value is 60 percent, you should add more memory until the value is consistently greater than 90 percent.

D. **Incorrect:** Determining which applications are not releasing memory does not affect the value of the buffer cache hit ratio, which is the percentage of pages found in the buffer cache without having to read from disk.

E. **Incorrect:** The Available Bytes counter indicates how many bytes of memory are currently available for use by processes. High values for the Available Bytes counter indicate that there is a memory surplus and you do not need to increase memory. The buffer cache hit ratio is the percentage of pages found in the buffer cache without having to read from disk and it is not set by evaluating the number of available bytes.

## 70-028.05.02.003

SQL Server is running on a multiprocessor system. You need to determine if the CPU usage rates are within an acceptable range. Which Performance Monitor counter should you use to determine the average amount of time all of the processors spend processing non-idle threads?

A. Processor: % User Time

B. Processor: % Privileged Time

C. System: % Total Processor Time

D. System: Processor Queue Length

E. Processor: % Processor Time

## 70-028.05.02.003

SQL Server is running on a multiprocessor system. You need to determine if the CPU usage rates are within an acceptable range. Which Performance Monitor counter should you use to determine the average amount of time all of the processors spend processing non-idle threads?

▶ **Correct Answer: C**

A. **Incorrect:** The Processor: % User Time counter indicates the percentage of time the processor spends executing user processes such as SQL Server.

B. **Incorrect:** The Processor: % Privileged Time counter indicates the percentage of time the processor spends executing Windows NT kernel commands such as processing SQL Server I/O requests.

C. **Correct:** The System: % Total Processor Time counter combines the average processor usage of all processors into a single counter.

D. **Incorrect:** The System: Processor Queue Length counter indicates the number of threads waiting for processor time.

E. **Incorrect:** The Processor: % Processor Time counter indicates the processor usage of *one* processor.

**70-028.05.02.004**

You are using Performance Monitor to monitor the CPU usage for the computer running SQL Server.

The required result is to determine the percentage of time the processor spends processing SQL Server I/O requests.

The first optional result is to determine the percentage of time the processor spends executing user processes.

The second optional result is to determine the number of threads waiting for processor time.

The proposed solution is to use Performance Monitor to activate the SQL Server: Buffer Manager: Buffer Cache Hit Ratio, the Processor: % User Time, and the System: Processor Queue Length counters.

What does the proposed solution provide?

A. The required result and all optional results.

B. The required result and one optional result.

C. The required result but none of the optional results.

D. The proposed solution does not provide the required result.

## 70-028.05.02.004

You are using Performance Monitor to monitor the CPU usage for the computer running SQL Server.

The required result is to determine the percentage of time the processor spends processing SQL Server I/O requests.

The first optional result is to determine the percentage of time the processor spends executing user processes.

The second optional result is to determine the number of threads waiting for processor time.

The proposed solution is to use Performance Monitor to activate the SQL Server: Buffer Manager: Buffer Cache Hit Ratio, the Processor: % User Time, and the System: Processor Queue Length counters.

What does the proposed solution provide?

## ▶ **Correct Answer: D**

A. **Incorrect:** See the explanation for answer D.

B. **Incorrect:** See the explanation for answer D.

C. **Incorrect:** See the explanation for answer D.

D. **Correct:** The Buffer Cache Hit Ratio, the % User Time, and the Processor Queue Length counters cannot determine the percentage of time the processor spends processing SQL Server I/O requests. To determine the percentage of time the processor spends processing SQL Server I/O requests, use the Processor: % Privileged Time counter. To determine the percentage of time the processor spends executing user processes, use the Processor: % User Time counter. To determine the number of threads waiting for processor time, use the System: Processor Queue Length counter.

## 70-028.05.02.005

Why should you monitor the Performance Monitor Memory: Page Faults/sec counter?

A. To ensure that disk activity is not caused by paging

B. To determine if SQL Server is consuming too much memory

C. To determine the average number of pages read from memory each second

D. To ensure that pages are not being stolen from SQL Server by the Virtual Memory Manager

## 70-028.05.02.005

Why should you monitor the Performance Monitor Memory: Page Faults/sec counter?

▶ **Correct Answer: A**

A. **Correct:** The Performance Monitor Memory: Pages/sec counter indicates the number of page faults caused by hard page faults when pages must be retrieved from disk *or* by writes to disk to free space in the working set. Since a high rate for the Pages/sec counter may indicate excessive paging, you should monitor the Memory: Page Faults/sec counter to make sure that paging does not cause the disk activity.

B. **Incorrect:** To monitor the amount of memory being used by SQL Server, you should examine the following performance counters: Process: Working Set, SQL Server: Buffer Manager: Buffer Cache Hit Ratio, SQL Server: Buffer Manager: Free Buffers, SQL Server: Memory Manager: Total Server Memory (KB).

C. **Incorrect:** The Performance Monitor Memory: Page Reads/sec is used to determine the average number of pages read from memory each second.

D. **Incorrect:** It is normal for Windows NT Virtual Memory Manager (VMM) to steal pages from SQL Server and other processes as it trims the working set sizes of those processes, causing page faults. A low level of page faults is normal, even if the computer has plenty of available memory.

# Further Reading

The *Microsoft SQL Server 7.0 System Administration Training* volume of the *Microsoft SQL Server 7.0 System Administration Training Kit,* Chapter 14, Lesson 2 discusses the use of the Windows NT Performance Monitor for SQL Server performance tuning.

Use Microsoft SQL Server Books Online (free download available at http://support.microsoft.com/download/support/mslfiles/sqlbol.exe) to search for "monitoring memory usage," "optimizing server performance using memory configuration options," "monitoring CPU use," and "server memory options" for details on the Windows NT Performance Monitor counters used for SQL Server performance tuning.

Download the White Paper "Microsoft SQL Server 7.0 Performance Tuning Guide" available under "support" at http://www.microsoft.com/sql for information about SQL Server 7.0 index selection, disk I/O subsystem tuning, and performance tuning tools.

The *Microsoft Windows NT Workstation 4.0 Resource Kit,* Chapter 10, contains detailed information about using Windows NT Performance Monitor counters.

*SQL Server System Administration.* New Riders, Indianapolis, IN, 1999. ISBN 1-56205-955-6. Chapter 11 contains a detailed discussion of performance tuning and optimization.

*Using Microsoft SQL Server 7.0.* Que, Indianapolis, IN, 1999. ISBN 0-7897-1628-3. Chapter 18 contains a detailed discussion of SQL Server optimization and tuning fundamentals.

O B J E C T I V E   5 . 3

# Limit resources used by queries.

Query cost is the estimated elapsed time, in seconds, required to execute a query on a specific hardware configuration. Setting a query cost limit allows you to control resources used by queries. There are two ways to set the query cost limit: for the entire server or for the current connection. To set the query cost limit for the entire server, use SQL Server Enterprise Manager or the sp_configure system stored procedure. To set the query cost limit for the current connection, you can only use the SET_QUERY_GOVERNOR_COST_LIMIT statement.

Specify a nonzero, nonnegative value to disallow execution of queries with an estimated running length exceeding that value. Specify 0 (the default) to set no query cost limit and to run all queries.

Questions related to this objective are designed to determine if you have an awareness of these issues. To successfully answer the questions for this objective, you need a firm understanding of several key terms. For definitions of these terms, refer to the Glossary in this book.

## Key Terms

- Configuration options

- Query

- Query cost

## 70-028.05.03.001

You log in to the local SQL Server as a member of the sysadmin role. You issue this Transact-SQL statement:

SET QUERY_GOVERNOR_COST_LIMIT 1

What effect does this command have?

A. No queries for the current connection are allowed to run.

B. Only one query can execute on the local server at a time.

C. All queries issued on the local server are allowed to run.

D. No queries estimated to require more than one minute can execute on the local server.

E. No queries estimated to require more than one second can execute for the current connection.

## 70-028.05.03.001

You log in to the local SQL Server as a member of the sysadmin role. You issue this Transact-SQL statement:

SET QUERY_GOVERNOR_COST_LIMIT 1

What effect does this command have?

▶ **Correct Answer: E**

A. **Incorrect:** The SET QUERY_GOVERNOR_COST_LIMIT 1 statement allows only queries for the current connection to run if they are estimated to run in less than one second. The estimated cost of the query must be less than the query cost value limit for the query to execute.

B. **Incorrect:** See the explanation for answer A.

C. **Incorrect:** The SET QUERY_GOVERNOR_COST_LIMIT 1 statement allows only queries for the current connection to run if they are estimated to run in less than one second. To run all queries for the local server, you must set the query cost value limit to 0 using the sp_configure system stored procedure or SQL Server Enterprise Manager. The estimated cost of the query must be less than the query cost value limit for the query to execute.

D. **Incorrect:** The SET QUERY_GOVERNOR_COST_LIMIT 1 statement allows only queries for the current connection to run if they are estimated to run in less than one second. The time value specified in the command indicates seconds, not minutes. The estimated cost of the query must be less than the query cost value limit for the query to execute.

E. **Correct:** The SET QUERY_GOVERNOR_COST_LIMIT 1 statement overrides the server-wide query cost value limit for the current session only, allowing queries to run if they are estimated to run in less than one second. The estimated cost of the query must be less than the query cost value limit for the query to execute.

## 70-028.05.03.002

You log in as a member of the sysadmin role to tune the local SQL Server. You enable the Query Governor option and set a maximum value of 15 for the server. What happens if a query with an estimated cost of 20 is executed?

A. It will not execute.

B. It will cause a bottleneck and terminate.

C. It will execute and terminate at 15 seconds.

D. It will execute and terminate at 15 minutes.

## 70-028.05.03.003

Which system stored procedure should you use to set the Query Governor Cost Limit option for the local server?

A. sp_dboption

B. sp_databases

C. sp_configure

D. sp_serveroption

E. sp_serveroptions

## 70-028.05.03.002

You log in as a member of the sysadmin role to tune the local SQL Server. You enable the Query Governor option and set a maximum value of 15 for the server. What happens if a query with an estimated cost of 20 is executed?

▶ **Correct Answer: A**

A. **Correct:** When the Query Governor option is enabled, queries with a cost above the specified cost value limit are stopped before they start. Since the cost value limit is set at 15, a query with an estimated cost value of 20 will not run.

B. **Incorrect:** When the Query Governor option is enabled, queries with a cost above the specified cost value limit are stopped before they start rather than run until a bottleneck or some predefined time limit is reached.

C. **Incorrect:** See the explanation for answer B.

D. **Incorrect:** See the explanation for answer B.

## 70-028.05.03.003

Which system stored procedure should you use to set the Query Governor Cost Limit option for the local server?

▶ **Correct Answer: C**

A. **Incorrect:** The sp_dboption system stored procedure displays or changes database options. The Query Governor Cost Limit option cannot be set using the sp_dboption system stored procedure.

B. **Incorrect:** The sp_databases system stored procedure lists databases that reside in the SQL Server installation or are accessible through a database gateway. The Query Governor Cost Limit option cannot be set using the sp_databases system stored procedure.

C. **Correct:** The sp_configure system stored procedure displays or changes global configuration settings for the current server, including the Query Governor Cost Limit option.

D. **Incorrect:** The sp_serveroption system stored procedure sets server options for remote servers and linked servers and also provides options for distributed queries that can be enabled or disabled on a per-linked-server basis. The Query Governor Cost Limit option cannot be set using the sp_serveroption system stored procedure.

E. **Incorrect:** The sp_serveroptions system stored procedure does not exist in SQL Server and cannot be used to set the Query Governor Cost Limit option.

**70-028.05.03.004**

You are tuning a database application by rewriting queries. Which SET stattement would you use to prevent yourself from executing a long-running query?

A. NOEXEC

B. NOCOUNT

C. ROWCOUNT

D. PARSEONLY

E. QUERY_GOVERNOR_COST_LIMIT

## 70-028.05.03.004

You are tuning a database application by rewriting queries. Which SET statement would you use to prevent yourself from executing a long-running query?

▶ **Correct Answer: E**

A. **Incorrect:** The SET NOEXEC statement compiles each query but does not execute it. SET NOEXEC is best used to have SQL Server validate the syntax and object names in Transact-SQL code when executing.

B. **Incorrect:** The SET NOCOUNT statement prevents the count (indicating the number of rows affected by a Transact-SQL statement) from being returned. SET NOCOUNT is best used to reduce network traffic and provide a performance boost for system stored procedures that do not return much actual data.

C. **Incorrect:** The SET ROWCOUNT statement causes SQL Server to stop processing a query after a specified number of rows are returned. SET ROWCOUNT is best used to limit the size of a result set.

D. **Incorrect:** The SET PARSEONLY statement checks the syntax of each Transact-SQL statement and returns any error messages without compiling or executing the statement. SET PARSEONLY is best used to have SQL Server validate the syntax and return error messages before compiling and executing.

E. **Correct:** The SET QUERY_GOVERNOR_COST_LIMIT statement is used to specify an upper limit for the time in which a query can run, overriding the limit specified in the server configuration for this session only. Use the statement to set your time limit for a query.

## 70-028.05.03.005

You log in to SQL Server as a member of the sysadmin role. You enable the Use Query Governor option to prevent queries exceeding the specified cost option for the local server. You specify a value of 10 for the query governor. What effect does this change have?

A. No queries for the current connection are allowed to run.

B. All queries issued on the local server are allowed to run.

C. Only 10 queries can execute on the local server at a time.

D. No queries estimated to require more than 10 seconds can execute on the local server.

E. No queries estimated to require more than 10 minutes can execute for the current connection.

## 70-028.05.03.005

You log in to SQL Server as a member of the sysadmin role. You enable the Use Query Governor option to prevent queries exceeding the specified cost option for the local server. You specify a value of 10 for the query governor. What effect does this change have?

▶ **Correct Answer: D**

A. **Incorrect:** Since you have set the query governor cost limit value to 10 at the server level, only queries for the current connection estimated to require less than 10 seconds are allowed to run.

B. **Incorrect:** Since you have set the query governor cost limit value to 10 at the server level, only queries issued on the local server estimated to require less than 10 seconds are allowed to run. To allow all queries issued on the local server to run, you must set the query governor cost limit value to 0 using the sp_configure system stored procedure or SQL Server Enterprise Manager.

C. **Incorrect:** Since you have set the query governor cost limit value to 10 at the server level, all queries issued on the local server estimated to require less than 10 seconds are allowed to run.

D. **Correct:** Since you have set the query governor cost limit value to 10 at the server level, only queries estimated to require less than 10 seconds are allowed to run on the local server.

E. **Incorrect:** Since you have set the query governor cost limit value to 10 at the server level, queries estimated to require less than 10 seconds are allowed to run for the current connection. The time value specified in the command indicates seconds, not minutes.

# Further Reading

Use Microsoft SQL Server Books Online (free download available at http://
support.microsoft.com/download/support/mslfiles/sqlbol.exe) to search for "query
tuning recommendations" and "query governor cost limit option" for details on using
the Query Governor option.

*SQL Server System Administration.* New Riders, Indianapolis, IN, 1999. ISBN
1-56205-955-6. Chapter 11 contains information about query design and optimization.

# Troubleshooting

The Troubleshooting domain examines issues involved in the diagnosis and resolution of problems relating to:

- Upgrading from SQL Server 6.*x*

- Backup and restore operations

- Replication

- Job or alert failures

- Distributed queries

- Client connectivity

- Access to SQL Server, databases, and database objects

## Tested Skills and Suggested Practices

- **Diagnosing and resolving problems in upgrading from SQL Server 6.*x*. Be able to diagnose and resolve problems that are the result of an upgrade.**

  - Practice 1: Learn the requirements for an upgrade from SQL Server 6.*x*. Read about the upgrade requirements for software, network protocols, SQL Server versions, disk space, and replication. Read about the tasks required for upgrading.

  - Practice 2: Read about how upgrade log files indicate the success or failure of various upgrade tasks. Learn how to use upgrade log files to troubleshoot the upgrade process.

- **Diagnosing and resolving problems in backup and restore operations. Be able to diagnose and resolve problems that are the result of backup and restore operations.**

■ Practice 1: Use Books Online to interpret error messages encountered as a result of backup and restore operations. Resolve problems using the recommended actions provided with each error message description.

- **Diagnosing and resolving replication problems. Be able to diagnose and resolve problems that are the result of replication.**

  ■ Practice 1: Learn which tools are used for diagnosing various replication problems. Use Books Online to resolve replication problems.

- **Diagnosing and resolving job or alert failures. Be able to diagnose and resolve problems that are the result of job or alert failures.**

  ■ Practice 1: Use Books Online to interpret error messages encountered as a result of job or alert failures. Resolve problems using the recommended actions provided with each error message description.

- **Diagnosing and resolving distributed query problems. Be able to diagnose and resolve problems that are the result of distributed queries.**

  ■ Practice 1: Learn which tools are used for diagnosing distributed query problems. Use Books Online to interpret error messages encountered as a result of distributed queries. Resolve problems using the recommended actions provided with each error message description.

- **Diagnosing and resolving client connectivity problems. Be able to diagnose and resolve problems with client connectivity.**

  ■ Practice 1: Learn how the SQL Server Client Network utility is used to configure network protocols on the client to communicate with a specific server.

  ■ Practice 2: Learn how clients must be configured to communicate with SQL Server running on Windows 95 or Windows 98.

- **Diagnosing and resolving problems in accessing SQL Server, databases, and database objects. Be able to diagnose and resolve problems in accessing SQL Server, databases, and database objects.**

  ■ Practice 1: Learn about the tools used to provide access to SQL Server, databases, and database objects, including login authentication, roles, groups, permissions, configuration options, database options, and installation settings.

O B J E C T I V E    6 . 1

# Diagnose and resolve problems in upgrading from SQL Server 6.x.

This objective examines two tools used to troubleshoot SQL Server upgrade problems:

- "Before Upgrading: Checklist" topic in Books Online

- Upgrade log files

When you encounter problems related to the upgrade process, review the "Before Upgrading: Checklist" topic in Books Online. The checklist provides the steps to take before performing an upgrade.

The SQL Server Upgrade Wizard creates a folder in the \Mssql7\Upgrade directory each time it runs. The folder name contains the servername, date, and time in the following format: \Mssql7\Upgrade\<Servername>_<date>_<time>. This folder contains log files that describe each upgrade step. The SQL Server Upgrade Wizard names some of the log files with an .OUT or an .ERR extension. Files with an .OUT extension indicate that no errors were encountered in the upgrade step. Files with an .ERR extension indicate that at least one error was encountered in the upgrade step.

In addition to the log files, the folder also contains a subfolder for each database that is upgraded. Each subfolder contains a set of files that describe all objects transferred in the database. The files are named in the following format: <servername>.<databasename>.<type>. The SQL Server Upgrade Wizard names some of the database files with an .OK or an .ERR extension. Files with an .OK extension indicate that all instances of that type of object were created successfully. Files with an .ERR extension indicate that at least one instance of that type of object was not created successfully.

Use the .ERR files to troubleshoot the upgrade process. In addition to viewing errors after the upgrade has completed using the upgrade subdirectories, you can view errors during the upgrade process in the Summary of Warnings section near the end of the upgrade, or in the Informational Files Found window in the SQL Server Upgrade Wizard.

Questions related to this objective are designed to determine if you have an awareness of these issues. To successfully answer the questions for this objective, you need a firm understanding of several key terms. For definitions of these terms, refer to the Glossary in this book.

## Key Terms

- SQL Server Upgrade Wizard

- Upgrade log files

### 70-028.06.01.001

You have a SQL Server 6.0 database that uses 25 MB of disk space and has several indexes. Service Pack 3 is installed. You are upgrading the database to SQL Server 7.0 on a target computer with 35 MB of available disk space. The upgrade stops. What could have caused the installation to stop?

A. There is not enough available disk space.

B. The SQL Server 6.0 database must first be upgraded to 6.5.

C. Service Pack 4 must first be installed on the SQL Server 6.0 computer.

D. Indexes must be dropped before a database can be upgraded to SQL Server 7.0.

### 70-028.06.01.002

You have limited disk space, so you plan to upgrade the SQL Server 6.5 products database using a tape backup. The computer that stores the products database also stores the sales database. You back up the products database to tape and use the SQL Server Upgrade Wizard to upgrade to 7.0. What is the state of the sales database?

A. It was deleted.

B. It is now a SQL Server 7.0 database.

C. It is a SQL Server 6.5 database accessible by both installations of SQL Server.

D. It is a SQL Server 6.5 database accessible only by SQL Server 7.0.

## 70-028.06.01.001

You have a SQL Server 6.0 database that uses 25 MB of disk space and has several indexes. Service Pack 3 is installed. You are upgrading the database to SQL Server 7.0 on a target computer with 35 MB of available disk space. The upgrade stops. What could have caused the installation to stop?

▶ **Correct Answer: A**

A. **Correct:** You should allow at least 1.5 times the space used by the existing SQL Server 6.0 database when upgrading to SQL Server 7.0. If there is not enough disk space available, the SQL Server Upgrade Wizard will stop.

B. **Incorrect:** It is not necessary to upgrade a SQL Server 6.0 database to SQL Server 6.5 before upgrading the database to SQL Server 7.0.

C. **Incorrect:** There is no Service Pack 4 for SQL Server 6.0. However, to upgrade a SQL Server 6.0 database, the SQL Server computer must have Windows NT Server Enterprise Edition 4.0 with Service Pack 4 or later, Windows NT Server 4.0 with Service Pack 4 or later, or Windows NT Workstation 4.0 with Service Pack 4 or later installed. The SQL Server computer must also have SQL Server 6.0 with Service Pack 3 or SQL Server 6.5 with Service Pack 3 or later.

D. **Incorrect:** You should not drop indexes before upgrading a database to SQL Server 7.0. The index information would be lost.

## 70-028.06.01.002

You have limited disk space, so you plan to upgrade the SQL Server 6.5 products database using a tape backup. The computer that stores the products database also stores the sales database. You back up the products database to tape and use the SQL Server Upgrade Wizard to upgrade to 7.0. What is the state of the sales database?

▶ **Correct Answer: A**

A. **Correct:** When you use the SQL Server Upgrade Wizard to upgrade using a tape backup, the data is exported to tape and all SQL Server 6.x devices, including databases, are deleted from the disk. All databases must be upgraded at the same time or they will be deleted.

B. **Incorrect:** See the explanation for answer A.

C. **Incorrect:** See the explanation for answer A.

D. **Incorrect:** See the explanation for answer A.

## 70-028.06.01.003

You plan to upgrade a SQL Server 6.5 database to a SQL Server 7.0 target computer. To ensure that the upgrade is successful, you are identifying any potential problems that might cause the SQL Server Upgrade Wizard to fail. Which system function should you run to ensure that its value is not NULL?

A. @@SPID

B. @@REMSERVER

C. @@SERVERNAME

D. @@SERVICENAME

## 70-028.06.01.004

You are upgrading the products database on the local server from SQL Server 6.0 to 7.0. Because of a lack of available disk space on the local server, you move the database to a backup server before upgrading. You complete the upgrade, but none of the user objects were created during the upgrade. What could have caused this error?

A. You do not have any of the Create permissions.

B. You did not first upgrade the database to SQL Server 6.5.

C. You did not create user login accounts on the backup server.

D. You did not first create user login accounts in SQL Server 7.0 before upgrading the database.

## 70-028.06.01.003

You plan to upgrade a SQL Server 6.5 database to a SQL Server 7.0 target computer. To ensure that the upgrade is successful, you are identifying any potential problems that might cause the SQL Server Upgrade Wizard to fail. Which system function should you run to ensure that its value is not NULL?

▶ **Correct Answer: C**

A. **Incorrect:** The @@SPID function returns the server process ID of the current user process. A NULL value does not indicate conditions that could cause the SQL Server Upgrade Wizard to fail.

B. **Incorrect:** The @@REMSERVER function returns the name of the remote SQL Server database server as it appears in the login record. A NULL value does not indicate conditions that could cause the SQL Server Upgrade Wizard to fail.

C. **Correct:** The @@SERVERNAME function returns the name of the local server running SQL Server. A NULL value indicates conditions that may cause the SQL Server Upgrade Wizard to fail. The computer name on which SQL Server runs must match the server name returned by @@SERVERNAME. You can change the server name returned by @@SERVERNAME using the sp_dropserver and sp_addserver system stored procedures.

D. **Incorrect:** The @@SERVICENAME function returns the registry key under which SQL Server is running. A NULL value does not indicate conditions that could cause the SQL Server Upgrade Wizard to fail.

## 70-028.06.01.004

You are upgrading the products database on the local server from SQL Server 6.0 to 7.0. Because of a lack of available disk space on the local server, you move the database to a backup server before upgrading. You complete the upgrade, but none of the user objects were created during the upgrade. What could have caused this error?

▶ **Correct Answer: C**

A. **Incorrect:** Create permissions allow you to create a database or an item in a database, such as a table or a stored procedure. Although object owners must have Create permissions to create new objects, it is not necessary to have Create permissions to upgrade the database and include user objects.

B. **Incorrect:** It is not necessary to upgrade a SQL Server 6.0 database to SQL Server 6.5 before upgrading it to SQL Server 7.0.

C. **Correct:** When you move a SQL Server 6.x database to a different server to perform an upgrade, login accounts for all users must be created in the new 6.x master database on the backup server.

D. **Incorrect:** It is not necessary to create user logins in SQL Server 7.0 before upgrading the database. Login and remote login registrations are transferred as part of the version upgrade process.

**70-028.06.01.005**

You have upgraded a SQL Server 6.5 database to a SQL Server 7.0 target computer. To ensure that the upgrade would be successful, you attempted to identify and correct potential problems. However, a user object was not created during the upgrade. How can you determine the cause of this failure?

A. View the UPGRADE.INI file in the WinNT directory.

B. View the STATUS.LOG file in the Upgrade directory.

C. View the log files with the .ERR extension in the Upgrade directory.

D. View the log files with the .OUT extension in the Upgrade directory.

## 70-028.06.01.005

You have upgraded a SQL Server 6.5 database to a SQL Server 7.0 target computer. To ensure that the upgrade would be successful, you attempted to identify and correct potential problems. However, a user object was not created during the upgrade. How can you determine the cause of this failure?

▶ **Correct Answer: C**

A. **Incorrect:** The UPGRADE.INI file in the WinNT directory is used to set defaults and run pretask and posttask applications.

B. **Incorrect:** The STATUS.LOG file in the Upgrade directory displays the current status of tasks being executed by the script interpreter.

C. **Correct:** Log files with the .ERR extension in the Upgrade directory list the errors encountered in each stage of the upgrade process, including objects whose creation statement failed during the upgrade and the reason for the failure.

D. **Incorrect:** Log files with the .OUT extension in the Upgrade directory list each stage of the upgrade process.

# Further Reading

The *Microsoft SQL Server 7.0 System Administration Training* volume of the *Microsoft SQL Server 7.0 System Administration Training Kit,* Chapter 4, Lesson 1 provides details on upgrade requirements. Lesson 2 covers using the SQL Server Upgrade Wizard. Lesson 3 provides information about troubleshooting upgrades.

Use Microsoft SQL Server Books Online (free download available at http://support.microsoft.com/download/support/mslfiles/sqlbol.exe) to search for "upgrading from an earlier version of SQL Server," "completing the SQL Server upgrade wizard," "before upgrading: checklist," and "upgrading log files" for details on troubleshooting SQL Server upgrades.

Download the white paper "Converting Databases to Microsoft SQL Server 7.0" available at http://support.microsoft.com/support/sql/papers.asp for information about using the SQL Server Upgrade Wizard.

# Diagnose and resolve problems in backup and restore operations.

This objective examines the tools used to troubleshoot SQL Server backup and restore problems:

- Error messages

- Error message descriptions in Books Online

- The "Troubleshooting Backing Up and Restoring" topic in Books Online

The most common problems encountered during backup and restore operations generate error messages, which include the error message number, the severity level, and a brief description of the problem. If you receive an error message while performing backup and restore operations, search Books Online for the error message number. Each Books Online reference provides an explanation of the error message and the action you should take to correct the error. In addition, the "Troubleshooting Backing Up and Restoring" topic lists problems you may encounter when backing up and restoring databases and transaction logs. Use this topic to find problem descriptions and suggestions for resolution.

Questions related to this objective are designed to determine if you have an awareness of these issues. To successfully answer the questions for this objective, you need a firm understanding of several key terms. For definitions of these terms, refer to the Glossary in this book.

# Key Terms

- Backup

- Backup device

- Backup file

- Backup media

- Database backup (also known as *full* or *complete* database backup)

- Database file

- Differential database backup

- Recovery

- Restore

- Roll back

- Roll forward

- Table

- Transaction log

- Transaction log backup

## 70-028.06.02.001

The primary database has failed and you need to enable the standby server. You attempt to back up the standby server and receive an error that the database is in warm-standby state. What is the most likely cause of this error?

A. The standby database has not been recovered.

B. The primary database has not been recovered.

C. The standby database is corrupt.

D. The primary database is corrupt.


## 70-028.06.02.002

The products database has failed. The last complete database backup was taken before you changed the sort order of the products database. You attempt to restore the backup and receive an error. What can you do to restore the backup?

A. Load the backup and restore the data with the appropriate sort order.

B. Use the BULK INSERT or DTS utilities to change the sort order of the backup.

C. Change the sort order of the products database, load the backup, and restore the data with the appropriate sort order.

D. Reinstall SQL Server on the local server using the same sort order as the backup, load the backup, and restore the data with the appropriate sort order.

## 70-028.06.02.001

The primary database has failed and you need to enable the standby server. You attempt to back up the standby server and receive an error that the database is in warm-standby state. What is the most likely cause of this error?

▶ **Correct Answer: A**

A. **Correct:** When you switch to your standby server, your failed server becomes the new standby server. The standby server cannot be backed up until it is recovered.

B. **Incorrect:** When you switch to your standby server, it replaces the old primary server. The error message is not caused by the primary server.

C. **Incorrect:** Although the standby database might be corrupted and may need to be recreated by copying the standby server, this is not the cause of the error stating that the database is in warm-standby state.

D. **Incorrect:** When you switch to your standby server, it replaces the old primary server. It does not cause the error stating that the database is in the warm-standby state.


## 70-028.06.02.002

The products database has failed. The last complete database backup was taken before you changed the sort order of the products database. You attempt to restore the backup and receive an error. What can you do to restore the backup?

▶ **Correct Answer: D**

A. **Incorrect:** A database cannot be restored unless its sort order matches the sort order running on the server.

B. **Incorrect:** A database cannot be restored unless its sort order matches the sort order running on the server. The BULK INSERT and DTS utilities are used to load data and are not used to change the sort order.

C. **Incorrect:** The sort order is set for the entire server, not for a specific database. In order to change the sort order for the server, you must rebuild the master and all user databases.

D. **Correct:** A database cannot be restored unless its sort order matches the sort order running on the server. To restore the backup, you must use BCP, BULK INSERT, or Data Transformation Services (DTS) to save the current products database. Then you must reinstall SQL Server and load the backup database. Finally, use BCP, BULK INSERT, or DTS to restore the database before changing to the needed sort order.

**70-028.06.02.003**

The products database fails. You back up the transaction log and restore the last complete database backup. You are attempting to apply the transaction log backup when you receive an error stating that the backup set cannot be restored because the database has not been rolled forward far enough. What is the most likely cause of this error?

A. The server found a gap in the transaction log backups.

B. The backup restored was not the last complete database backup performed.

C. The last complete backup was not restored using the RECOVERY option.

D. The transaction log backup performed after the database failed is corrupt.

**70-028.06.02.003**

The products database fails. You back up the transaction log and restore the last complete database backup. You are attempting to apply the transaction log backup when you receive an error stating that the backup set cannot be restored because the database has not been rolled forward far enough. What is the most likely cause of this error?

▶ **Correct Answer: A**

A. **Correct:** You received error 4305, which indicates that the restore operation found a gap between the last restore and the transaction log that you attempted to apply. You must locate the missing, earlier transaction log backups and apply these first. Transaction logs must be restored in the same order in which they were backed up.

B. **Incorrect:** See the explanation for answer A.

C. **Incorrect.** See the explanation for answer A.

D. **Incorrect.** See the explanation for answer A.

## 70-028.06.02.004

The products database fails. You back up the transaction log and restore the last complete database backup. There are two transaction log backups to apply. To restore the first transaction log backup in the sequence, you issue this command:

RESTORE LOG products
FROM products_log1
WITH RECOVERY

You receive an error when you attempt to apply the second log using this command:

RESTORE LOG products
FROM products_log2
WITH RECOVERY

What should you do to fully restore the products database?

A. Reissue the first and second command using the NORECOVERY option.

B. Restore the complete database backup and the last transaction log backup only.

C. Restore the complete database backup and all the transaction logs using the NORECOVERY option.

D. Restore the complete database backup and use the NORECOVERY option on all but the final RESTORE command when restoring the transaction log backups.

## 70-028.06.02.004

The products database fails. You back up the transaction log and restore the last complete database backup. There are two transaction log backups to apply. To restore the first transaction log backup in the sequence, you issue this command:

```
RESTORE LOG products
FROM products_log1
WITH RECOVERY
```

You receive an error when you attempt to apply the second log using this command:

```
RESTORE LOG products
FROM products_log2
WITH RECOVERY
```

What should you do to fully restore the products database?

► **Correct Answer: D**

A. **Incorrect:** The RESTORE statement NORECOVERY option instructs the restore operation not to roll back any uncommitted (incomplete) transactions. When restoring a database backup and multiple transaction logs, SQL Server requires the use of the NORECOVERY option on all but the final RESTORE statement. If you reissue the first and second commands using the NORECOVERY option, the database will remain unavailable.

B. **Incorrect:** Transaction logs must be restored in the order in which they were backed up. Restoring the complete database backup and the last transaction log backup would return error 4305, which indicates that the restore operation found a gap between the last restore and the transaction log that you attempted to apply. You must locate the missing, earlier transaction log backups and apply these first.

C. **Incorrect:** The RESTORE statement NORECOVERY option instructs the restore operation not to roll back any uncommitted (incomplete) transactions. When restoring a database backup and multiple transaction logs, SQL Server requires the use of the NORECOVERY option on all but the final RESTORE statement. If you restore the complete database backup and all the transaction logs using the NORECOVERY option, the database will remain unavailable.

D. **Correct:** The RESTORE statement NORECOVERY option instructs the restore operation not to roll back any uncommitted (incomplete) transactions. When restoring a database backup and multiple transaction logs, SQL Server requires the use of the NORECOVERY option on all but the final RESTORE statement. The database will remain unavailable until the RECOVERY option is used on the final transaction log backup.

**70-028.06.02.005**

You create a new database and perform a complete database backup. You insert data into the database using a SELECT INTO statement and attempt to perform a transaction log backup, but you receive an error stating that a transaction log backup is not allowed. What is the most likely cause of this error?

A. The Truncate Log On Checkpoint database option is enabled.

B. A backup device is not defined for the new database.

C. No database operations occurred that require a transaction log backup.

D. A backup operation cannot be performed at the same time as a SELECT INTO operation.

## 70-028.06.02.005

You create a new database and perform a complete database backup. You insert data into the database using a SELECT INTO statement and attempt to perform a transaction log backup, but you receive an error stating that a transaction log backup is not allowed. What is the most likely cause of this error?

▶ **Correct Answer: A**

A. **Correct:** When the Truncate Log On Checkpoint database option is enabled, transaction log backups cannot be performed. The database can be backed up only by a complete or differential database backup. The error message states that BACKUP LOG is not allowed while the Truncate Log On Checkpoint option is enabled.

B. **Incorrect:** You may specify a backup device during the transaction log backup. However, the backup is still not allowed.

C. **Incorrect:** You used the SELECT INTO statement to insert data into the database. SELECT INTO creates a new table and inserts the rows resulting from the query into it. It is desirable to perform a transaction log backup when a large number of changes to the database occur over a relatively short period of time, resulting in the last database backup becoming out of date quickly.

D. **Incorrect:** While a backup operation cannot be performed at the same time as a SELECT INTO operation, the error message does not state that a transaction log backup is not allowed at all. The error message informs you that the SELECT INTO operation must be serialized and tells you to reissue the transaction log backup after the SELECT INTO operation is completed.

# Further Reading

The *Microsoft SQL Server 7.0 System Administration Training* volume of the *Microsoft SQL Server 7.0 System Administration Training Kit,* Chapter 10, Lesson 4 provides details on using a standby server.

Use Microsoft SQL Server Books Online (free download available at http://support.microsoft.com/download/support/mslfiles/sqlbol.exe) to search for "trouble-shooting backing up and restoring" for details on problems you may encounter when backing up and restoring databases and transaction logs. Search for "how to set up, maintain, and bring online a standby server" for information about implementing standby servers.

O B J E C T I V E   6 . 3

# Diagnose and resolve replication problems.

This objective examines the tools used to troubleshoot SQL Server replication problems:

- To view replication agent information, including error details, agent history, and session details, use Replication Monitor.

- To troubleshoot problems with replication alerts and replication jobs, use SQL Server Agent.

- To troubleshoot problems with Subscriber connectivity, use SQL Server Query Analyzer.

- To reference the replication security mechanisms, use the "Managing Replication Security" topic in Books Online.

- To troubleshoot problems with replication agent performance, use Windows NT Performance Monitor.

- To validate the data being updated at a Subscriber as the replication process is occurring, use the sp_publication and sp_article_validation system stored procedures.

- To resolve replication problems, use the "Troubleshooting Replication" topic in Books Online.

A good starting point for diagnosing replication problems is to view the agent history on the Replication Monitor Agent History dialog box. Here you can determine which actions failed and the reasons for failure. Although the message details in agent history may not always identify the problem, they may point to issues you can investigate in more detail using the other troubleshooting tools.

Questions related to this objective are designed to determine if you have an awareness of these issues. To successfully answer the questions for this objective, you need a firm understanding of several key terms. For definitions of these terms, refer to the Glossary in this book.

# Key Terms

- Distribution Agent

- Distributor

- Log Reader Agent

- Merge Agent

- Merge replication

- Publication

- Publisher

- Pull subscription

- Push subscription

- Replication

- Replication agents

- Snapshot Agent

- Snapshot replication

- Subscriber

- Synchronization

- Transactional replication

## 70-028.06.03.001

You are configuring replication between a local and a remote server. You have configured both servers, but replication is not working. You verify that the network between the two servers is functioning properly. What should you do next to diagnose the problem?

A. Use SQL Server Query Analyzer to test the connectivity.

B. Increase the HistoryVerboseLevel in Replication Monitor to the highest possible value.

C. Verify that the account that SQL Server is using for replication has access to the other server.

D. View the SQL Server Error Log and SQL Server Agent Error Log to determine which server generated the error.

## 70-028.06.03.001

You are configuring replication between a local and a remote server. You have configured both servers, but replication is not working. You verify that the network between the two servers is functioning properly. What should you do next to diagnose the problem?

▶ **Correct Answer: C**

A. **Incorrect:** SQL Server Query Analyzer is a graphical user interface for designing and testing Transact-SQL statements, batches, and scripts interactively. The Query Analyzer is not used to test connectivity between the local and remote server.

B. **Incorrect:** Setting the HistoryVerboseLevel to its highest value increases the amount of history logged by a replication agent and provides a more detailed understanding of actions and failures at each point in the replication process. However, if replication is not working, no history is logged by the replication agents.

C. **Correct:** Many replication problems relate to connectivity or security. After verifying that the network is functioning properly, verify that the accounts are configured properly and have been given the appropriate permissions.

D. **Incorrect:** The SQL Server Error Log provides information about SQL Server events. The SQL Server Agent Error Log provides information about warnings and errors specific to SQL Server Agent. These logs are not used to determine which server caused the error, and it is more likely that the problem is related to connectivity or security rather than a particular server.

**70-028.06.03.002**

Merge replication between a local Distributor and a remote Subscriber is not functioning properly. A replication task is failing, and you need to determine the cause of the failure. Which tool should you use to view the history of the Merge Agent?

A.  SQL Server Profiler

B.  Windows NT Event Viewer

C.  SQL Server Replication Monitor

D.  SQL Server Performance Monitor

**70-028.06.03.002**

Merge replication between a local Distributor and a remote Subscriber is not functioning properly. A replication task is failing, and you need to determine the cause of the failure. Which tool should you use to view the history of the Merge Agent?

▶ **Correct Answer: C**

A. **Incorrect:** The SQL Server Profiler is a tool that captures a continuous record of server activity in real time. The Profiler is the best tool for monitoring database activity, including user access methods, user activity, object access, application use, and performance bottlenecks. The SQL Server Profiler does not provide the task history of the Merge Agent.

B. **Incorrect:** The Windows NT Event Viewer provides information about errors, warnings, and the successes or failures of tasks. Windows NT Event Viewer does not provide the task history of the Merge Agent.

C. **Correct:** The Replication Monitor provides details about the current activity and the task history of the replication agents, including the Merge Agent.

D. **Incorrect:** SQL Server Performance Monitor integrates Windows NT Performance Monitor with SQL Server, providing up-to-the-minute activity and performance statistics as well as a means to diagnose system problems. Performance Monitor does not provide the task history of the Merge Agent.

## 70-028.06.03.003

To replicate data to remote offices, your company uses snapshot replication with pull subscriptions. Each Subscriber and the Distributor are running Windows 95 and using the default installation of SQL Server. You receive an error when the replication agents attempt to access the Snapshot folder on the Distributor. What should you do to correct this problem?

A. Share the folder manually.

B. Upgrade the Subscribers to Windows 98.

C. Upgrade the Distributor to Windows 98.

D. Create a push subscription to update the Publisher.

E. Use SQL Server Query Analyzer to test the connectivity.

## 70-028.06.03.003

To replicate data to remote offices, your company uses snapshot replication with pull subscriptions. Each Subscriber and the Distributor are running Windows 95 and using the default installation of SQL Server. You receive an error when the replication agents attempt to access the Snapshot folder on the Distributor. What should you do to correct this problem?

▶ **Correct Answer: A**

    A. **Correct:** To allow pull subscriptions on the Distributor server running Windows 95, you must change the Snapshot folder to a network path accessible by replication agents running at the Publisher and Subscribers by sharing the folder manually.

    B. **Incorrect:** Upgrading the Subscribers to Windows 98 will not make the Snapshot folder on the Distributor accessible to the replication agents.

    C. **Incorrect:** Upgrading the Distributor to Windows 98 will not make the Snapshot folder on the Distributor accessible to the replication agents.

    D. **Incorrect:** Push subscriptions do not update the Publisher and will not make the Snapshot folder on the Distributor accessible to the replication agents.

    E. **Incorrect:** SQL Server Query Analyzer is a graphical user interface for designing and testing Transact-SQL statements, batches, and scripts interactively. The Query Analyzer is not used to make the Snapshot folder on the Distributor accessible to the replication agents.

## 70-028.06.03.004

When attempting to replicate data from a SQL Server 7.0 database to a SQL Server 6.5 database, you receive an error message that Msreplication_subscriptions is an invalid object. You run the sp_addpublisher70 system stored procedure at the Subscriber, but it does not correct the problem. Which are possible solutions to the problem? (Choose all that apply.)

A. Execute the REPLP70.SQL script at the SQL Server 6.5 Subscriber.

B. Verify the syntax used in the sp_addpublisher70 system stored procedure.

C. Create a publication at the SQL Server 7.0 Publisher and push the subscription to the SQL Server 6.5 Publisher.

D. Verify that the login used to connect to the subscription has the necessary permissions.

E. Verify that the SQL Server 6.5 Subscriber is registered at the SQL Server 7.0 Enterprise Manager.

## 70-028.06.03.005

Your company uses merge replication to allow all the sites to make changes to customer data. What should you do if the Merge Agent fails because of a timeout?

A. Increase the network connection timeout.

B. Add a Publisher to the replication model.

C. Increase the QueryTimeOut value in the Merge Agent profile.

D. Decrease the HistoryVerboseLevel value in the Merge Agent profile.

## 70-028.06.03.004

When attempting to replicate data from a SQL Server 7.0 database to a SQL Server 6.5 database, you receive an error message that Msreplication_subscriptions is an invalid object. You run the sp_addpublisher70 system stored procedure at the Subscriber, but it does not correct the problem. Which are possible solutions to the problem? (Choose all that apply.)

▶ **Correct Answers: A, B, C, and E**

    A. **Correct:** Executing the REPLP70.SQL script at the SQL Server 6.5 Subscriber creates the sp_addpublisher70 system stored procedure on the SQL Server 6.5 Subscriber, which then adds a SQL Server 7.0 Publisher at the SQL Server 6.5 Subscriber and may provide a solution to the problem.

    B. **Correct:** You should verify the syntax used in the sp_addpublisher70 system stored procedure: "sp_addpublisher 70 *<publisher server name>*, *<NT account used by Dist. agent>*"

    C. **Correct:** Creating a publication at the SQL Server 7.0 Publisher and adding a push subscription to the SQL Server 6.5 Publisher may provide a solution to the problem.

    D. **Incorrect:** Since the error message stated that MSreplication_ subscriptions is an invalid object, verifying login permissions is not a solution to the problem.

    E. **Correct:** Registering the SQL Server 6.5 Subscriber at the SQL Server 7.0 Enterprise Manager may provide a solution to the problem.

## 70-028.06.03.005

Your company uses merge replication to allow all the sites to make changes to customer data. What should you do if the Merge Agent fails because of a timeout?

▶ **Correct Answer: C**

    A. **Incorrect:** The network connection timeout involves the connection between SQL Server and the network and will not help a Merge Agent failure due to a timeout.

    B. **Incorrect:** Since your company uses merge replication, adding another Publisher to the replication model will not help a Merge Agent failure due to a timeout.

    C. **Correct:** If the Merge Agent fails because of a timeout, increase the QueryTimeOut value in the Merge Agent profile. The QueryTimeOut value is the number of seconds before the query times out.

    D. **Incorrect.** The HistoryVerboseLevel value in the Merge Agent profile specifies the amount of history logged during a merge operation. Decreasing the HistoryVerboseLevel value will not help a Merge Agent failure due to a timeout.

# Further Reading

The *Microsoft SQL Server 7.0 System Administration Training* volume of the *Microsoft SQL Server 7.0 System Administration Training Kit,* Chapter 17, Lesson 1 provides details on monitoring and troubleshooting replication.

Use Microsoft SQL Server Books Online (free download available at http:// support.microsoft.com/download/support/mslfiles/sqlbol.exe) to search for "trouble-shooting replication" for information about handling replication problems.

O B J E C T I V E   6 . 4

# Diagnose and resolve job or alert failures.

If you experience problems with alerts, view the "Troubleshooting Alerts" topic in Books Online. This topic lists problems you may encounter with alerts. Use this topic to find problem descriptions and suggestions for resolution.

Questions related to this objective are designed to determine if you have an awareness of these issues. To successfully answer the questions for this objective, you need a firm understanding of several key terms. For definitions of these terms, refer to the Glossary in this book.

# Key Terms

- Alert
- Application log
- Event log
- Fail-safe operator
- Job
- NET SEND
- Operator
- SQL Server Agent

**70-028.06.04.001**

You created an alert to fire when the transaction log for the products database is 75 percent full. The alert fires, but the operator notification is not timely. The alert is not complex and it notifies only one operator. What could be the cause for the delay?

A. The CPU usage is too high.

B. The operator is not on duty when the alert fires.

C. There is an e-mail, pager, or NET SEND address error.

D. The Delay Between Responses setting for the alert is too high.

**70-028.06.04.002**

An alert is firing, but the operator is not receiving notification. You verify that the e-mail, pager, and NET SEND addresses are correct. What should you check? (Choose all that apply.)

A. That the alert is enabled

B. The SQL Server Agent error log

C. The operator's on-duty schedule

D. The Delay Between Responses setting for the alert

E. That the counter value is above the defined threshold value for at least 20 seconds

## 70-028.06.04.001

You created an alert to fire when the transaction log for the products database is 75 percent full. The alert fires, but the operator notification is not timely. The alert is not complex and it notifies only one operator. What could be the cause for the delay?

▶ **Correct Answer: D**

A.  **Incorrect:** High CPU usage may allow the Windows NT application log to fill rapidly with the same error but it is not the cause of untimely notifications.

B.  **Incorrect:** The operator's on-duty schedule may determine whether or not notifications are received but it has no effect on untimely notifications.

C.  **Incorrect:** E-mail, pager, or NET SEND address problems may determine whether or not notifications are received but they have no effect on untimely notifications.

D.  **Correct:** If an alert is firing but the notification is not timely, it is likely that the Delay Between Responses setting for the alert is too high. The Delay Between Responses setting specifies the wait period, in seconds, between responses to an alert.

## 70-028.06.04.002

An alert is firing, but the operator is not receiving notification. You verify that the e-mail, pager, and NET SEND addresses are correct. What should you check? (Choose all that apply.)

▶ **Correct Answers: B and C**

A.  **Incorrect:** If an alert is firing, it is enabled.

B.  **Correct:** If an alert is firing but the operator is not receiving notification, you should check the SQL Server Agent error log for e-mail problems.

C.  **Correct:** If an alert is firing but the operator is not receiving notification, you should check the operator's on-duty schedule. The operator must be on duty to receive the alert.

D.  **Incorrect:** You should check the Delay Between Responses setting if the notifications for an alert are untimely, but the Delay Between Responses setting is not the cause of an operator notification problem.

E.  **Incorrect:** You should check the counter value if the alert is not firing, but the counter value is not the cause of an operator notification problem.

## 70-028.06.04.003

An alert is enabled but not firing. The SQLServerAgent and EventLog services are running, and the event appears in the Windows NT Event Viewer window. What should you do to diagnose the problem? (Choose all that apply.)

A. Test the e-mail, pager, and NET SEND addresses.

B. Review the SQL Server Agent error log for e-mail problems.

C. Verify that the history values for the alert are changing.

D. Verify that the Delay Between Responses setting for the alert is set appropriately.

E. Verify that the counter value is maintained for at least 20 seconds.

## 70-028.06.04.003

An alert is enabled but not firing. The SQLServerAgent and EventLog services are running, and the event appears in the Windows NT Event Viewer window. What should you do to diagnose the problem? (Choose all that apply.)

▶ **Correct Answers: C and E**

A. **Incorrect:** Testing e-mail, pager, or NET SEND addresses may determine whether or not notifications are received but will have no effect on alert firing problems.

B. **Incorrect:** Checking the SQL Server Agent error log for e-mail problems will not help you diagnose an alert firing problem. You should check this error log when an alert is firing but an operator is not receiving notification.

C. **Correct:** If an alert is not firing, you must check that: 1) the SQLServerAgent and EventLog services are running, 2) the event appears in the Windows NT Event Viewer window, 3) the alert is enabled, 4) the history values of the alert are changing, and 5) the counter value is maintained for a minimum of 20 seconds. SQL Server Agent polls the performance counters at 20-second intervals.

D. **Incorrect:** The Delay Between Responses setting for the alert may cause untimely notification for an alert but it is not the cause of an alert firing problem.

E. **Correct:** See the explanation for answer C.

## 70-028.06.04.004

You set an alert to fire if the lock wait time is over 15 seconds. What could happen if the SQL Server: Locks object counter value does not maintain the value for at least 20 seconds?

A. The alert may use all of your resources.

B. The alert will generate an alert only within the Windows NT registry.

C. The alert may cause a backlog of events in the Windows NT application log.

D. The alert may not fire because SQL Server Agent may fail to see the spike.

## 70-028.06.04.005

You created an alert to fire when the transaction log for the products database is 75 percent full. The alert fires, but the operator notification is not timely. The alert response is complex and notifies several operators. What should you do to minimize the delay?

A. Send the notification to one group e-mail address rather than to each individual operator.

B. Increase the value of the Delay Between Responses setting for the alert.

C. View the SQL Server Agent error log for e-mail problems.

D. Verify that the e-mail, pager, and NET SEND addresses are correct.

## 70-028.06.04.004

You set an alert to fire if the lock wait time is over 15 seconds. What could happen if the SQL Server: Locks object counter value does not maintain the value for at least 20 seconds?

▶ **Correct Answer: D**

A. **Incorrect:** If the SQL Server: Locks object counter value does not maintain the value for at least 20 seconds, the alert will not use all of your resources.

B. **Incorrect:** If the SQL Server: Locks object counter value does not maintain the value for at least 20 seconds, the alert will not generate an alert within the Windows NT registry.

C. **Incorrect:** If the SQL Server: Locks object counter value does not maintain the value for at least 20 seconds, the alert will not cause a backlog of events in the Windows NT application log.

D. **Correct:** If the SQL Server: Locks object counter value does not maintain the value for at least 20 seconds, the alert may not fire because SQL Server Agent polls the performance counters at 20-second intervals. If performance is polled before the value is set, SQL Server Agent may fail to see the spike. For the alert to fire, the counter value must be maintained for a minimum of 20 seconds.

## 70-028.06.04.005

You created an alert to fire when the transaction log for the products database is 75 percent full. The alert fires, but the operator notification is not timely. The alert response is complex and notifies several operators. What should you do to minimize the delay?

▶ **Correct Answer: A**

A. **Correct:** If an alert can notify multiple operators, you should send as few notifications as possible to speed up response time. Rather than sending notifications to operators separately, send notification to one group e-mail address.

B. **Incorrect:** If an alert is firing but notification is not timely, you should reduce the Delay Between Responses value for the alert to ease the delay.

C. **Incorrect:** Checking the SQL Server Agent error log for e-mail problems may reveal a cause for the delay. However, since the alert can notify multiple operators, you may achieve a faster response time by sending notification to one group e-mail address rather than to each individual operator. You should usually check this error log when an alert is firing but an operator is not receiving notification.

D. **Incorrect:** E-mail, pager, or NET SEND address problems may determine whether or not notifications are received but they have no effect on the timeliness of notifications.

# Further Reading

The *Microsoft SQL Server 7.0 System Administration Training* volume of the *Microsoft SQL Server 7.0 System Administration Training Kit,* Chapter 13, Lesson 4 covers the troubleshooting of jobs, alerts, and notifications.

Use Microsoft SQL Server Books Online (free download available at http://support.microsoft.com/download/support/mslfiles/sqlbol.exe) to search for "troubleshooting alerts" for details on handling problems with alerts.

OBJECTIVE   6.5

# Diagnose and resolve distributed query problems.

Since distributed queries access data from multiple heterogeneous data sources using OLE DB, finding the source of a problem may be complex. On an error condition involving an OLE DB provider, SQL Server displays two sets of error messages: *provider error messages*, which are surrounded by square brackets and are returned by the OLE DB provider, and *SQL Server error messages*.

This objective examines the tools used to troubleshoot SQL Server distributed query problems:

- SQL Server error messages

- SQL Server error message descriptions in Books Online

- The "Distributed Queries Error Messages" topic in Books Online

- OLE DB provider error messages

- SQL Server Profiler

If you receive an error message while performing a distributed query, search Books Online for the error message number. Each Books Online reference provides an explanation of the error message and the action you should take to correct the problem. In addition, the "Distributed Queries Error Messages" topic lists errors you may encounter when performing distributed queries. Use this topic to find problem descriptions and suggestions for resolution.

Use SQL Server Profiler to trace the OLE DB errors event class, which may allow you to access more detailed information about an OLE DB error encountered during a distributed query.

Questions related to this objective are designed to determine if you have an awareness of these issues. To successfully answer the questions for this objective, you need a firm understanding of several key terms. For definitions of these terms, refer to the Glossary in this book.

## Key Terms

- Authentication

- Column

- Data source

- Data source name (DSN)

- Distributed query

- Index

- Linked server

- Local server

- Login (account)

- Metadata

- OLE DB

- OLE DB provider

- Remote server

- Table

**70-028.06.05.001**

The customer data is stored in a local SQL server, and the sales data is stored in a remote Oracle server. You issue a distributed query to compare the sales figures for each department with the size and location of each customer in each department. The distributed query fails because the OLE DB data source could not be initialized. What are the most likely causes of this failure? (Choose all that apply.)

A. The tables or columns included in the SELECT statement do not exist.

B. There is not a valid login and password configured for the linked server.

C. The initialization parameters for the linked server are incorrect for this provider.

D. The OLE DB provider does not support the necessary interface for the SELECT statement.

E. The login used to connect to the remote server does not have the required permissions on the table.

## 70-028.06.05.001

The customer data is stored in a local SQL server, and the sales data is stored in a remote Oracle server. You issue a distributed query to compare the sales figures for each department with the size and location of each customer in each department. The distributed query fails because the OLE DB data source could not be initialized. What are the most likely causes of this failure? (Choose all that apply.)

▶ **Correct Answers: B and C**

   A. **Incorrect:** See the explanation for answer B.

   B. **Correct:** The error message for the failed query (number 7303) indicates that there is not a valid login and password configured for the linked server or that the initialization parameters for the linked server are incorrect for this provider.

   C. **Correct:** See the explanation for answer B.

   D. **Incorrect:** See the explanation for answer B.

   E. **Incorrect:** See the explanation for answer B.

## 70-028.06.05.002

The sales tax data is stored in a local SQL server that uses Windows NT authentication, and the sales data is stored in a remote Oracle server. You issue a distributed query to compute the sales tax payable for each sale processed. The distributed query fails and you receive this error message:

```
Could not perform a Windows NT authenticated login because delegation is not
available.
```

Which system stored procedure should you use to correct this problem?

A. sp_addlogin

B. sp_catalogs

C. sp_remoteoption

D. sp_addlinkedserver

E. sp_addlinkedsrvlogin

## 70-028.06.05.002

The sales tax data is stored in a local SQL server that uses Windows NT authentication, and the sales data is stored in a remote Oracle server. You issue a distributed query to compute the sales tax payable for each sale processed. The distributed query fails and you receive this error message:

```
Could not perform a Windows NT authenticated login because delegation is not
available.
```

Which system stored procedure should you use to correct this problem?

▶ **Correct Answer: E**

A. **Incorrect:** The error message for the failed query (number 7413) indicates that a distributed query is being attempted for a Windows NT authenticated login without an explicit login mapping. You need to map the Windows NT authenticated login to a remote login and password. The sp_addlogin system stored procedure only allows you to create a new SQL Server login that provides connection to a SQL server using SQL Server authentication.

B. **Incorrect:** The error message for the failed query (number 7413) indicates that a distributed query is being attempted for a Windows NT authenticated login without an explicit login mapping. You need to map the Windows NT authenticated login to a remote login and password. The sp_catalogs system stored procedure displays the list of catalogs in the specified linked server but will not correct the login problem.

C. **Incorrect:** The error message for the failed query (number 7413) indicates that a distributed query is being attempted for a Windows NT authenticated login without an explicit login mapping. You need to map the Windows NT authenticated login to a remote login and password. The sp_remoteoption system stored procedure allows you to display or change options for a remote login defined on the local server running SQL Server but it does not allow you to correct the login mapping.

D. **Incorrect:** The sp_addlinkedserver system stored procedure allows you to create a linked server but it will not correct the login problem. You need to map the Windows NT authenticated login to a remote login and password.

E. **Correct:** The error message for the failed query (number 7413) indicates that a distributed query is being attempted for a Windows NT authenticated login without an explicit login mapping. To correct this problem, you must use sp_addlinkedsrvlogin to map the Windows NT authenticated login to a remote login and password.

## 70-028.06.05.003

The forecast data is stored in a local SQL server, and the geography data is stored in a remote Oracle server. You issue a distributed query to compare the forecast data for each department with the geography of each region. The distributed query fails and you receive this error message:

```
Could not process object 'weather_data'. The OLE DB provider Oracle indicates that
the object has no columns.
```

You verify that the WEATHER_DATA table exists and that it has three columns. What is the most likely cause of the failure?

A. There is an error in the syntax of the query string.

B. You do not have the required permissions on the WEATHER_DATA table.

C. There is not a valid login and password configured for the linked server.

D. The OLE DB provider does not support the necessary interface for the statement.

## 70-028.06.05.004

The production data is stored on a local SQL server, and the sales data is stored on a remote SQL server. You issue a distributed query to compare the sales figures to the number of products produced by each facility. The distributed query fails, and you receive an error message stating that an error occurred while preparing the query for execution against the OLE DB provider. What should you do to correct this problem?

A. Fix the syntax errors in the query string.

B. Grant the necessary permissions to the user account.

C. Use the sp_addlinkedsrvlogin system stored procedure to update the login mapping.

D. Correct the initialization parameters specified in the sp_addlinkedserver system stored procedure.

## 70-028.06.05.003

The forecast data is stored in a local SQL server, and the geography data is stored in a remote Oracle server. You issue a distributed query to compare the forecast data for each department with the geography of each region. The distributed query fails and you receive this error message:

```
Could not process object 'weather_data'. The OLE DB provider Oracle indicates that
the object has no columns.
```

You verify that the WEATHER_DATA table exists and that it has three columns. What is the most likely cause of the failure?

▶ **Correct Answer: B**

A. **Incorrect:** See the explanation for answer B.

B. **Correct:** The error message for the failed query (number 7357) indicates that the login used to connect to the provider does not have the required permissions for the table or columns.

C. **Incorrect:** See the explanation for answer B.

D. **Incorrect:** See the explanation for answer B.

## 70-028.06.05.004

The production data is stored on a local SQL server, and the sales data is stored on a remote SQL server. You issue a distributed query to compare the sales figures to the number of products produced by each facility. The distributed query fails, and you receive an error message stating that an error occurred while preparing the query for execution against the OLE DB provider. What should you do to correct this problem?

▶ **Correct Answer: A**

A. **Correct:** Since the error message for the failed query (number 7321) indicates a possible syntax error in the pass-through query's query string parameter, you should check the query string and correct any syntax errors.

B. **Incorrect:** The error message for the failed query (number 7321) indicates a possible syntax error in the pass-through query's query string parameter and cannot be corrected by granting permissions. The query string must be checked and corrected.

C. **Incorrect:** The error message for the failed query (number 7321) indicates a possible syntax error in the pass-through query's query string parameter and cannot be corrected by updating the login mapping using the sp_addlinkedsrvlogin system stored procedure. The query string must be checked and corrected.

D. **Incorrect:** The error message for the failed query (number 7321) indicates a possible syntax error in the pass-through query's query string parameter and cannot be corrected by changing the initialization parameters specified in the sp_addlinkedserver system stored procedure. The query string must be checked and corrected.

**70-028.06.05.005**

The customer data is stored in a local SQL server, and the sales data is stored in a remote Oracle server. You issue a distributed query to compare the sales figures for each department with the size and location of each customer in each department. The distributed query fails because a registry entry could not be located for the OLE DB provider. You verify that the Oracle server has been registered correctly. What is the most likely cause of this failure?

A. The tables or columns included in the SELECT statement do not exist.

B. The OLE DB provider does not support the necessary interface for the statement.

C. The *rmtsrvname* parameter in the sp_addlinkedsrvlogin system stored procedure is incorrect.

D. The *provider_name* parameter in the sp_addlinkedserver system stored procedure is incorrect.

## 70-028.06.05.005

The customer data is stored in a local SQL server, and the sales data is stored in a remote Oracle server. You issue a distributed query to compare the sales figures for each department with the size and location of each customer in each department. The distributed query fails because a registry entry could not be located for the OLE DB provider. You verify that the Oracle server has been registered correctly. What is the most likely cause of this failure?

▶ **Correct Answer: D**

A. **Incorrect:** See the explanation for answer D.

B. **Incorrect:** See the explanation for answer D.

C. **Incorrect:** See the explanation for answer D.

D. **Correct:** The error message for the failed query (number 7403) indicates that the name used in the *provider_name* parameter of the sp_addlinkedserver system stored procedure is incorrect.

# Further Reading

Use Microsoft SQL Server Books Online (free download available at http://support.microsoft.com/download/support/mslfiles/sqlbol.exe) to search for "distributed queries error messages" for troubleshooting tips and techniques for distributed queries against various OLE DB providers.

# Diagnose and resolve client connectivity problems.

The SQL Server Client Network utility lets you configure network protocols on the client to communicate with a specific server. The server uses client configuration information in the following manner:

- If the server name has been specified in the Server Alias Configurations list on the client, the client connects using the Net-Library and connection parameters specified for that configuration.

- If the server name does not match a server specified in the Server Alias Configurations list, then the default Net-Library (specified on the client) is used.

- If no default Net-Library has been defined on the client, the Named Pipes Net-Library is used.

Clients running Windows NT, Windows 95, or Windows 98 default to using the Named Pipes Net-Library. You may need to connect using an alternate Net-Library if you are connecting from a client using the default Net-Library (Named Pipes) to SQL Server running on Windows 95 or Windows 98; if you must specify a client configuration for communicating with a specific server; or if you are connecting to a server configured to listen on another port.

Questions related to this objective are designed to determine if you have an awareness of these issues. To successfully answer the questions for this objective, you need a firm understanding of several key terms. For definitions of these terms, refer to the Glossary in this book.

## Key Terms

- DB-Library

- Net-Library (network library)

- Protocol

- Protocol stack

**70-028.06.06.001**

You use NET VIEW to test the connection between a Named Pipes client and a Named Pipes server. The connection is open, but you cannot connect the client to SQL Server. Which two utilities could you use to test the network and local named pipes? (Choose two.)

A. OSQL

B. ISQL

C. REGREBLD

D. MAKEPIPE

E. READPIPE

F. SQLFTWIZ

## 70-028.06.06.001

You use NET VIEW to test the connection between a Named Pipes client and a Named Pipes server. The connection is open, but you cannot connect the client to SQL Server. Which two utilities could you use to test the network and local named pipes? (Choose two.)

▶ **Correct Answers: D and E**

    A. **Incorrect:** The OSQL utility allows you to enter Transact-SQL statements, system procedures, and script files using ODBC to communicate with SQL Server. The OSQL utility is not used to test the network or local named pipes.

    B. **Incorrect:** The ISQL utility allows you to enter Transact-SQL statements, system procedures, and script files using DB-Library to communicate with SQL Server. The ISQL utility is not used to test the network or local named pipes.

    C. **Incorrect:** The REGREBLD utility allows you to back up or restore the SQL Server registry entries if they become corrupted. The REGREBLD utility is not used to test the network or local named pipes.

    D. **Correct:** If the connection between the client and the server is open, but you still cannot connect to SQL Server, you should test the integrity of network and local named pipes using the MAKEPIPE and READPIPE utilities. Use MAKEPIPE on the server for the Windows NT operating system. Use READPIPE on the client for the Windows NT, Windows 95, Windows 98, and MS-DOS operating systems.

    E. **Correct:**  See the explanation for answer D.

    F. **Incorrect:** The SQLFTWIZ utility allows you to execute the Full-Text Indexing Wizard using a command prompt utility. The SQLFTWIZ utility is not used to test the network or local named pipes.

**70-028.06.06.002**

You are attempting to connect a client running the IPX/SPX protocol stack to a server that is running the TCP/IP protocol stack. The client is using the client Multiprotocol Net-Library and the server is listening on the server Multiprotocol Net-Library. The client cannot connect to the server. What is the most likely cause of this problem?

A. The client and server must use the default Net-Library.

B. The client and server must be using the same Net-Library.

C. The client and server must be running the same protocol stack.

D. A server alias was not used to specify the default Net-Library.

**70-028.06.06.003**

You are attempting to connect several Windows 98 clients to a SQL Server running on Windows 98. You did not alter the default settings when installing SQL Server on the server or the clients. The clients are unable to connect to the SQL Server. What is the most likely cause of this problem?

A. The DB-Library options were not set appropriately.

B. The default Net-Library for the client should be changed.

C. The default Net-Library for the server should be changed.

D. The server and clients are not using the same network protocol.

## 70-028.06.06.002

You are attempting to connect a client running the IPX/SPX protocol stack to a server that is running the TCP/IP protocol stack. The client is using the client Multiprotocol Net-Library and the server is listening on the server Multiprotocol Net-Library. The client cannot connect to the server. What is the most likely cause of this problem?

▶ **Correct Answer: C**

    A. **Incorrect:** When connecting a client to a server running SQL Server, the client and server must be using the same Net-Library and running the same protocol stack. It is not necessary to use the default Net-Library.

    B. **Incorrect:** The client and server are already using the same Net-Library. However, when connecting a client to a server running SQL Server, the client and server must also be running the same protocol stack.

    C. **Correct:** When connecting a client to a server running SQL Server, the client and server must be using the same Net-Library and running the same protocol stack.

    D. **Incorrect:** When connecting a client to a server running SQL Server, the client and server must be using the same Net-Library and running the same protocol stack. It is not necessary to specify a server alias to specify the default Net-Library.

## 70-028.06.06.003

You are attempting to connect several Windows 98 clients to a SQL Server running on Windows 98. You did not alter the default settings when installing SQL Server on the server or the clients. The clients are unable to connect to the SQL Server. What is the most likely cause of this problem?

▶ **Correct Answer: B**

    A. **Incorrect:** See the explanation for answer B.

    B. **Correct:** The default Net-Library on Windows 9x clients is Named Pipes. However, SQL Server running on Windows 98 does not support Named Pipes. Therefore, if you want to connect to the server that runs Windows 98, changing the default Net-Library for the client solves the problem.

    C. **Incorrect:** The SQL Server running on Windows 98 does not support Named Pipes.

    D. **Incorrect:** See the explanation for answer B.

## 70-028.06.06.004

You are unable to connect a Windows 95 client to a SQL server running on Windows 95. You determine that Named Pipes is not supported on the server's Windows 95 platform. Which management tool should you use to change the default client Net-Library?

A.  SQL Server Setup

B.  ODBC Data Source Administrator

C.  SQL Server Client Network utility

D.  SQL Server Network utility

## 70-028.06.06.005

You are unable to connect a Windows 98 client that uses the NWLink IPX/SPX net-library to a SQL server running Windows NT. Which management tool should you use to set up a new Net-Library configuration entry for the server?

A.  SQL Server Setup

B.  ODBC Data Source Administrator

C.  SQL Server Client Network utility

D.  SQL Server Network utility

## 70-028.06.06.004

You are unable to connect a Windows 95 client to a SQL server running on Windows 95. You determine that Named Pipes is not supported on the server's Windows 95 platform. Which management tool should you use to change the default client Net-Library?

▶ **Correct Answer: C**

    A. **Incorrect:** SQL Server Setup allows you to select and activate *server* Net-Libraries during setup. You cannot change the default *client* Net-Library using SQL Server Setup.

    B. **Incorrect:** The ODBC Data Source Administrator allows you to configure ODBC data sources on computers running Windows NT, Windows 95, or Windows 98. You cannot change the default client Net-Library using ODBC Data Source Administrator.

    C. **Correct:** The SQL Server Client Network utility allows you to change the default *client* Net-Library for the SQL Server connection.

    D. **Incorrect:** SQL Server Network utility allows you to reconfigure *SQL Server* to listen on additional server Net-Libraries. You cannot change the default *client* Net-Library using the SQL Server Network utility.

## 70-028.06.06.005

You are unable to connect a Windows 98 client that uses the NWLink IPX/SPX net-library to a SQL server running Windows NT. Which management tool should you use to set up a new Net-Library configuration entry for the server?

▶ **Correct Answer: D**

    A. **Incorrect:** SQL Server Setup allows you to select and activate server Net-Libraries during setup. It is not necessary to run SQL Server Setup to set up a new Net-Library configuration entry for the server.

    B. **Incorrect:** The ODBC Data Source Administrator allows you to configure ODBC data sources on computers running Windows NT, Windows 95, or Windows 98. You cannot set up a new Net-Library configuration for the server using ODBC Data Source Administrator.

    C. **Incorrect:** The SQL Server Client Network utility allows you to set up a new *client* Net-Library configuration for the SQL Server connection.

    D. **Correct:** The SQL Server Network utility allows you to reconfigure *SQL Server* to listen on additional server Net-Libraries such as NWLink IPX/SPX.

# Further Reading

Use Microsoft SQL Server Books Online (free download available at http://support.microsoft.com/download/support/mslfiles/sqlbol.exe) to search for "setting up client configuration entries," "managing clients," and "configuring net-libraries and network protocols" and related topics for details on resolving connectivity problems.

OBJECTIVE 6.7

# Diagnose and resolve problems in accessing SQL Server, databases, and database objects.

This objective examines the items used to provide access to SQL Server, databases, and database objects:

- Login authentication

- Roles

- Groups

- Permissions

- Configuration options

- Database options

- Installation settings

Questions related to this objective are designed to determine if you have an awareness of these issues. To successfully answer the questions for this objective, you need a firm understanding of several key terms. For definitions of these terms, refer to the Glossary in this book.

# Key Terms

- Group

- Permission

- Sort order

- SQL Server Agent

- Table

## 70-028.06.07.001

You change the sort order after installing SQL Server. Some users are unable to access their databases. Which action will resolve this problem?

A. Rebuilding all databases

B. Upgrading to SQL Server Enterprise Edition

C. Executing the sp_configure system stored procedure

D. Reinstalling Windows NT Server and SQL Server, ensuring that both are configured with the same code page

## 70-028.06.07.002

Your company network is growing, and you have recently added 10 Windows NT Workstation client computers to your domain and configured them to access SQL Server 7.0. The UPS devices for these new computers have not yet arrived. A power failure occurs on the client side while users of the 10 new computers are connected to SQL Server. Before the new computers are restarted, you notice that their sessions have been orphaned and that locks are blocking other connections to SQL Server. Which command should you use to close the orphaned SQL Server sessions?

A. KILL

B. DUMP

C. SHUTDOWN

D. DROP VIEW

## 70-028.06.07.001

You change the sort order after installing SQL Server. Some users are unable to access their databases. Which action will resolve this problem?

► **Correct Answer: A**

A. **Correct:** The sort order is a set of rules that determines how SQL Server collates and presents data in response to database queries. If the sort order is changed after SQL Server is installed, all databases must be rebuilt and the data must be reloaded.

B. **Incorrect:** Upgrading to SQL Server Enterprise Edition allows you to support large databases with a large number of users but it does not allow users to access their databases after the sort order has been changed.

C. **Incorrect:** Executing the sp_configure system stored procedure does not allow users to access their databases after the sort order has been changed.

D. **Incorrect:** A code page determines the types of characters recognized by SQL Server. It is not necessary or even desirable for the SQL Server code page to match the Windows NT server code page.

## 70-028.06.07.002

Your company network is growing, and you have recently added 10 Windows NT Workstation client computers to your domain and configured them to access SQL Server 7.0. The UPS devices for these new computers have not yet arrived. A power failure occurs on the client side while users of the 10 new computers are connected to SQL Server. Before the new computers are restarted, you notice that their sessions have been orphaned and that locks are blocking other connections to SQL Server. Which command should you use to close the orphaned SQL Server sessions?

► **Correct Answer: A**

A. **Correct:** Use the KILL command to close an orphaned session. All resources held by the session are then released.

B. **Incorrect:** The DUMP command makes a backup copy of a database or of the transaction log.

C. **Incorrect:** The SHUTDOWN command immediately stops SQL Server.

D. **Incorrect:** The DROP VIEW command removes a view from the current database.

## 70-028.06.07.003

SQL Server is experiencing deadlocks on a continuing basis, and the associated rollbacks are impacting performance. Which trace flag should you use to investigate this situation?

A. 106

B. 326

C. 1204

D. 1704

## 70-028.06.07.004

You create a user to update employee records. You grant the user the Update permission on the EMPLOYEE table. The user issues this command:

UPDATE employee
   SET salary = (salary * 1.25)
     WHERE deptid = 1504

The statement fails and the user receives a permissions error. What is the most likely cause for this error?

A. There is no DEPTID value equal to 1504.

B. The UPDATE statement has a syntax error.

C. The EMPLOYEE table does not have a salary column.

D. The user needs the Select permission for the EMPLOYEE table.

## 70-028.06.07.003

SQL Server is experiencing deadlocks on a continuing basis, and the associated rollbacks are impacting performance. Which trace flag should you use to investigate this situation?

▶ **Correct Answer: C**

A. **Incorrect:** Trace flag 106 disables line number information for syntax errors.

B. **Incorrect:** Trace flag 326 prints information about the estimated and actual cost of sorts.

C. **Correct:** Trace flag 1204 returns the type of locks participating in the deadlock and the current command affected. You can investigate the situation since all messages appear in the error log and in the console screen where SQL Server was started.

D. **Incorrect:** Trace flag 1704 prints information when a temporary table is created or dropped.

## 70-028.06.07.004

You create a user to update employee records. You grant the user the Update permission on the EMPLOYEE table. The user issues this command:

UPDATE employee
    SET salary = (salary * 1.25)
        WHERE deptid = 1504

The statement fails and the user receives a permissions error. What is the most likely cause for this error?

▶ **Correct Answer: D**

A. **Incorrect:** A missing department ID value in the EMPLOYEE table does not return a permissions error.

B. **Incorrect:** Incorrect syntax for the UPDATE statement does not return a permissions error.

C. **Incorrect:** A missing salary column in the EMPLOYEE table does not return a permissions error.

D. **Correct:** Since the UPDATE statement contains a WHERE clause, the Select permission is required to update the EMPLOYEE table. If the user does not have the Select permission, a permissions error is returned.

**70-028.06.07.005**

The human resources department at your company is connected to SQL Server. You accidentally drop the Windows NT HR group account in Windows NT. The HR group must be able to connect to SQL Server, so you recreate the group account in Windows NT; however, the HR group is still unable to connect to SQL Server. Why are members of the HR group unable to connect to SQL Server?

A. The HR group login was not recreated in exactly the same manner as it was initially created.

B. The guest user account has been deleted.

C. The group login must be dropped from SQL Server and recreated.

D. The sp_grantdbaccess system stored procedure must be used to add a group login account for the newly created Windows NT group.

## 70-028.06.07.005

The human resources department at your company is connected to SQL Server. You accidentally drop the Windows NT HR group account in Windows NT. The HR group must be able to connect to SQL Server, so you recreate the group account in Windows NT; however, the HR group is still unable to connect to SQL Server. Why are members of the HR group unable to connect to SQL Server?

▶ **Correct Answer: C**

A. **Incorrect:** It is not necessary to recreate groups in exactly the same manner in which they are initially created.

B. **Incorrect:** Guest accounts are not required except for the master and tempdb databases.

C. **Correct:** If you drop and recreate a group account in Windows NT, you must also drop and recreate the group login account in SQL Server, since SQL Server uses the Windows NT security identifier (SID) to identify the group. When the group is dropped and recreated in Windows NT, the SID changes.

D. **Incorrect:** The sp_grantdbaccess system stored procedure is used to associate the group members with a user ID in each database they need to access, not to connect the users to SQL Server.

# Further Reading

The *Microsoft SQL Server 7.0 System Administration Training* volume of the *Microsoft SQL Server 7.0 System Administration Training Kit,* Chapter 2, Lesson 1 provides information about sort order. Chapter 14, Lesson 2 discusses the tools for monitoring SQL Server, including trace flags. Chapter 11, Lesson 1 contains details on recreating group accounts. Chapter 12, Lesson 1 provides information about using the UPDATE statement.

Use Microsoft SQL Server Books Online (free download available at http://support.microsoft.com/download/support/mslfiles/sqlbol.exe) to search for "sort order" for details on changing sort order. Search for "orphaned sessions" for information about handling orphaned sessions. Search for "trace flags" to find the trace flag to use to diagnose performance issues. Search for "update" for details on using the UPDATE statement. Search for "groups" for details on recreating group accounts. Search for "accessing and changing data fundamentals" for information about providing access to databases and database objects.

# The Microsoft Certified Professional Program

The Microsoft Certified Professional (MCP) program is designed to comprehensively assess and maintain software-related skills. Microsoft has developed several certifications to provide industry recognition of a candidate's knowledge and proficiency with Microsoft products and technologies. This appendix provides suggestions to help you prepare for an MCP exam and describes the process for taking the exam. The appendix also contains an overview of the benefits associated with certification and gives you an example of the exam track you might take for MCSE certification.

## Preparing for an MCP Exam

This section contains tips and information to help you prepare for an MCP certification exam. Besides study and test-taking tips, this section provides information on how and where to register, test fees, and what to expect upon arrival at the testing center.

## Studying for an Exam

The best way to prepare for an MCP exam is to study, learn, and master the technology or operating system on which you will be tested. The Readiness Review can help complete your understanding of the software or technology by assessing your practical knowledge and helping you focus on additional areas of study. For example, if you are pursuing the Microsoft Certified Systems Engineer (MCSE) certification, you must learn and use the tested Microsoft operating system. You can then use the Readiness Review to understand the skills that test your knowledge of the operating system, perform suggested practices with the operating system, and ascertain additional areas where you should focus your study by using the electronic assessment.

▶    **To prepare for any certification exam**

1. Identify the objectives for the exam.

   The Readiness Review lists and describes the objectives you will be tested on during the exam.

2. Assess your current mastery of those objectives.

   The Readiness Review electronic assessment tool is a great way to test your grasp of the objectives.

3. Practice the job skills for the objectives you have not mastered, and read more information about the subjects tested in each of these objectives.

   You can take the electronic assessment multiple times until you feel comfortable with the subject material.

# Your Practical Experience

MCP exams test the specific skills needed on the job. Since in the real world you are rarely called upon to recite a list of facts, the exams go beyond testing your knowledge of a product or terminology. Instead, you are asked to *apply* your knowledge to a situation, analyze a technical problem, and decide on the best solution. Your hands-on experience with the software and technology will greatly enhance your performance on the exam.

# Test Registration and Fees

You can schedule your exam up to six weeks in advance, or as late as one working day before the exam date. Sylvan Prometric and Virtual University Enterprises (VUE) administer all the Microsoft Certified Professional exams. To take an exam at an authorized Prometric Testing Center, in the United States call Sylvan at 800-755-EXAM (3926). To register online, or for more registration information, visit Sylvan's Web site at http://www.slspro.com. For information about taking exams at a VUE testing center, visit the VUE information page at http://www.vue.com, or call 888-837-8616 in the United States. When you register, you will need the following information:

- Unique identification number (This is usually your Social Security or Social Insurance number. The testing center also assigns an identification number, which provides another way to distinguish your identity and test records.)

- Mailing address and phone number

- E-mail address

- Organization or company name

- Method of payment (Payment must be made in advance, usually with a credit card or check.)

Testing fees vary from country to country, but in the United States and many other countries the exams cost approximately $100 (U.S.). Contact the testing vendor for exact pricing. Prices are subject to change, and in some countries, additional taxes may be applied.

When you schedule the exam, you will be provided with instructions regarding the appointment, cancellation procedures, identification requirements, and information about the testing center location.

# Taking an Exam

If this is your first Microsoft certification exam, you may find the following information helpful upon arrival at the testing center.

## Arriving at the Testing Center

When you arrive at the testing center, you will be asked to sign a log book and show two forms of identification, including one photo identification (such as a driver's license or company security identification). Before you may take the exam, you will be asked to sign a Non-Disclosure Agreement and a Testing Center Regulations form, which explains the rules you will be expected to comply with during the test. Upon leaving the exam room at the end of the test, you will again sign the log book.

## Exam Details

Before you begin the exam, the test administrator will provide detailed instructions about how to complete the exam and how to use the testing computer or software. Because the exams are timed, if you have any questions, ask the exam administrator before the exam begins. Consider arriving 10 to 15 minutes early so you will have time to relax and ask questions before the exam begins. Some exams may include additional materials or exhibits (such as diagrams). If any exhibits are required for your exam, the test administrator will provide you with them before you begin the exam and collect them from you at the end of the exam.

The exams are all closed book. You may not use a laptop computer or have any notes or printed material with you during the exam session. You will be provided with a set amount of blank paper for use during the exam. All paper will be collected from you at the end of the exam.

### The Exam Tutorial

The test administrator will show you to your test computer and will handle any preparations necessary to start the testing tool and display the exam on the computer. Before you begin your exam, you can take the exam tutorial, which is designed to familiarize you with computer-administered tests by offering questions similar to those on the exam. Taking the tutorial does not affect your allotted time for the exam.

### Exam Length and Available Time

The number of questions on each exam varies, as does the amount of time allotted for each exam. Generally, unless the certification exam uses computer adaptive testing, exams consist of 50 to 70 questions and take approximately 90 minutes to complete. Specific information about the number of exam questions and available time will be provided to you when you register.

## Tips for Taking the Exam

Since the testing software lets you move forward and backward through the exam, answer the easy questions first. Then go back and spend the remaining time on the harder questions.

When answering the multiple-choice questions, eliminate the obviously incorrect answers first. There are no trick questions on the test, so the correct answer will always be among the list of possible answers.

Answer all the questions before you quit the exam. An unanswered question is scored as an incorrect answer. If you are unsure of the answer, make an educated guess.

## Your Rights as a Test Taker

As an exam candidate, you are entitled to the best support and environment possible for your exam. In particular, you are entitled to a quiet, uncluttered test environment and knowledgeable and professional test administrators. You should not hesitate to ask the administrator any questions before the exam begins, and you should also be given time to take the online testing tutorial. Before leaving, you should be given the opportunity to submit comments about the testing center, the staff, or the test itself.

# Getting Your Exam Results

After you have completed an exam, you will immediately receive your score online and be given a printed Examination Score Report, which also breaks down the results by section. Passing scores on the different certification exams vary. You do not need to send these scores to Microsoft. The test center automatically forwards them to Microsoft within five working days, and if you pass the exam, Microsoft sends a confirmation to you within two to four weeks.

If you do not pass a certification exam, you may call the testing vendor to schedule a time to retake the exam. Before reexamination, you should review the appropriate sections of the Readiness Review and focus additional study on the topic areas where your exam results could be improved. Please note that you must pay the full registration fee again each time you retake an exam.

# About the Exams

Microsoft Certified Professional exams follow recognized standards for validity and reliability. They are developed by technical experts who receive input from job-function and technology experts.

## How MCP Exams Are Developed

To ensure the validity and reliability of the certification exams, Microsoft adheres to a rigorous exam-development process that includes an analysis of the tasks performed in specific job functions. Microsoft then translates the job tasks into a comprehensive set of objectives that measure knowledge, problem-solving abilities, and skill level. The objectives are prioritized and then reviewed by technical experts to create the certification exam questions. (These objectives are also the basis for developing the Readiness Review series.) Technical and job-function experts review the exam objectives and questions several times before releasing the final exam.

## Computer Adaptive Testing

Microsoft is developing more effective ways to determine who meets the criteria for certification by introducing innovative testing technologies. One of these testing technologies is computer adaptive testing (CAT). This testing method is currently being used on the Internet Information Server 4.0 (70-087) exam. When taking this exam, test takers start with an easy-to-moderate question. Those who answer the question correctly get a more difficult follow-up question. If that question is answered correctly, the difficulty of the subsequent question also increases. Conversely, if the first question is answered incorrectly, the following question will be easier. This process continues until the testing system determines the test taker's ability.

With this system, everyone may answer the same percentage of questions correctly, but because people with a higher ability can answer more difficult questions correctly, they will receive a higher score. To learn more about computer adaptive testing and other testing innovations, visit http://www.microsoft.com/mcp.

## If You Have a Concern About the Exam Content

Microsoft Certified Professional exams are developed by technical and testing experts, with input and participation from job-function and technology experts. Microsoft ensures that the exams adhere to recognized standards for validity and reliability. Candidates generally consider them to be relevant and fair. If you feel that an exam question is inappropriate or if you believe the correct answer shown to be incorrect, write or call Microsoft at the e-mail address or phone number listed for the Microsoft Certified Professional Program in the "References" section of this appendix.

Although Microsoft and the exam administrators are unable to respond to individual questions and issues raised by candidates, all input from candidates is thoroughly researched and taken into consideration during development of subsequent versions of the exams. Microsoft is committed to ensuring the quality of these exams, and your input is a valuable resource.

# Overview of the MCP Program

Becoming a Microsoft Certified Professional is the best way to show employers, clients, and colleagues that you have the knowledge and skills required by the industry. Microsoft's certification program is one of the industry's most comprehensive programs for assessing and maintaining software-related skills, and the MCP designation is recognized by technical managers worldwide as a mark of competence.

# Certification Programs

Microsoft offers a variety of certifications so you can choose the one that meets your job needs and career goals. The MCP program focuses on measuring a candidate's ability to perform a specific job function, such as one performed by a systems engineer or a solution developer. Successful completion of the certification requirements indicates your expertise in the field. Microsoft certifications include:

- Microsoft Certified Systems Engineer (MCSE)

- Microsoft Certified Systems Engineer + Internet (MCSE + I)

- Microsoft Certified Professional (MCP)

- Microsoft Certified Professional + Internet (MCP + I)

- Microsoft Certified Professional + Site Building (MCP + Site Building)

- Microsoft Certified Database Administrator (MCDBA)

- Microsoft Certified Solution Developer (MCSD)

# Microsoft Certified Systems Engineer (MCSE)

Microsoft Certified Systems Engineers have a high level of expertise with Microsoft Windows NT and the Microsoft BackOffice integrated family of server software and can plan, implement, maintain, and support information systems with these products. MCSEs are required to pass four operating system exams and two elective exams. The Administering Microsoft SQL Server 7.0 exam earns elective credit toward this certification.

## MCSE Exam Requirements

You can select a Microsoft Windows NT 3.51 or Microsoft Windows NT 4.0 track for the MCSE certification. From within the track you have selected, you must pass four core operating system exams and then pass two elective exams. Visit the Microsoft Certified Professional Web site for details about current exam requirements, exam alternatives, and retired exams. This road map outlines the path an MCSE candidate would pursue for Windows NT 4.0.

## Microsoft Windows NT 4.0 Core Exams

You must pass four core exams and two elective exams. You may choose among Windows 95, Windows NT Workstation 4.0, or Windows 98 for one of the core exams. The core exams are as follows:

- Exam 70-067: Implementing and Supporting Microsoft Windows NT Server 4.0

- Exam 70-068: Implementing and Supporting Microsoft Windows NT Server 4.0 in the Enterprise

- Exam 70-064: Implementing and Supporting Microsoft Windows 95, or exam 70-073: Microsoft Windows NT Workstation 4.0, or exam 70-098: Implementing and Supporting Microsoft Windows 98

- Exam 70-058: Networking Essentials

## MCSE Electives

The elective exams you choose are the same for all Windows NT tracks. You must choose two exams from the following list.

- Exam 70-013: Implementing and Supporting Microsoft SNA Server 3.0, or exam 70-085: Implementing and Supporting Microsoft SNA Server 4.0 (If both SNA Server exams are passed, only one qualifies as an MCSE elective.)

- Exam 70-019: Designing and Implementing Data Warehouses with Microsoft SQL Server 7.0

- Exam 70-018: Implementing and Supporting Microsoft Systems Management Server 1.2, or exam 70-086: Implementing and Supporting Microsoft Systems Management Server 2.0 (If both SMS exams are passed, only one qualifies as an MCSE elective.)

- Exam 70-027: Implementing a Database Design on Microsoft SQL Server 6.5, or exam 70-029: Designing and Implementing Databases with Microsoft SQL Server 7.0 (If both SQL Server exams are passed, only one qualifies as an MCSE elective.)

- Exam 70-026: System Administration for Microsoft SQL Server 6.5, or exam 70-028: Administering Microsoft SQL Server 7.0 (If both exams from this group are passed, only one qualifies as an MCSE elective.)

- Exam 70-053: Internetworking Microsoft TCP/IP on Microsoft Windows NT (3.5-3.51), or exam 70-059: Internetworking with Microsoft TCP/IP on Microsoft Windows NT 4.0 (If both TCP/IP exams are passed, only one qualifies as an MCSE elective.)

- Exam 70-056: Implementing and Supporting Web Sites Using Microsoft Site Server 3.0

- Exam 70-076: Implementing and Supporting Microsoft Exchange Server 5, or exam 70-081: Implementing and Supporting Microsoft Exchange Server 5.5 (If both Exchange Server exams are passed, only one qualifies as an MCSE elective.)

- Exam 70-077: Implementing and Supporting Microsoft Internet Information Server 3.0 and Microsoft Index Server 1.1, or exam 70-087: Implementing and Supporting Microsoft Internet Information Server 4.0 (If both Internet Information Server exams are passed, only one qualifies as an MCSE elective.)

- Exam 70-078: Implementing and Supporting Microsoft Proxy Server 1.0, or exam 70-088: Implementing and Supporting Microsoft Proxy Server 2.0 (If both Proxy Server exams are passed, only one qualifies as an MCSE elective.)

- Exam 70-079: Implementing and Supporting Microsoft Internet Explorer 4.0 by Using the Internet Explorer Administration Kit

Note that certification requirements may change. In addition, some retired certification exams may qualify for credit towards current certification programs. For the latest details on core and elective exams, go to http://www.microsoft.com/mcp and review the appropriate certification.

### Novell, Banyan, and Sun Exemptions

The Microsoft Certified Professional program grants credit for the networking exam requirement for candidates who are certified as Novell CNEs, Master CNEs, or CNIs; Banyan CBSs or CBEs; or Sun Certified Network Administrators for Solaris 2.5 or 2.6. Go to the Microsoft Certified Professional Web site at http://www.microsoft.com/mcp/certstep/exempt.htm for current information and details.

## Other Certification Programs

In addition to the MCSE certification, Microsoft has created other certification programs that focus on specific job functions and career goals.

### Microsoft Certified Systems Engineer + Internet (MCSE + I)

An individual with the MCSE + Internet credential is qualified to enhance, deploy, and manage sophisticated intranet and Internet solutions that include a browser, a proxy server, host servers, a database, and messaging and commerce components. Microsoft Certified Systems Engineers with a specialty in the Internet are required to pass seven operating system exams and two elective exams.

### Microsoft Certified Professional (MCP)

Microsoft Certified Professionals have demonstrated in-depth knowledge of at least one Microsoft product. An MCP has passed a minimum of one Microsoft operating system exam and may pass additional Microsoft Certified Professional exams to further qualify his or her skills in a particular area of specialization. A Microsoft Certified Professional has extensive knowledge about specific products but has not completed a job-function certification. The MCP credential provides a solid background for other Microsoft certifications.

### Microsoft Certified Professional + Internet (MCP + I)

A person receiving the Microsoft Certified Professional + Internet certification is qualified to plan security, install and configure server products, manage server resources, extend servers to run CGI scripts or ISAPI scripts, monitor and analyze performance, and troubleshoot problems.

### Microsoft Certified Professional + Site Building (MCP + Site Building)

Microsoft has recently created a certification designed for Web site developers. Individuals with the Microsoft Certified Professional + Site Building credential are qualified to plan, build, maintain, and manage Web sites using Microsoft technologies and products. The credential is appropriate for people who manage sophisticated, interactive Web sites that include database connectivity, multimedia, and searchable content. Microsoft Certified Professionals with a specialty in site building are required to pass two exams that measure technical proficiency and expertise.

### Microsoft Certified Database Administrator (MCDBA)

The Microsoft Certified Database Administrator credential is designed for professionals who implement and administer Microsoft SQL Server databases. Microsoft Certified Database Administrators are required to pass four core exams and one elective exam.

### Microsoft Certified Solution Developer (MCSD)

The Microsoft Certified Solution Developer credential is the premium certification for professionals who design and develop custom business solutions with Microsoft development tools, technologies, and platforms. The MCSD certification exams test the candidate's ability to build Web-based, distributed, and commerce applications by using Microsoft's products, such as Microsoft SQL Server, Microsoft Visual Studio, and Microsoft Transaction Server.

# Certification Benefits

Obtaining Microsoft certification has many advantages. Industry professionals recognize Microsoft Certified Professionals for their knowledge and proficiency with Microsoft products and technologies. Microsoft helps to establish the program's recognition by promoting the expertise of MCPs within the industry. By becoming a Microsoft Certified Professional, you will join a worldwide community of technical professionals who have validated their expertise with Microsoft products.

In addition, you will have access to technical and product information directly from Microsoft through a secured area of the MCP Web site. You will be invited to Microsoft conferences, technical training sessions, and special events. MCPs also receive *Microsoft Certified Professional Magazine,* a career and professional development magazine.

Your organization will receive benefits when you obtain your certification. Research shows that Microsoft certification provides organizations with increased customer satisfaction and decreased support costs through improved service, increased productivity, and greater technical self-sufficiency. It also gives companies a reliable benchmark for hiring, promoting, and career planning.

# Skills 2000 Program

Microsoft launched the Skills 2000 initiative to address the gap between the number of open jobs in the computing industry and the number of skilled professionals to fill them. The program, launched in 1997, builds upon the success of Microsoft's training and certification programs to reach a broader segment of the work force. Many of today's computing professionals consider the current skills gap to be their primary business challenge.

Skills 2000 aims to significantly reduce the skills gap by reaching out to individuals currently in the computing work force, as well as those interested in developing a career in information technology (IT). The program focuses on finding and placing skilled professionals in the job market today with Microsoft Solution Provider organizations. Microsoft will also facilitate internships between MSPs and students developing IT skills. In addition, Skills 2000 targets academic instructors at high schools, colleges, and universities by offering free technical training to teachers and professors who are educating the work force of tomorrow.

For more information about the Skills 2000 initiative, visit the Skills 2000 site at http://www.microsoft.com/skills2000/. This site includes information about starting a career in the IT industry, IT-related articles, and a career aptitude tool.

# Volunteer Technical Contributors

To volunteer for participation in one or more of the exam development phases, please sign up using the Technical Contributors online form on the MCP Web site: http://www.microsoft.com/mcp/examinfo/certsd.htm.

# References

To find out more about Microsoft certification materials and programs, to register with an exam administrator, or to get other useful resources, check the following references. For Microsoft references outside the United States or Canada, contact your local Microsoft office.

### Microsoft Certified Professional Program
To find information about Microsoft certification exams and information to help you prepare for any specific exam, go to http://www.microsoft.com/mcp, send e-mail to mcp@msprograms.com, or call 800-636-7544.

The MCP online magazine provides information for and about Microsoft Certified Professionals. The magazine is also a good source for exam tips. You can view the online magazine at http://www.mcpmag.com.

### Microsoft Developer Network
The Microsoft Developer Network (MSDN) subscription center is your official source for software development kits, device driver kits, operating systems, and information about developing applications for Microsoft Windows and Windows NT. You can visit MSDN at http://msdn.microsoft.com or call 800-759-5474.

### Microsoft Press

Microsoft Press offers comprehensive learning and training resources to help you get the most from Microsoft technology. For information about books published by Microsoft Press, go to http://mspress.microsoft.com or call 800-MSPRESS.

### Microsoft Press ResourceLink

Microsoft Press ResourceLink is an online information resource for IT professionals who deploy, manage, or support Microsoft products and technologies. ResourceLink gives you access to the latest technical updates, tools, and utilities from Microsoft and is the most complete source of technical information about Microsoft technologies available anywhere. You can reach Microsoft Press ResourceLink and find out about a trial membership at http://mspress.microsoft.com/reslink.

### Microsoft TechNet IT Home

Microsoft TechNet IT Home is a resource designed for IT professionals. The Microsoft TechNet Web site is designed for anyone who evaluates, deploys, maintains, develops, or supports IT systems. Microsoft TechNet can help you stay on top of technology trends. See the TechNet Web site for more information at http://www.microsoft.com/technet/.

### Microsoft Training and Certification

You can find lists of various study aids for the training and certification in Microsoft products at http://www.microsoft.com/train_cert.

### Self Test Software

Self Test Software provides the Readiness Review online assessment. For an additional fee, Self Test Software will provide test questions for this exam and other certification exams. For further information, go to http://www.stsware.com/microsts.htm.

### Sylvan Prometric Testing Centers

To register to take a Microsoft Certified Professional exam at any of the Sylvan Prometric testing centers around the world, go online at http://www.slspro.com. In the United States, you can call 800-755-EXAM.

### Virtual University Enterprises (VUE)

You can register for a certification exam with VUE by using online registration, by registering in person at a VUE testing center, or by calling 888-837-8616 in the United States. Visit http://www.vue.com/ms for testing sites, available examinations, and other registration numbers.

# Glossary

## A

**alert** A user-defined response to a SQL Server event. Alerts can either execute a defined task or send an e-mail and/or pager message to a specified operator.

**American National Standards Institute (ANSI)** An organization of American industry and business groups that develops trade and communication standards for the United States. Through membership in International Organization for Standardization (ISO) and International Electrotechnical Commission (IEC), ANSI coordinates American standards with corresponding international standards. ANSI published the ANSI SQL-92 standard in conjunction with the ISO/IEC SQL-92 standard.

**anonymous subscription** A pull subscription that allows a server known to the Publisher only for the duration of the connection to receive a subscription to a publication. Anonymous subscriptions require less overhead than standard pull subscriptions because information about them is not stored at the Publisher or the Distributor.

**ANSI** *See* American National Standards Institute (ANSI).

**ANSI SQL-92** *See* SQL-92.

**API** *See* application programming interface (API).

**application log** A Windows NT file that records events. It can be viewed only by using Windows NT Event Viewer. When SQL Server is configured to use the Windows NT application log, each SQL Server session writes new events to that log. (Unlike the SQL Server error log, a new application log is not created each time you start SQL Server.)

**application programming interface (API)** A set of routines available in an application, such as DB-Library, for use by software programmers when designing an application interface.

**application role** A SQL Server role that provides security for a particular application, ensuring that users gain access to SQL Server databases through specific applications only. Application roles are assigned to applications, not users, and are activated when the user enters a password for the application.

**argument** A switch supported by a function that allows you to specify a particular behavior. Sometimes called an *option* or a *parameter*.

**article** The basic unit of replication. An article contains data originating from a table or stored procedure marked for replication. One or more articles are contained within a publication.

**authentication** Identifies the user and verifies the permission to connect with SQL Server. A user's name and password are compared against an authorized list; if the system detects a match, access is granted to the extent specified in the permission list for that user.

**authentication mode** Identifies the method of authentication—either SQL Server and Windows NT (Mixed mode) or Windows NT only—used by the SQL Server.

**automatic recovery** Recovery that occurs every time SQL Server is restarted. Automatic recovery protects your database if there is a system failure. In each database, the automatic recovery mechanism checks the transaction log. If the log has committed transactions that have not been written to the database, it performs those transactions again. This action is known as *rolling forward*. If the log has uncommitted transactions that have not been written to the database, it removes those transactions from the log. This action is known as *rolling back*.

# B

**back up** To create a copy of a database, transaction log, file, or filegroup in a database on another device or file. A backup is made to tape, named pipe, or hard disk. Backups are made using either SQL Server Enterprise Manager or the BACKUP statement.

**backup device** A tape, disk file, or named pipe used in a backup or restore operation.

**backup file** A file that stores a complete or partial database, transaction log, or file and/or filegroup backup.

**backup media** The disk, tape, or named pipe used to store the backup set.

**backup set** The output (a file or group of files) of a single backup operation, stored on disk or tape.

**bcp (bulk copy program) utility** A command-prompt utility that copies SQL Server data to or from an operating system file in a user-specified format.

**binary sort order** Sorts characters by the value of the character in the installed character set. Binary order is the simplest and fastest sort order.

**bottleneck** A component of the system that restricts the performance of the entire system.

**bulk copy** The transfer of large amounts of data into or out of a SQL Server table or view.

# C

**cache** A buffer used to hold data during input/output (I/O) transfers between disk and random access memory (RAM).

**call-level interface (CLI)** The interface supported by ODBC for use by an application. *See also* Open Database Connectivity (ODBC).

**character set** Determines the types of characters that SQL Server recognizes in the char, varchar, and text data types. A character set is a set of 256 letters, digits, and symbols specific to a country or language. The printable characters of the first 128 values are the same for all character sets. The last 128 characters, sometimes referred to as extended characters, are unique to each character set. A character set is related to, but separate from, Unicode characters. A character set is also referred to as a *code page*.

**CLI** *See* call-level interface (CLI).

**client** A front-end application that uses the services provided by a server. The computer that hosts the application is referred to as the *client computer*. SQL Server client software enables computers to connect to a computer running SQL Server over a network.

**cluster** A group of servers that can operate as a single server.

**code page** *See* character set.

**column** In a SQL database table, the area, sometimes called a field, in each row that stores the data about an attribute of the object modeled by the table. Individual columns are characterized by their maximum length and the type of data that can be placed in them. A column contains an individual data item within a row.

**COM** *See* component object model (COM).

**component object model (COM)** The programming model on which several SQL Server and database application programming interfaces (APIs), such as SQL-DMO, OLE-DB, and ADO, are based.

**configuration options** Global configuration settings for the current server.

**contention** On a network, competition among stations for the opportunity to use a communications line or network resource.

**Create Trace Wizard** Guides you through the process of creating a trace.

**Current Activity window** Provides a graphic snapshot of the currently running SQL Server processes, including user activity, blocked processes, and locks.

# D

**data column** Describes the data that is collected for each of the event classes captured in a trace.

**data migration** The process of making existing data work on a different computer or operating system.

**data source** The source of data for an object such as a cube or dimension. Also, the specification of the information necessary to access source data. Sometimes refers to a DataSource object. *See also* data source name (DSN).

**data source name (DSN)** The name assigned to an ODBC data source. Applications can use data source names (DSNs) to request a connection to a system ODBC data source, which specifies the computer name and (optionally) the database to which the DSN maps. A DSN can also refer to an OLE DB connection.

**data transfer** The process of copying data to or from a computer running SQL Server.

**data transformation** A set of operations applied to source data before it can be stored in the destination using Data Transformation Services (DTS). For example, DTS allows calculating new values from one or more source columns, or breaking a single column into multiple values to be stored in separate destination columns. Data transformation is performed during the process of copying data into a data warehouse.

**Data Transformation Services (DTS)** A SQL Server component used to import, export, and transform data from different data sources.

**data type** An attribute that specifies the type of information that can be stored in a column or variable. System-supplied data types are provided by SQL Server; user-defined data types can also be created.

**database** A collection of information, tables, and other objects organized and presented to serve a specific purpose, such as to facilitate searching, sorting, and recombining data.

**database backup** Records the complete database, including pages containing data and the information used to rebuild database files and filegroups. Also known as *full* or *complete database backup*.

**Database Consistency Checker (DBCC)** Statements used to check the logical and physical consistency of a database. Maintenance statements maintain tasks on a database, index, or filegroup. Miscellaneous statements perform various tasks such as enabling row-level locking or removing a dynamic-link library (DLL) from memory. Status statements perform status checks. Validation statements validate operations on a database, table, index, catalog, filegroup, system table, or allocation of database pages.

**database file** A file in which a database is stored. One database can be stored in several files. SQL Server uses three types of database files: data files (which store data), log files (which store transaction logs), and backup files (which store backups of a database).

**database object** One of the components of a database: a table, index, trigger, view, key, constraint, default, rule, user-defined data type, or stored procedure.

**database options** Determine the characteristics of each database. Only the system administrator or database owner can modify these options.

**database owner** A member of the database administrator role of a database. There is only one database owner. The owner has full permissions in that database and determines the access and capabilities provided to other users.

**DB-Library** A series of high-level language (including C) libraries that provide the application programming interface (API) for the client in a client/server system. DB-Library sends requests from a client to a server. DB-Library allows the developer to incorporate Transact-SQL statements into an application to retrieve and update data in a SQL Server database.

**dbo account** A special user account created automatically in each database to which the sa login account and all members of the sysadmin server role are mapped. Any object that a system administrator creates automatically belongs to dbo. The dbo account cannot be removed from any database.

**deadlock** A situation when two users, each having a lock on one piece of data, attempt to acquire a lock on the other's piece. Each user waits for the other to release the lock. SQL Server detects deadlocks and terminates one user's process.

**default database** The database the user is connected to immediately after logging in to SQL Server.

**default filegroup** Contains the pages for all tables and indexes that do not have a filegroup specified when they are created.

**deny** Removes a permission from a user account and prevents the account from gaining permission through membership in groups or roles within the permission.

**dependencies** The views and procedures that depend on the specified table or view.

**diacritical mark** A mark that appears with a letter to indicate a specific phonetic value.

**dictionary sort order** Sorts characters by the order in which they appear in the dictionary.

**differential database backup** Records only those changes made to the database since the last complete database backup. A differential backup is smaller and faster to restore than a database backup, and it has minimal effect on performance.

**distribute** To move transactions or snapshots of data from the Publisher to Subscribers, where they are applied to the destination tables in the subscription databases.

**distributed query** A single query that accesses data from heterogeneous data sources.

**Distribution Agent** The replication component that moves the transactions and snapshot jobs held in distribution database tables to Subscribers.

**distribution database** A store-and-forward database that holds all transactions waiting to be sent to Subscribers. The distribution database receives transactions sent to it from the Publisher by the Log Reader Agent and holds them until the Distribution Agent moves them to the Subscribers.

**Distributor** The server containing the distribution database. The Distributor receives all changes to published data, stores the changes in its distribution database, and transmits them to Subscribers. The Distributor may or may not be the same computer as the Publisher.

**DLL** *See* dynamic-link library (DLL).

**domain** In Windows NT security, a collection of computers grouped for viewing and administrative purposes that share a common security database. A domain provides access to the centralized user accounts and group accounts maintained by the domain administrator. Each domain has a unique name.

**DTS** *See* Data Transformation Services (DTS).

**DTS Designer** Allows experienced users to create complex Data Transformation Services (DTS) packages that import, export, and transform heterogeneous data using graphics tools on a designer work surface.

**DTS Export Wizard** Guides you through the process of creating Data Transformation Services (DTS) packages to export data from a SQL Server database to heterogeneous data sources.

**DTS Import Wizard** Guides you through the process of creating Data Transformation Services (DTS) packages to import heterogeneous data to a SQL Server database.

**dynamic-link library (DLL)** An executable routine containing a specific set of functions stored in a .DLL file and loaded on demand when needed by the program that calls it.

# E

**encryption** A method for keeping sensitive information confidential by changing data into an unreadable form.

**event** Any significant occurrence in the system or in an application that requires users to be notified or requires an entry to be added to a log.

**event categories** Collections that describe the type of event class.

**event class** An event generated within the SQL Server engine, such as the start of the execution of a stored procedure, a successful or failed connection to SQL Server, a transaction, or a lock time-out.

**event log** A file that contains both SQL Server error messages and messages for all activities on the computer.

**Everyone group** In Windows NT, includes all local and remote users who have connected to the computer, including those who connect as guests. You cannot control who becomes a member of the Everyone group; however, you can assign permissions and rights.

# F

**failover** In clustering, the transferring of all resources owned by a failed node to another node.

**fail-safe operator** The operator notified about an alert after all pager notifications to the designated operators have failed.

**fault tolerance** Ensures data integrity when hardware failures occur.

**file** A complete, named collection of information. Where a database is stored; one database can be stored in several files. SQL Server uses three types of files: *data files* (which store data), *log files* (which store transaction logs), and *backup files* (which store backups of a database).

**file backup** Records all pages in a specified file.

**filegroup** A named collection of one or more files that forms a single unit of allocation and administration.

**filegroup backup** Records all pages in a specified filegroup.

**filter** A set of criteria applied to records to show a subset of the records or to sort the records.

**filtering** Designates selected rows or columns of a table for replication as an article.

**fixed database role** Any of the predefined roles defined at the database level existing in each database.

**fixed server role** Any of the predefined roles defined at the server level existing outside individual databases.

**fragmentation** Occurs when data modifications are made. You can reduce fragmentation and improve read-ahead performance by dropping and recreating a clustered index.

**full-text catalog** Stores a database's full-text index.

**full-text index** The portion of a full-text catalog that stores all of the full-text words and their locations for a given table.

**full-text service** The SQL Server component that performs the full-text querying.

**function** A set of instructions that operates as a single logical unit, can be called by name, accepts input parameters, and returns information. In Transact-SQL, a function is a unit of syntax consisting of a keyword and, usually, a set of parameters. There are several categories of Transact-SQL functions: *string, math, system, niladic, text and image, date, aggregate*, and *conversion*.

# G

**grant** Applies to a user account a permission that allows the account to perform an activity or work with data.

**group** Administrative unit within Windows NT that contains Windows NT users or other groups.

**guest account** A special user account created automatically in each database for logins without a database user account. Guest accounts can be added and removed at any time from any database except master and tempdb.

# H

**heterogeneous data** Any non-SQL Server data. Heterogeneous data can be accessed in place through OLE-DB, Linked Servers, ODBC, and the OPENROWSET and OPENQUERY commands.

Heterogeneous data can be imported through Data Transformation Services (DTS), the bcp utility, and the BULK INSERT command, among others.

**homogeneous data** Data that comes from one or more SQL Server databases.

**horizontal filtering** Creates an article that replicates only selected rows from the base table. Subscribers receive only the subset of horizontally filtered data. You can use horizontal filtering to partition your base table horizontally.

# I

**IEC** *See* International Electrotechnical Commission (IEC).

**implied permission** Permission to perform an activity specific to a fixed role or database ownership. Implied permissions cannot be granted, revoked, or denied.

**index** In a relational database, a database object that provides fast access to data in the rows of a table, based on key values. Indexes provide quick access to data and can enforce uniqueness on the rows in a table. SQL Server supports clustered and nonclustered indexes.

**Index Tuning Wizard** Allows you to select and create an optimal set of indexes and statistics for a SQL Server database without requiring an expert understanding of the structure of the database, the workload, or the internals of SQL Server.

**input/output (I/O)** Read or write actions a computer performs. Reading is done with input devices such as the keyboard and the mouse, as well as disk files, while writing is usually done via the display and the printer for the user and via disk files or communications ports for the computer.

**International Electrotechnical Commission (IEC)** One of two international standards bodies responsible for developing international data communications standards. The International Electrotechnical Commission works closely with the International Organization for Standardization (ISO) to define standards of computing. They jointly published the ISO/IEC SQL-92 standard for SQL.

**International Organization for Standardization (ISO)** One of two international standards bodies responsible for developing international data communications standards. The International Organization for Standardization works closely with the International Electrotechnical Commission (IEC) to define standards of computing. They jointly published the ISO/IEC SQL-92 standard for SQL.

**interprocess communication (IPC)** A system by which threads and processes can transfer data and messages among themselves. Interprocess communication is used to offer and receive services from other programs.

**IPC** *See* interprocess communication (IPC).

**ISO** *See* International Organization for Standardization (ISO).

# J

**job** An implementation of an administrative action that contains one or more steps. The term *job* replaces the SQL Server 6.5 term *task*.

**job step** An action that the job takes on a database or a server.

# L

**latches** Short-term synchronization objects protecting actions that need not be locked for the life of a transaction. Latches are primarily used to protect a row while it is being read for a connection.

**latency** The amount of time that elapses between when a change is completed on the Publisher and

when it appears in the destination database on the Subscriber.

**linked server** An abstraction of an OLE DB data source that looks like another server to the local SQL Server. A linked server has an associated OLE DB provider that manages the data source.

**local group** A Windows NT group containing user accounts and global groups from the domain group it is created in, and any trusted domain. Local groups cannot contain other local groups.

**local server** The server to which the user is logged. If remote servers are set up for the local server, users can access remote servers from their local server.

**lock** A restriction on access to a resource in a multiuser environment. SQL Server locks users out of a specific record, field, or file automatically to maintain security or to prevent concurrent data manipulation problems.

**Log Reader Agent** The transactional replication component that moves transactions marked for replication from the transaction log on the Publisher to the distribution database.

**logical name** A name used by SQL Server to identify a file. A logical name for a file must correspond to the rules for identifiers and can have as many as 30 characters.

**login (account)** The identity with which a user establishes a connection to SQL Server.

# M

**MAPI (Messaging Application Programming Interface)** The Microsoft interface specification that allows different messaging and workgroup applications (including e-mail, voice mail, and fax) to work through a single client. Both SQL Mail and SQLAgentMail use MAPI.

**master database**  The database that controls user databases and the operation of SQL Server as a whole. It is installed automatically with SQL Server and it keeps track of user accounts, remote user accounts, and remote servers that this server can interact with. It also tracks ongoing processes, configurable environment variables, system error messages, databases on SQL Server, storage space allocated to each database, tapes and disks available on the system, and active locks.

**master domain**  A domain trusted by all other domains on the network that acts as the central administrative unit for user and group accounts.

**media**  The physical material—such as paper, disk, or tape—used for storing computer-based information.

**media failure**  The failure of one or more of the disk drives holding a database, resulting in a complete loss of data unless an earlier copy of the data can be restored.

**media header**  The first record in a disk or tape file, containing information such as media identification, layout structure, and date of last update.

**media set**  All media involved in a backup operation.

**Merge Agent**  In merge replication, the component that applies initial snapshot jobs held in publication database tables to Subscribers. It also merges incremental data changes that have occurred since the initial snapshot was created.

**merge replication**  A type of replication that allows sites to make autonomous changes to replicated data and, at a later time, merges changes made at all sites. Merge replication does not guarantee transactional consistency.

**metadata**  Information about the properties of data, such as the type of data in a column (numeric, text, and so on) or the length of a column; information about the structure of data; information that specifies the design of objects, such as cubes or dimensions.

**Microsoft Search service**  A full-text indexing and search engine.

**migration**  The process of making existing applications and data work on a different computer or operating system.

**mirror set**  A fully redundant or "shadow" copy of data. Mirror sets provide fault tolerance.

**model database**  A database that provides the template for new user databases. Each time a database is created, SQL Server makes a copy of the model and then extends it to the size requested. A new database cannot be smaller than the model.

**msdb database**  A database used by SQL Server, SQL Server Enterprise Manager, and SQL Server Agent to store data, including job, alert, task, and replication scheduling information, as well as backup and restore history information.

**MSDTC (Microsoft Distributed Transaction Coordinator) service**  Coordinates transactions across all the servers enlisted in a distributed transaction and updates the completion of the transaction to ensure that all of the updates on all the servers are made permanent.

**MSSQLServer service**  The database server for SQL Server.

# N

**named pipe**  An interprocess communication (IPC) mechanism that SQL Server and Open Data Services use to provide communication between clients and servers. Named pipes permit access to shared network resources.

**NET SEND**  A notification method that specifies the recipient (computer or user) of a network message. This method is not supported on Windows 95 or Windows 98 operating systems.

**Net-Library (network library)** A library of functions for managing network connections and routing. Each network library allows SQL Server to use a particular network protocol.

**node** A physical machine in a cluster.

**nonlogged operations** Operations that are not logged to prevent the transaction log from filling rapidly and running out of disk space. Operations include: bulk load operations, the SELECT INTO statements, the WRITETEXT statements, and the UPDATETEXT statements. The Select Into/Bulk Copy database option must be set for the operations to be nonlogged.

# O

**object** One of the components of a database: a table, index, trigger, view, key, constraint, default, rule, user-defined data type, or stored procedure. Also called a *database object*.

**Object Linking and Embedding (OLE)** An application programming interface (API) for sharing objects among applications. OLE is built on the component object model (COM).

**object permission** Based on a table, view, or stored procedure. Controls the ability to execute the SELECT, INSERT, UPDATE, and DELETE statements against the table or view.

**ODBC** *See* Open Database Connectivity (ODBC).

**OLAP** *See* online analytical processing (OLAP).

**OLE** *See* Object Linking and Embedding (OLE).

**OLE DB** A COM-based application programming interface (API) for accessing data. OLE DB supports accessing any format data storage (databases, spreadsheets, text files, and so on) for which an OLE DB provider is available.

**OLE DB provider** A software component that exposes an OLE DB interface. Each OLE DB provider is specific to a particular storage mechanism (for example, SQL Server databases, Access databases, or Excel spreadsheets).

**online analytical processing (OLAP)** A technology that uses multidimensional structures to provide rapid access to data for analysis. The source data for OLAP is commonly stored in data warehouses in a relational database.

**Open Database Connectivity (ODBC)** A database-material application programming interface (API) aligned with the American National Standards Institute (ANSI) and International Organization for Standardization (ISO) standards for database call-level interface (CLI). ODBC supports access to any database for which an ODBC driver is available.

**operator** A person in an organization who may be notified by SQL Server when an event occurs.

**optimize** To improve performance.

**owner password** A password for the Data Transformation Services (DTS) package that protects any sensitive user name and server password information in the package from unauthorized users.

# P

**package** A Data Transformation Services (DTS) object that defines one or more tasks to be executed in a coordinated sequence to import, export, or transform data.

**page faults** Occur when a program requests a page of code or data not in its working set (the portion of physical memory used by a particular application). A hard page fault occurs when the requested page must be retrieved from disk. A soft page fault occurs when the requested page is found elsewhere in physical memory.

**paging file** A special file on a PC's hard disk. With virtual memory under Windows NT, some of the program code and other information is kept in RAM while other information is temporarily swapped into virtual memory to the paging file. When that information is required again, Windows NT pulls it back into RAM and, if necessary, swaps other information to virtual memory.

**Performance Monitor** *See* Windows NT Performance Monitor.

**permissions** Assignments made to users, groups, or roles that specify the users permitted to access and manipulate database objects. *Object permissions* determine who may access a database object and how it may be accessed. *Statement permissions* determine who may create databases or database objects or who may back up databases and transaction logs. *Implied permissions* allow database access and manipulation based on a user's membership in a predefined system role or ownership of database objects.

**permission state** The status of a permission—grant, revoke, or deny.

**permission type** The classification of a permission by function—object, statement, or implied.

**physical name** The path where a file or mirrored file is located. The default is the path of the MASTER.DAT file followed by the first eight characters of the file's logical name.

**primary data file** The starting point of the database and the pointer to the rest of the files in the database. Every database has one primary data file. The recommended file extension for primary data files is .MDF.

**primary filegroup** Contains the primary data file and any other files not put into another filegroup. All pages for the system tables are allocated in the primary filegroup.

**protocol** A set of rules or standards designed to enable computers to connect with one another and exchange information.

**protocol stack** The set of protocols that work together on different levels to enable communication on a network.

**public role** A special database role to which every database user belongs. The public role captures all default permissions for users in a database; cannot have users, groups, or roles assigned to it because they belong to the role by default; and is contained in every database, including master, msdb, tempdb, model, and all user databases. The public role cannot be dropped.

**publication** A group of articles available for replication as a unit. A publication can contain one or more published tables or stored procedure articles from one user database. Each user database can have one or more publications.

**publication database** A database source of replicated data. A database containing tables for replication.

**publish** To make data available for replication.

**Publisher** A server that makes data available for replication. A Publisher maintains publication databases and sends copies of all changes of the published data to the Distributor.

**pubs database** A sample database provided with SQL Server.

**pull subscription** A type of subscription in which the initiation of data movement is made at the Subscriber. The Subscriber maintains a subscription by requesting—or *pulling*—the appropriate data changes from a Publisher. The Distribution Agent is maintained at the Subscriber, thereby reducing the amount of overhead at the Distributor.

**push subscription** A type of subscription in which the initiation of data movement is made at the Publisher. The Publisher maintains a subscription by sending—or *pushing*—the appropriate data changes to one or more Subscribers. The Distribution Agent is maintained at the Distributor.

# Q

**query** A specific request for data retrieval, modification, or deletion.

**query cost** The estimated elapsed time, in seconds, required to execute a query on a specific hardware configuration.

# R

**RAID (redundant array of independent disks)** A method used to standardize and categorize fault-tolerant disk systems. Six levels gauge various mixes of performance, reliability, and cost.

**read performance** The speed and accuracy with which data is read.

**recovery** The operation of rolling back all uncompleted transactions and rolling forward all completed transactions. Recovery is required to restore the integrity of the database. Restoring a database backup or applying a transaction log backup recovers the database automatically at the end of the restore operation. Additionally, recovery occurs in a database each time the database is opened (for example, when SQL Server starts).

**remote procedure call (RPC)** The invocation of a stored procedure on a remote server from a procedure on a server.

**remote server** A SQL server on the network that can be accessed through a user's local server. SQL Server Setup can install, upgrade, or configure remote servers.

**replication** Duplication of table schema and data or stored procedure definitions and calls from a source database to a destination database, usually on separate servers.

**replication agents** Components assigned to each step of replication that keep a history of actions performed. The four replication agents are: Snapshot Agent, Log Reader Agent, Distribution Agent, and Merge Agent.

**replication model** Consists of Publishers, Distributors, and Subscribers; articles and publications; and push and pull subscriptions.

**replication settings** The articles, subscriptions, and publications of each selected database, including the distribution database.

**replication types** Include snapshot, transactional, and merge. Provide different capabilities and attributes for latency, autonomy, data consistency, conflicts, and network resources during replication.

**resource domain** A trusting domain that establishes a one-way trust relationship with the master domain, enabling users with accounts in the master database to use resources in all the other domains.

**restore** An operation that returns the database to the state it was in when the backup was created. Any incomplete transactions in the database backup (transactions that were not complete when the backup operation completed originally) are rolled back to ensure the database remains consistent.

**revoke** Removes a previously granted or denied permission from a user account in the current database. The user account may or may not have the permission through membership in groups or roles.

**role** An administrative unit within SQL Server that allows you to organize users into a unit to which you can apply permissions. Roles are used in SQL Server the way groups are used in Windows NT. Roles may contain SQL Server logins, Windows NT logins, groups, or other roles. *See also* group.

**roll back** The ability to remove partially completed transactions after a database or other system failure.

**roll forward** The ability to recover from disasters, such as media failure, by reading the transaction log and reapplying all readable and complete transactions.

# S

**sa (system administrator) login** A login authorized to perform all functions in SQL Server. Certain critical administrative functions can be performed only by the sa login. The system administrator (sa) login is provided for backward compatibility with earlier versions of SQL Server.

**scalability** The ability to grow by increasing the speed or capacity of a system.

**schema** A description of a database generated by the data definition language (DDL) of the database management system (DBMS). In online analytical processing (OLAP) services, a schema is a description of multidimensional objects such as cubes, dimensions, and so forth.

**script** A collection of Transact-SQL statements used to perform an operation. Transact-SQL scripts are stored as files, usually with the .SQL extension.

**secondary data files** All data files other than the primary data file. Some databases may not have any secondary data files, while others may have multiple secondary data files across multiple physical disk drives. The recommended file extension for secondary data files is .NDF.

**server group** A collection of one or more servers organized to improve administrative capabilities.

**Server Network utility** Used to manage the server Net-Libraries and specify the network protocol stacks on which the server will listen for client requests. It can be also used to specify that SQL Server will listen on a non-default network address.

**service** A process that performs a specific system function and often provides an application programming interface (API) for other processes to call. It runs independently on a computer running Windows NT, unlike a program that requires a logged-on user to start or stop the program.

**setup initialization file** A text file, using the Windows .INI file format, that stores configuration information allowing SQL Server to be installed without a user having to be present to respond to prompts from the Setup program.

**severity level number** The severity level of an error. Valid levels are from 1 through 25. Only the system administrator can add a message with a severity level from 19 through 25.

**Snapshot Agent** The replication component that prepares snapshot files of published tables and stored procedures, stores the files on the Distributor, and records information about synchronization status in the distribution database.

**snapshot replication** A type of replication that takes a snapshot of current data in a publication at a Publisher and replaces the entire replica at a Subscriber on a periodic basis, in contrast to publishing changes when they occur.

**SNMP (Simple Network Management Protocol)** An application protocol that offers network management services. Using SNMP, you can monitor SQL Server across different platforms (for example, Windows NT, Windows 95 or Windows 98, and UNIX).

**sort order** A set of rules that determines how SQL Server compares, collates, and presents character data in response to database queries.

**SQL** *See* structured query language (SQL).

**SQL-92** The latest version of the standard for SQL, published in 1992. The international standard is ISO/IEC 9075:1992 Database Language SQL. The American National Standards Institute (ANSI) also published a corresponding standard (Data Language SQL X3.135-1192), so SQL-92 is sometimes referred to as ANSI SQL in the United States.

**SQL Executive settings** Tasks scheduled by SQL Executive.

**SQL Mail** A component of SQL Server that includes extended stored procedures and allows SQL Server to send and receive mail messages through the built-in Windows NT Messaging Application Programming Interface (MAPI). A mail message can consist of short text strings, the output from a query, or an attached file.

**SQL Server Agent** Used to create and manage local or multiserver jobs, alerts, and operators. Job schedules are defined in the Job Properties dialog box. SQL Server Agent communicates with SQL Server to execute the job according to the job's schedule.

**SQL Server Enterprise Manager** A graphical application that allows for easy, enterprise-wide configuration and management of SQL Server and SQL Server objects. You can also use SQL Server Enterprise Manager to manage logins, permissions, and users; create scripts; manage devices and databases; back up databases and transaction logs; and manage tables, views, stored procedures, triggers, indexes, rules, defaults, and user-defined data types.

**SQL Server Profiler** A SQL Server tool that captures a continuous record of server activity in real time. SQL Server Profiler can monitor many different server events and event categories; filter these events with user-specified criteria; and output a trace to the screen, a file, or another SQL Server.

**SQL Server Query Analyzer** A SQL Server utility that allows you to enter Transact-SQL statements and stored procedures in a graphical user interface. SQL Server Query Analyzer also provides the capability for graphically analyzing the execution of queries.

**SQL Server Service Manager** A SQL Server utility that provides a graphical way to start, pause, and stop the MSDTC, MSSQLServer, and SQLServerAgent services. SQL Server is integrated with the service control management of Windows NT, so you can start, pause, and stop SQL Server, MSDTC, and SQL Server Agent from the Services application in Control Panel or from the Server Manager application.

**SQL Server Upgrade Wizard** Automates the process of upgrading SQL Server 6.*x* databases to SQL Server 7.0.

**SQL statement** A SQL or Transact-SQL statement, such as SELECT or DELETE, that performs some action on data.

**SQLAgentMail** A service provided by the SQLServerAgent service that sends e-mail when an alert is triggered or a scheduled task succeeds or fails. SQLAgentMail is configured and operated separately from SQL Mail.

**SQLServerAgent service** Used to create and manage local or multiserver jobs, alerts, and operators and to notify system administrators of problems that have occurred with the server.

**standby server** A second server that can be brought online in the event of failure of the primary production server.

**startup option** Settings and command-line switches that affect SQL Server parameters at startup.

**statement permission** Controls the execution of Transact-SQL statements that create database objects or perform certain administrative tasks. Can be granted, revoked, or denied.

**stored procedure** A precompiled collection of Transact-SQL statements stored under a name and processed as a unit. Stored procedures are available for managing SQL Server and displaying information about databases and users. SQL Server–supplied stored procedures are called system stored procedures.

**stripe set** Refers to the saving of data across identical partitions on different drives. Stripe sets do not provide fault tolerance.

**structured query language (SQL)** A database query and programming language originally developed by IBM for mainframe computers. It is widely used for accessing data, querying, updating, and managing relational database systems. There is now an ANSI-standard SQL definition for all computer systems.

**subscribe** To agree to receive a publication. A destination database on a Subscriber subscribes to replicated data from a publication database on a Publisher.

**Subscriber** A server that receives copies of published data. Subscribers can make updates to data (but a Subscriber making updates is not the same as a Publisher). A Subscriber can, in turn, become a Publisher to other Subscribers.

**subscription database** The database that receives tables and data replicated from a publication database.

**synchronization** The process of maintaining the same schema and data in a publication at a Publisher and in the replica of a publication at a Subscriber.

**sysadmin role** Allows logins to perform any task within SQL Server.

**system administrator** The person responsible for the overall administration of SQL Server.

**system databases** The four databases provided on a newly installed SQL Server installation: master, tempdb, model, and msdb databases. In addition, you can also install the sample database, pubs, which is provided as a learning tool and is the basis for most of the examples in the SQL Server documentation.

**system stored procedures** A SQL Server–supplied, precompiled collection of Transact-SQL statements. System stored procedures are provided as shortcuts for retrieving information from system tables or as mechanisms for accomplishing database administration and other tasks that involve updating system tables.

**system tables** Store SQL Server configuration information and definitions of all the objects, users, and permissions in SQL Server databases. Server-level configuration information is stored in system tables found only in the master database. Every database contains system tables defining the users, objects, and permissions contained by the database.

# T

**table** An object in a database that stores data as a collection of rows and columns.

**tape backup** A backup operation to any tape device supported by Windows NT. If you are creating a tape backup file, you must first install the tape device by using Windows NT. The tape device must be physically attached to the SQL Server you are backing up.

**tempdb database** A database that provides a storage area for temporary tables, temporary stored procedures, and other temporary working storage needs. No special permissions are required to use tempdb (that is, to create temporary tables or to execute commands that may require storage space in the tempdb database). All temporary tables are stored in tempdb, no matter what database the user who creates them is using.

**thread** A mechanism that allows one or more paths of execution through the same instance of an application. Each device requires one thread and each remote site requires two threads. SQL Server uses the native thread services of Windows NT. There are separate threads for each network, a separate thread for database checkpoints, and a pool of threads for all users.

**trace event criteria** Parameters used to restrict (filter) the event data captured within the trace.

**trace file** A file used by SQL Server Profiler to record monitored events.

**transaction** A group of database operations combined into a logical unit of work that is either wholly committed or rolled back. A transaction is atomic, consistent, isolated, and durable.

**transaction log** A database file in which all changes to the database are recorded. It is used by SQL Server during automatic recovery.

**transaction log backup** Records only the transactions that have modified a database since the last complete database, differential database, or transaction log backup.

**transactional replication** A type of replication that marks selected transactions in the Publisher's database transaction log for replication and then distributes them asynchronously to Subscribers as incremental changes, while maintaining transactional consistency.

**Transact-SQL** The standard language for communicating between applications and SQL Server. The Transact-SQL language is an enhancement to Structured Query Language (SQL), the ANSI-standard relational database language. It provides a comprehensive language for defining tables; for inserting, updating, or deleting information stored in tables; and for controlling access to data in those tables. Extensions such as stored procedures make Transact-SQL a full programming language.

**trusted connection** Authenticated connections between clients and servers. Windows NT Authentication requires network protocols that support trusted connections.

**tuning** Minimizing the response time for each query and maximizing the throughput of the entire database server by minimizing network traffic, disk I/O, and CPU time.

# U

**unattended installation** The installation of SQL Server on a computer using a setup initialization file, which eliminates the need to respond to prompts. An unattended installation may also be referred to as an automated installation.

**Unicode** Unicode defines a set of letters, numbers, and symbols that SQL Server recognizes in the nchar, nvarchar, and ntext data types. It is related to but separate from character sets. Unicode has more than 65,000 possible values compared to a character set's 256, and it takes twice as much space to store. Unicode includes characters for most languages.

**Unicode collation** Acts as a sort order for Unicode data. It is a set of rules that determines how SQL Server compares, collates, and presents Unicode data in response to database queries.

**upgrade log files** Files that describe the results of each step in the upgrade process from SQL Server 6.$x$ to 7.0.

**user (account)** Controls permissions for activities performed in a database.

**user password**  A password for the Data Transformation Services (DTS) package that allows a user to execute a package but not view the package definition. If you set a user password, you must also set an owner password.

**user-defined database role**  A SQL Server role that allows you to create your own group of database users with a set of common permissions.

**user-defined error message**  A customized error message created by the user that is raised from a user-specified condition.

# V

**vertical filtering**  Creates an article that replicates only selected columns from the base table. Subscribers receive only the subset of vertically filtered data. The primary key columns in a table cannot be filtered out of an article in a transactional publication. You can use vertical filtering to partition your base table vertically.

**view**  An alternate way of looking at data from one or more tables in the database. A view is a virtual table, usually created as a subset of columns from one or more tables.

# W

**Windows NT Performance Monitor**  A Windows NT component that provides a way for system administrators to monitor the performance of SQL Server. SQL Server statistics include lock performance, current size of transaction logs, user connections, and server performance. You can even set alerts to initiate a specified action when a specified threshold is reached.

**working set**  The portion of physical memory that a running program can use, as assigned by the operating system. When a process needs code or data that is not in its working set, a page fault occurs and the Virtual Memory Manager adds the new pages to the working set. When memory is plentiful, more pages are added and working sets are larger. When memory is scarce, fewer pages are added and working sets are smaller.

**workload file**  A SQL script or a SQL Server Profiler trace saved to a file or table containing SQL batch or remote procedure call (RPC) event classes and the Event Class and Text data columns, used by the Index Tuning Wizard to build a recommendation of the optimal set of indexes that should be in place.

# Index

## Special Characters and Numbers

## A

# Microsoft Press Resource Kits—powerhouse resources to minimize costs while maximizing performance

# Ready solutions *for the* IT administrator

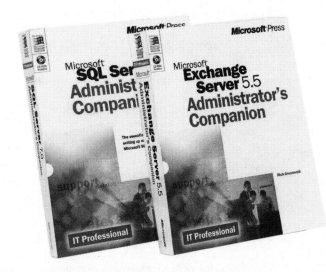

**K**eep your IT systems up and running with ADMINISTRATOR'S COMPANIONS from Microsoft Press. These expert guides serve as both tutorial and reference for critical deployment and maintenance tasks for Microsoft products and technologies. Packed with real-world expertise, hands-on numbered procedures, and handy workarounds, ADMINISTRATOR'S COMPANIONS deliver ready answers for on-the-job results.

# There's no *substitute* for *experience.*

**N**ow you can apply the best practices from real-world implementations of Microsoft technologies with NOTES FROM THE FIELD. Based on the extensive field experiences of Microsoft Consulting Services, these valuable technical references outline tried-and-tested solutions you can use in your own company, right now.

| **Deploying Microsoft® SQL Server™ 7.0 (Notes from the Field)** | **Optimizing Network Traffic (Notes from the Field)** | **Managing a Microsoft Windows NT® Network (Notes from the Field)** | ***Coming Soon!*** <br> **Deploying Microsoft Office 2000 (Notes from the Field)** |
|---|---|---|---|
| **U.S.A.** $39.99 | **U.S.A.** $39.99 | **U.S.A.** $39.99 | **U.S.A.** $39.99 |
| U.K. £37.49 | U.K. £37.49 [V.A.T. included] | U.K. £37.49 [V.A.T. included] | U.K. £37.49 [V.A.T. included] |
| Canada $59.99 | Canada $59.99 | Canada $59.99 | Canada $59.99 |
| ISBN 0-7356-0726-5 | ISBN 0-7356-0648-X | ISBN 0-7356-0647-1 | ISBN 0-7356-0727-3 |

# MICROSOFT LICENSE AGREEMENT
Book Companion CD

**IMPORTANT—READ CAREFULLY:** This Microsoft End-User License Agreement ("EULA") is a legal agreement between you (either an individual or an entity) and Microsoft Corporation for the Microsoft product identified above, which includes computer software and may include associated media, printed materials, and "online" or electronic documentation ("SOFTWARE PRODUCT"). Any component included within the SOFTWARE PRODUCT that is accompanied by a separate End-User License Agreement shall be governed by such agreement and not the terms set forth below. By installing, copying, or otherwise using the SOFTWARE PRODUCT, you agree to be bound by the terms of this EULA. If you do not agree to the terms of this EULA, you are not authorized to install, copy, or otherwise use the SOFTWARE PRODUCT; you may, however, return the SOFTWARE PRODUCT, along with all printed materials and other items that form a part of the Microsoft product that includes the SOFTWARE PRODUCT, to the place you obtained them for a full refund.

## SOFTWARE PRODUCT LICENSE

The SOFTWARE PRODUCT is protected by United States copyright laws and international copyright treaties, as well as other intellectual property laws and treaties. The SOFTWARE PRODUCT is licensed, not sold.

1. **GRANT OF LICENSE.** This EULA grants you the following rights:

    a. **Software Product.** You may install and use one copy of the SOFTWARE PRODUCT on a single computer. The primary user of the computer on which the SOFTWARE PRODUCT is installed may make a second copy for his or her exclusive use on a portable computer.

    b. **Storage/Network Use.** You may also store or install a copy of the SOFTWARE PRODUCT on a storage device, such as a network server, used only to install or run the SOFTWARE PRODUCT on your other computers over an internal network; however, you must acquire and dedicate a license for each separate computer on which the SOFTWARE PRODUCT is installed or run from the storage device. A license for the SOFTWARE PRODUCT may not be shared or used concurrently on different computers.

    c. **License Pak.** If you have acquired this EULA in a Microsoft License Pak, you may make the number of additional copies of the computer software portion of the SOFTWARE PRODUCT authorized on the printed copy of this EULA, and you may use each copy in the manner specified above. You are also entitled to make a corresponding number of secondary copies for portable computer use as specified above.

    d. **Sample Code.** Solely with respect to portions, if any, of the SOFTWARE PRODUCT that are identified within the SOFTWARE PRODUCT as sample code (the "SAMPLE CODE"):

    i. **Use and Modification.** Microsoft grants you the right to use and modify the source code version of the SAMPLE CODE, *provided* you comply with subsection (d)(iii) below. You may not distribute the SAMPLE CODE, or any modified version of the SAMPLE CODE, in source code form.

    ii. **Redistributable Files.** Provided you comply with subsection (d)(iii) below, Microsoft grants you a nonexclusive, royalty-free right to reproduce and distribute the object code version of the SAMPLE CODE and of any modified SAMPLE CODE, other than SAMPLE CODE, or any modified version thereof, designated as not redistributable in the Readme file that forms a part of the SOFTWARE PRODUCT (the "Non-Redistributable Sample Code"). All SAMPLE CODE other than the Non-Redistributable Sample Code is collectively referred to as the "REDISTRIBUTABLES."

    iii. **Redistribution Requirements.** If you redistribute the REDISTRIBUTABLES, you agree to: (i) distribute the REDISTRIBUTABLES in object code form only in conjunction with and as a part of your software application product; (ii) not use Microsoft's name, logo, or trademarks to market your software application product; (iii) include a valid copyright notice on your software application product; (iv) indemnify, hold harmless, and defend Microsoft from and against any claims or lawsuits, including attorney's fees, that arise or result from the use or distribution of your software application product; and (v) not permit further distribution of the REDISTRIBUTABLES by your end user. Contact Microsoft for the applicable royalties due and other licensing terms for all other uses and/or distribution of the REDISTRIBUTABLES.

2. **DESCRIPTION OF OTHER RIGHTS AND LIMITATIONS.**

    - **Limitations on Reverse Engineering, Decompilation, and Disassembly.** You may not reverse engineer, decompile, or disassemble the SOFTWARE PRODUCT, except and only to the extent that such activity is expressly permitted by applicable law notwithstanding this limitation.

    - **Separation of Components.** The SOFTWARE PRODUCT is licensed as a single product. Its component parts may not be separated for use on more than one computer.

    - **Rental.** You may not rent, lease, or lend the SOFTWARE PRODUCT.

- **Support Services.** Microsoft may, but is not obligated to, provide you with support services related to the SOFTWARE PRODUCT ("Support Services"). Use of Support Services is governed by the Microsoft policies and programs described in the user manual, in "online" documentation, and/or in other Microsoft-provided materials. Any supplemental software code provided to you as part of the Support Services shall be considered part of the SOFTWARE PRODUCT and subject to the terms and conditions of this EULA. With respect to technical information you provide to Microsoft as part of the Support Services, Microsoft may use such information for its business purposes, including for product support and development. Microsoft will not utilize such technical information in a form that personally identifies you.

- **Software Transfer.** You may permanently transfer all of your rights under this EULA, provided you retain no copies, you transfer all of the SOFTWARE PRODUCT (including all component parts, the media and printed materials, any upgrades, this EULA, and, if applicable, the Certificate of Authenticity), **and** the recipient agrees to the terms of this EULA.

- **Termination.** Without prejudice to any other rights, Microsoft may terminate this EULA if you fail to comply with the terms and conditions of this EULA. In such event, you must destroy all copies of the SOFTWARE PRODUCT and all of its component parts.

3. **COPYRIGHT.** All title and copyrights in and to the SOFTWARE PRODUCT (including but not limited to any images, photographs, animations, video, audio, music, text, SAMPLE CODE, REDISTRIBUTABLES, and "applets" incorporated into the SOFTWARE PRODUCT) and any copies of the SOFTWARE PRODUCT are owned by Microsoft or its suppliers. The SOFTWARE PRODUCT is protected by copyright laws and international treaty provisions. Therefore, you must treat the SOFTWARE PRODUCT like any other copyrighted material **except** that you may install the SOFTWARE PRODUCT on a single computer provided you keep the original solely for backup or archival purposes. You may not copy the printed materials accompanying the SOFTWARE PRODUCT.

4. **U.S. GOVERNMENT RESTRICTED RIGHTS.** The SOFTWARE PRODUCT and documentation are provided with RESTRICTED RIGHTS. Use, duplication, or disclosure by the Government is subject to restrictions as set forth in subparagraph (c)(1)(ii) of the Rights in Technical Data and Computer Software clause at DFARS 252.227-7013 or subparagraphs (c)(1) and (2) of the Commercial Computer Software—Restricted Rights at 48 CFR 52.227-19, as applicable. Manufacturer is Microsoft Corporation/One Microsoft Way/Redmond, WA 98052-6399.

5. **EXPORT RESTRICTIONS.** You agree that you will not export or re-export the SOFTWARE PRODUCT, any part thereof, or any process or service that is the direct product of the SOFTWARE PRODUCT (the foregoing collectively referred to as the "Restricted Components"), to any country, person, entity, or end user subject to U.S. export restrictions. You specifically agree not to export or re-export any of the Restricted Components (i) to any country to which the U.S. has embargoed or restricted the export of goods or services, which currently include, but are not necessarily limited to, Cuba, Iran, Iraq, Libya, North Korea, Sudan, and Syria, or to any national of any such country, wherever located, who intends to transmit or transport the Restricted Components back to such country; (ii) to any end user who you know or have reason to know will utilize the Restricted Components in the design, development, or production of nuclear, chemical, or biological weapons; or (iii) to any end user who has been prohibited from participating in U.S. export transactions by any federal agency of the U.S. government. You warrant and represent that neither the BXA nor any other U.S. federal agency has suspended, revoked, or denied your export privileges.

## DISCLAIMER OF WARRANTY

**NO WARRANTIES OR CONDITIONS.** MICROSOFT EXPRESSLY DISCLAIMS ANY WARRANTY OR CONDITION FOR THE SOFTWARE PRODUCT. THE SOFTWARE PRODUCT AND ANY RELATED DOCUMENTATION ARE PROVIDED "AS IS" WITHOUT WARRANTY OR CONDITION OF ANY KIND, EITHER EXPRESS OR IMPLIED, INCLUDING, WITHOUT LIMITA-TION, THE IMPLIED WARRANTIES OF MERCHANTABILITY, FITNESS FOR A PARTICULAR PURPOSE, OR NONINFRINGEMENT. THE ENTIRE RISK ARISING OUT OF USE OR PERFORMANCE OF THE SOFTWARE PRODUCT REMAINS WITH YOU.

**LIMITATION OF LIABILITY.** TO THE MAXIMUM EXTENT PERMITTED BY APPLICABLE LAW, IN NO EVENT SHALL MICROSOFT OR ITS SUPPLIERS BE LIABLE FOR ANY SPECIAL, INCIDENTAL, INDIRECT, OR CONSEQUENTIAL DAM-AGES WHATSOEVER (INCLUDING, WITHOUT LIMITATION, DAMAGES FOR LOSS OF BUSINESS PROFITS, BUSINESS INTERRUPTION, LOSS OF BUSINESS INFORMATION, OR ANY OTHER PECUNIARY LOSS) ARISING OUT OF THE USE OF OR INABILITY TO USE THE SOFTWARE PRODUCT OR THE PROVISION OF OR FAILURE TO PROVIDE SUPPORT SERVICES, EVEN IF MICROSOFT HAS BEEN ADVISED OF THE POSSIBILITY OF SUCH DAMAGES. IN ANY CASE, MICROSOFT'S ENTIRE LIABILITY UNDER ANY PROVISION OF THIS EULA SHALL BE LIMITED TO THE GREATER OF THE AMOUNT ACTUALLY PAID BY YOU FOR THE SOFTWARE PRODUCT OR US$5.00; PROVIDED, HOWEVER, IF YOU HAVE ENTERED INTO A MICROSOFT SUPPORT SERVICES AGREEMENT, MICROSOFT'S ENTIRE LIABILITY REGARDING SUPPORT SERVICES SHALL BE GOVERNED BY THE TERMS OF THAT AGREEMENT. BECAUSE SOME STATES AND JURISDICTIONS DO NOT ALLOW THE EXCLUSION OR LIMITATION OF LIABILITY, THE ABOVE LIMITATION MAY NOT APPLY TO YOU.

## MISCELLANEOUS

This EULA is governed by the laws of the State of Washington USA, except and only to the extent that applicable law mandates govern-ing law of a different jurisdiction.

Should you have any questions concerning this EULA, or if you desire to contact Microsoft for any reason, please contact the Microsoft subsidiary serving your country, or write: Microsoft Sales Information Center/One Microsoft Way/Redmond, WA 98052-6399.

# System Requirements

To use the Readiness Review compact disc, you need a computer equipped with the following minimum configuration:

- 486 or higher Intel-based processor (486 must be running in Enhanced Mode)

- Microsoft Windows 95, Windows 98, or Windows NT 4.0 or later

- 4 MB of RAM

- 15 MB of available hard disk space

- CD-ROM drive

- Mouse or other pointing device (recommended)

# Register Today!

Return this
*MCSE Readiness Review – Exam 70-028: Administering
Microsoft® SQL Server™ 7.0*
registration card today

## Microsoft® Press

**mspress.microsoft.com**

---

OWNER REGISTRATION CARD                                                   0-7356-0672-2

## *MCSE Readiness Review – Exam 70-028: Administering Microsoft® SQL Server™ 7.0*

_____  _____  _____
FIRST NAME                          MIDDLE INITIAL                LAST NAME

_____
INSTITUTION OR COMPANY NAME

_____
ADDRESS

_____

_____  _____  _____
CITY                                                                STATE               ZIP

_____  ( )_____
E-MAIL ADDRESS                                                      PHONE NUMBER

U.S. and Canada addresses only. Fill in information above and mail postage-free.
Please mail only the bottom half of this page.

*For information about Microsoft Press® products, visit our Web site at* **mspress.microsoft.com**

**Microsoft**®*Press*

## BUSINESS REPLY MAIL
FIRST-CLASS MAIL   PERMIT NO. 108   REDMOND WA

**POSTAGE WILL BE PAID BY ADDRESSEE**

NO POSTAGE
NECESSARY
IF MAILED
IN THE
UNITED STATES

MICROSOFT PRESS
PO BOX 97017
REDMOND, WA  98073-9830